ROBOTICA

In every era of communications technology – whether print, radio, television, or Internet – some form of government censorship follows to regulate the medium and its messages. Today we are seeing the phenomenon of "machine speech" enhanced by the development of sophisticated artificial intelligence. Ronald K. L. Collins and David M. Skover argue that the First Amendment must provide defenses and justifications for covering and protecting robotic expression. It is irrelevant that a robot is not human and cannot have intentions; what matters is that a human experiences robotic speech as meaningful. This is the constitutional recognition of "intentionless free speech" at the interface of the robot and receiver. *Robotica* is the first book to develop the legal arguments for these purposes. Aimed at law and communication scholars, lawyers, and free speech activists, this work explores important new problems and solutions at the interface of law and technology.

RONALD K. L. COLLINS is the Harold S. Shefelman Distinguished Scholar at the University of Washington School of Law.

DAVID M. SKOVER is the Fredric C. Tausend Professor of Constitutional Law at Seattle University School of Law.

Robotica

SPEECH RIGHTS AND ARTIFICIAL INTELLIGENCE

RONALD K. L. COLLINS
University of Washington

DAVID M. SKOVER
Seattle University

CAMBRIDGE
UNIVERSITY PRESS

CAMBRIDGE
UNIVERSITY PRESS

University Printing House, Cambridge CB2 8BS, United Kingdom

One Liberty Plaza, 20th Floor, New York, NY 10006, USA

477 Williamstown Road, Port Melbourne, VIC 3207, Australia

314–321, 3rd Floor, Plot 3, Splendor Forum, Jasola District Centre, New Delhi – 110025, India

79 Anson Road, #06–04/06, Singapore 079906

Cambridge University Press is part of the University of Cambridge.

It furthers the University's mission by disseminating knowledge in the pursuit of education, learning, and research at the highest international levels of excellence.

www.cambridge.org
Information on this title: www.cambridge.org/9781108428064
DOI: 10.1017/9781108649445

First published 2018

Printed in the United States of America by Sheridan Books, Inc.

A catalogue record for this publication is available from the British Library.

ISBN 978-1-108-42806-4 Hardback
ISBN 978-1-108-44871-0 Paperback

Contents

About the Authors

Ronald K. L. Collins is the Harold S. Shefelman Scholar at the University of Washington Law School. Before coming to the law school, Collins served as a law clerk to Justice Hans A. Linde on the Oregon Supreme Court, a Supreme Court Fellow under Chief Justice Warren Burger, and a scholar at the Washington, DC, office of the Newseum's First Amendment Center.

Collins has written constitutional briefs that were submitted to the Supreme Court and various other federal and state high courts. In addition to the books that he coauthored with David Skover, he is the editor of *Oliver Wendell Holmes: A Free Speech Reader* (2010) and coauthor with Sam Chaltain of *We Must Not Be Afraid to Be Free* (2011). His last solo book was *Nuanced Absolutism: Floyd Abrams and the First Amendment* (2013). Collins is the book editor of *SCOTUSblog* and writes a weekly blog (First Amendment News), which appears on the *Concurring Opinions* website.

David M. Skover is the Fredric C. Tausend Professor of Constitutional Law at Seattle University School of Law. He teaches, writes, and lectures in the fields of federal constitutional law, federal jurisdiction, and mass communications theory and the First Amendment.

Skover graduated from the Woodrow Wilson School of International and Domestic Affairs at Princeton University. He received his law degree from Yale Law School, where he was an editor of the *Yale Law Journal*. Thereafter, he served as a law clerk for Judge Jon O. Newman at the Federal District Court for the District of Connecticut and the US Court of Appeals for the Second Circuit. In addition to the books that he coauthored with Ronald Collins, he is the coauthor with Pierre Schlag of *Tactics of Legal Reasoning* (1986).

Together, Collins and Skover have authored *The Death of Discourse* (1996 and 2005), *The Trials of Lenny Bruce: The Fall & Rise of an American Icon* (2002 and

2012), *Mania: The Outraged & Outrageous Lives That Launched a Cultural Revolution* (2013), *On Dissent: Its Meaning in America* (2013), *When Money Speaks: The McCutcheon Decision, Campaign Finance Laws, and the First Amendment* (2014), and *The Judge: 26 Machiavellian Lessons* (2017). They have also coauthored numerous scholarly articles in various journals including the *Harvard Law Review, Stanford Law Review, Michigan Law Review*, and the *Supreme Court Review*, among other publications. *The Trials of Lenny Bruce* (revised and expanded) and *Mania, On Dissent, When Money Speaks* and *The Judge* are available in e-book form.

About the Commentators

Jane Bambauer is a Professor of Law at the University of Arizona's James E. Rogers College of Law. Her research assesses the social costs and benefits of Big Data and questions the wisdom of many well-intentioned privacy laws. Her articles have appeared in the *Stanford Law Review, Michigan Law Review, California Law Review*, and the *Journal of Empirical Legal Studies*. Professor Bambauer's own data-driven research explores biased judgment, legal education, and legal careers. She holds a BS in mathematics from Yale College and a JD from Yale Law School.

Ryan Calo is the Lane Powell and D. Wayne Gittinger Associate Professor of Law at the University of Washington. He is a faculty codirector of the University of Washington Tech Policy Lab, a unique, interdisciplinary research unit that spans the School of Law, Information School, and Paul G. Allen School of Computer Science and Engineering. Professor Calo holds courtesy appointments at the University of Washington Information School and the Oregon State University School of Mechanical, Industrial, and Manufacturing Engineering. His research on law and emerging technology appears in leading law reviews (*California Law Review, University of Chicago Law Review*, and *Columbia Law Review*) and technical publications (*Nature, Artificial Intelligence*) and is frequently referenced by the mainstream media (*New York Times, Wall Street Journal*).

James Grimmelmann is a professor at Cornell Tech and Cornell Law School. His research focuses on how laws regulating software affect freedom, wealth, and power. He helps lawyers and technologists understand each other and writes about digital copyright, search engines, privacy on social networks, online governance, and other topics in computer and Internet law. He is the author or coauthor of *Internet Law: Cases and Problems* (7th edn., 2017) and two other casebooks, multiple amicus briefs, more than forty scholarly articles, and numerous op-eds and essays.

Bruce E. H. Johnson is a partner at Davis Wright Tremaine in Seattle, Washington. He is a veteran litigator who represents information industry clients on issues involving media and communications law as well as technology and intellectual property matters. His expertise includes advising on First Amendment law issues, particularly involving commercial speech, commercial transactions, and consumer rights. Mr. Johnson is the author of Washington's Reporter's Shield Law enacted in 2007, and Washington's Uniform Correction or Clarification of Defamation Act enacted in 2013. Mr. Johnson is the coauthor with Steven G. Brody of *Advertising and Commercial Speech: A First Amendment Guide* (2nd edn., 2004).

Helen Norton is a professor at the University of Colorado (Boulder) School of Law, where she holds the Ira C. Rothgerber, Jr. Chair in Constitutional Law. Her scholarly and teaching interests include constitutional law, civil rights, and employment discrimination law. She served as leader of President-elect Obama's transition team charged with reviewing the Equal Employment Opportunity Commission in 2008 and is frequently invited to testify before Congress and federal agencies on civil rights law and policy issues. Before entering academia, Professor Norton served as Deputy Assistant Attorney General for Civil Rights at the US Department of Justice and as Director of Legal and Public Policy at the National Partnership for Women & Families. Among other publications, her scholarly writings have appeared in the *Duke Law Journal* and the *Supreme Court Review*; her latest article on artificial intelligence appeared in the *Northwestern University Law Review*.

Acknowledgments

Each of us has cause to think with deep gratitude of those who have lighted the flame within us.

             – Albert Schweitzer

Robotica would not have been possible without the efforts of many who fueled our intellectual flames. We gratefully recognize them here.

First and foremost: This book would never have been conceptualized had it not been for Ryan Calo, who through his teaching, writings, and conversations opened our minds to the world of robotics. In time, that led us to think about robotic expression and free speech. In that sense, Ryan's inspiration influenced us as it has many others.

Next is John Berger, our editor at Cambridge University Press, who has always believed in our book projects through the years and who has once again put his support fully behind this work. Our thanks to him and to the entire Cambridge University Press production team.

We also owe a debt of gratitude to our long-time friend, editor, and publisher Alex Lubertozzi. We were fortunate to meet him in 2002 when he edited the first edition of *The Trials of Lenny Bruce* at Sourcebooks. Since then, his publishing house, *Top Five Books*, has released the second edition of *The Trials of Lenny Bruce* (2012) and issued *Mania: The Outraged & Outrageous Lives That Launched a Cultural Revolution* (2013) and *When Money Speaks: The McCutcheon Decision, Campaign Finance Laws, and the First Amendment* (2014). Alex's assistance was invaluable for this project, as he designed the ingenious book cover art for *Robotica* and assisted in the production of the manuscript. It's been a wondrous ride with you, Alex!

A full measure of thanks goes, as well, to our reliable research librarians – Kelly Kunsch at Seattle University School of Law and Mary Whisner and her colleagues at the University of Washington Law School.

An early version of Part II of this book was presented at the 2015 Conference on Governance of Emerging Technologies in Scottsdale, Arizona, in May of 2015. Our thanks to the organizers of that conference who selected our paper for presentation and to the conference participants who engaged with our work there.

Last, but certainly not least, a cornucopia of gratitude goes to our commentators – Jane Bambauer, Ryan Calo, James Grimmelmann, Bruce Johnson, and Helen Norton. Their challenging observations on our work added immeasurably to the value of this book. By their sifting and weighing, they pushed us to better explain and defend our thesis at higher levels of analysis, and they enabled our readers to see beyond the first-level critiques that might be leveled at *Robotica*.

The Thesis

Prologue

Technology and Communication

And the word was made functional. As you will soon discover, that statement is rich with historical, philosophical, technological, legal, and constitutional meaning. Yet that meaning escapes us. Just as fish take water as a given, we take much for granted regarding the technologies that enable our communication. It is precisely that awareness of the technological underpinnings of communication that informs our discussion of robotics and free speech. And it is that eye-opening awareness – at once historical and futuristic – that points to new ways of thinking about free expression in an advanced technological world. Before turning to all that, a few words must be said about the obvious and about how we communicate.

It is a preoccupation that traces back many millennia: how to project the human voice and vision so that they carry over distance and time. The primitive world of orality was cabined by the confines of face-to-face communication. Such communication was largely limited to the time and place of its utterance and to its immediate recipients. Technology was needed to *amplify* and *transmit* the human voice and vision so that messages might reach a larger audience. Equally important, of course, was the need to *preserve* such messages. Here again, technology served to make the preservation of communication possible. Technology also furthered at least one other significant communicative function: it enabled the human mind to *broaden* the domain of knowledge and thereafter share that information with countless other humans, both living and yet to be born. In all of these ways and others, technology made it both possible and desirable to move beyond the limits of orality.

How did people communicate before the invention of writing some 3,200 years BC in places such as Mesopotamia, Egypt, and China? And what if we turn the communicative clock back 40,000 years to the early days of "writing" with numbers (e.g., notches carved in wood, bone, and stone to tally items)? Then there were the Paleolithic cave paintings that date back to around the same period. What is common to all of these early forms of communication is that they did not rely on

3

orality to convey their messages. They all utilized some technology to make their mark – some tool used in conjunction with a primitive form of "art" or "science." For example, technology gave some messages a form of permanence (e.g., the 35,400 year-old pig paintings found in Indonesian island caves), or it allowed messages to be transported over great distances (e.g., ancient Egyptian hieroglyphs placed on papyrus or wood). Other primitive communicative systems fostered more mass communication (e.g., smoke signals or drumming). In the cases of mathematical, scientific, and philosophical writing, technology brought something more to the communicative realm: it improved and expanded the domains of knowledge in ways that could thereafter be utilized and shared with others.

The *function* of such ancient technologies (be they stones, signs, or smoke) was to expand and enrich communication and the thinking process. In these ways, technology was vital to communication. The evolution of communication is thus inseparable from technology. Of course, the major jump in our evolutionary history was the invention of the printing press, which revolutionized everything from how people comprehended their world to how they understood their God. Later still, the technologies of the telegraph, telephone, motion pictures, radio, and television expanded the evolutionary arc of knowledge and communication. The advent of the World Wide Web and digitalized information (available on a range of communicative platforms from computers to tablets to cell phones) revolutionized life, law, and even civilization itself as never before.

It is axiomatic: with every revolutionary change brought about by a new communicative technology, there will be new threats to the established order, whether political, religious, economic, or social. Some of those threats will be real, others imagined. Some harms will be grave, others trivial. Some injuries, although significant, will be tolerated because the overall benefits of the technologies far outweigh their costs. In other words, the utility of communicative technologies can be so essential to our daily lives that we cannot function without them.

Additionally, the relationship of technology and communication raises many relevant questions: How has law adapted to such changes in communication? Did it give any staying power to these changes? How did it attempt to regulate them? And to what extent did it resort to censorship in order to counter the new communicative culture? This last question is a vital one, because censorship has long tracked the evolution of new and emerging technologies. If a communicative medium is mass in its reach, largely decentralized in its structure, instantaneous in its delivery, and potentially transformative in its messages, censorship (in any variety of forms) is almost certain to follow.

This is all backdrop to the larger concern of this small book, namely, robotic communication and its relationship to our system of freedom of expression. To explore that realm is to ask yet more questions. Is algorithmic data "speech" for First Amendment purposes? What values does communication spawned by artificial intelligence advance? In what ways, if any, can the traditional paradigms of our free speech jurisprudence apply to robotic expression? Given answers to these questions, it is important to ask what are the likely speech harms we might confront in such a brave new technological world? And what of the utility of robotic communication? Will it be so great as to prompt us to legal and cultural concessions that might otherwise strike us as intolerable or, worse still, inhumane?

Our epilogue closes with a philosophical comparison of John Milton's *Areopagitica* (1644) with our own *Robotica*. Whereas the former defended the technology of print against censorship, our tract situates the communicative technology of robotics within the domain of our First Amendment freedoms – all of this duly mindful of the necessity to rein in such liberty upon a convincing demonstration of immediate and serious harm.

True to our objectives, this book is concise in its presentation and modest in its scope. To be sure, more could (and will) be said. For now, it is enough to begin the process of thinking anew about the relationship between communication and technology.

So let us start our inquiry. As your eyes scan the lines of our text, prepare to return to the world of orality, a world in which spoken language encoded and transmitted information. Think about it: even in the world of the spoken word, could communication exist without some form of technology? To ask that kind of epistemological question about ancient forms of communication is to tilt one's mind to the future and to the dawn of Robotica.

Part I

The Progress and Perils of Communication

The relationship between technology and communication is illuminated by an ancient myth told by Plato in his *Phaedrus*. It illustrates how a new mode of expression furthers the progress of human knowledge while destabilizing the customary ways of speaking and thinking. In the process, the governing impulse is to defend the old ways against the new technology.

Plato's account held that among the ancient Egyptian gods, there was one named Theuth who first discovered writing, among other things. Theuth revealed his invention to the Egyptian king Thamus and urged him to teach the art of writing to all his subjects. "O King," Theuth explained, "here is something that, once learned, will make the Egyptians wiser and will improve their memory." Thamus was unmoved by the high regard that the father of writing had for his creation. "In fact," the king contended, "it will introduce forgetfulness into the soul of those who learn it: they will not practice using their memory because they will put their trust in writing, which is external and depends on signs that belong to others, instead of trying to remember from the inside, completely on their own." To push his point further, Thamus argued that writing would provide only "the appearance of wisdom, not its reality." For the invention will expose his subjects to "many things without being properly taught, and they will imagine that they have come to know much while for the most part they will know nothing."[1]

For our purposes, the significance of this myth is multidimensional. At the outset, it reveals that Theuth's writing represents a fundamental change in the method of communication. It takes the living word out of the mouth and places it onto the dead-letter script. Essentially, King Thamus understood that writing is more than a technique of memory; it is a technology external to the human user. Once writing is embraced, orality operates in its shadows. It becomes "speech-in-the-light-of-writing – a tool self-consciously adopted."[2]

Moreover, this artificial technology conflicts with the old ways of learning and knowing about the world. The art of memory as practiced by those entrusted with preserving a society's oral history – spiritual, political, social, and cultural – is eclipsed when writing inscribes that history more accurately, efficiently, and enduringly. To be sure, and as Socrates stressed in Plato's dialogue, when something is gained by a technology, something is lost. One does not have to dismiss Socrates' attack on writing to appreciate his point about the advantages of oral dialectical engagement. Even so, it is well to remember that Plato smiled kindly on Theuth's invention insofar as he retold the Egyptian myth and memorialized Socrates' reactions to it *in writing*. Tellingly, Plato parted company from his teacher because the functional value of writing outweighed categorical adherence to the oral way.

Viewed from this perspective, Plato might be seen as an outlaw in the king's regime. Essentially, Thamus' animosity to the technology of writing would rationalize censorship. Once reading and writing are widespread, the king's subjects would be empowered to think on their own and might no longer respect the ruling authority of oral tradition. Interestingly, what is at issue here is not a censorship of messages but a censorship of a medium.

In reading all that follows, bear these six points in mind. First, a new technology of communication not only affects how information is disseminated and preserved, but it changes how information is conceptualized and processed in human affairs. Second, any new and useful mode of communication will likely pose some real danger to the existing order. Third, the prospect of peril will likely prompt some type of censorship. Fourth, the dangers of a particular message may be inextricably tied up with the chosen method of communication. Fifth, whether a new technology ultimately prevails in life and law may well depend more on its functionality than on fidelity to established norms. Finally, once the new world of communication reaches its zenith, it is impractical to return to the old. As will become apparent later, these considerations significantly inform why and how we value the freedoms of expression in the long arc of time culminating in the Age of Robotica.

OVERCOMING ORALITY

In the beginning was the word, the *spoken* word. Of course, that is not quite true. The spoken word presumes the existence of some technique of communicating; we call that language. And "language" may or may not have been simply oral. For example, visual signifiers (e.g., smoke signals) or aural signifiers (e.g., the pounding of drums) were forms of communication in primitive societies. If for the sake of convenience and clarity we confine orality to spoken communication, we can better appreciate its deficiencies.

For communication to be truly effective, it must conquer distance; it must triumph over time; and it must surmount the obstacles of uncertainty. Standing alone, pure speech is ill suited to achieve these things. Something *more* – be it a technique and/or technology – is necessary. Think of it this way: the *technique* of ritual utterances, for example, could improve memory and thereby reduce the problems of uncertainty; by the same token, resort to the *technology* of "drums" could alleviate the problem of communicating over distances. Understood against this backdrop, the story of how humans overcame the deficiencies of orality provides a conceptual canvas on which to view the evolution of communication. In that process, communication improved and knowledge expanded but not without real risks to the customs that made oral society what it was *said* to be. Aided by print technology (digital or otherwise), let us sketch out some of the characteristics of the oral culture.

Primary orality, as we portray it, is a culture of communication based more heavily on spoken language than anything else. For thousands of years before Plato wrote the *Phaedrus* and for some 2,100 years thereafter, the oral culture was dominant. It prevailed until literacy and the use of the vernacular in writing became more widespread between the eleventh and seventeenth centuries. And in that oral world, communication and knowledge tended more toward the customary, the provincial, the participatory, the ceremonial, the adaptable, and the contextual.

Preliterate societies depended heavily on ritual and ceremony, including religious ceremony, to manage transactions and oversee social relations.[3] For example, before written documents were used to make conveyances, parties exchanged symbolic objects or engaged in rituals to signify their transactions and to commit the events to the memory of witnesses. As Professor M. T. Clanchy explains:

> [T]he witnesses 'heard' the donor utter the words of the grant and 'saw' him make the transfer by a symbolic object, such as a knife or a turf from the land ... Such a gesture was intended to impress the event on the memory of all those present. If there were a dispute subsequently, resort was had to the recollection of the witnesses.[4]

Whether the ritual involved an oral recitation accompanied by the transfer of a twig, turf, glove, or ring or the touching of an altar cloth or bell rope,[5] the longest measure was the living memory. To preserve the security of a transaction, the oral culture relied on generational memory. "Since memory was obviously likely to be the more enduring the longer its possessors were destined to remain on this earth, the contracting parties often brought children with them."[6] Visual and oral drama imbued the event with significance.

Oral solemnities also played an integral part in conflict resolution in preliterate cultures. For example, in their move away from blood feuds, the Northern and Western European tribal orders of the sixth to tenth centuries often used "trials by ritual oaths" to settle conflicts between households and clans.[7] Opposing parties would appear before public assemblies and exchange a series of oaths and offer "supporting proof" in the testimony of a number of kin or neighbors, known as "oath helpers" or "compurgators," who would also recite ritual oaths. Professor Harold Berman describes the significance of oathtaking as "legal speech" in an oral society: "All [oaths] were cast in poetic form, with abundant use of alliteration ... The dramatic and poetic elements ... elevated legal speech above ordinary speech."[8]

Among the Germanic peoples, the same public assemblies that issued judgments in trials by oaths also issued oral proclamations, known as "dooms."[9] The dooms, though not legislation in any contemporary sense, nevertheless pronounced the community's rightful ways. In Icelandic societies, the oral norms were announced once a year by the highest official, the "lawspeaker."[10] Professional "remembrancers" in other preliterate societies served a similar role of preserving and transmitting their legends and customs.[11]

What ritual sanctified, what ceremony legitimated, and what remembrancers recounted were the habits and norms of the people. "[T]he accustomed ways of life ... were passed from generation to generation by unwritten tradition."[12] By nature, custom was evolutionary, collective, and comparatively participatory;[13] oral norms emerged more from patterns of social relations among the ordinary folk than from deliberate and defined regulation by any governmental authority. Spoken custom was "tied to the movement of life itself in the flow of time."[14]

Because they flowed with life, oral traditions were far less likely to be rigid than later handwritten and typographic social orders would be. While oral culture had formalistic[15] and exclusionary qualities,[16] adaptability was its dominant feature. The fact that customs had to be recalled and repeated rather than recorded and read made them relatively malleable.[17] "Remembered truth was ... flexible and up to date, because no ancient custom would be proved to be older than the memory of the oldest living wise man."[18] The medieval Italian lawyer Azo insinuated the fluidity of custom when he stated, "A custom can be called *long* ... if it was introduced within ten or twenty years, *very long* if it dates from thirty years, and *ancient* if it dates from forty years."[19] Thus, it is anachronistic to characterize the lawspeaker or remembrancer as a professional historian who studied and recounted the past objectively.[20] With memory as the only safeguard of their traditions, members of oral societies could give the sanction of "ancient" custom to practices or beliefs that were relatively new.[21]

In an environment in which custom had a "creative energy,"[22] the oral tradition was "living" – localized, situated, and contextualized. Bound to no written text, custom could operate as the mirror and mold of the community's purposes. Essentially, the other significant attributes of the oral tradition derived from its contextual nature: The custom, the ceremony, the participation, and the adaptability in the oral way of knowing and communicating reflected and shaped the common consciousness.

In all of this, what is central is that the oral peoples depended heavily on *technique* to overcome the limitations of memory and to preserve and propagate the domain of their knowledge. Memory could not be self-dependent, however, if only because individual memories might be hopelessly inaccurate and multiple memories might chaotically conflict. Importantly, then, the truth-keeper – the lawspeaker or the remembrancer – legitimated the most significant narratives and norms of the oral culture. In that sense, the truth-keeper served as a medium for the society's most valuable messages. By mastering the techniques of memory, that figure performed, in effect, as a human *technology*. Thus understood, the concept of a truth-keeper validates the etymology of the word "technology" – *techno* meaning art, craft, or skill and *logy* meaning speech or discourse. In other words, skill in the service of speech.

The very character of any significant medium carries a certain power. That power may differ for diverse media, but the common thread is the capacity to influence or shape the way people understand their world or communicate with one another. For the oral societies, the keepers of truth largely determined the contours of political, religious, or social "histories." Given such power, they could either dismiss or repress conflicting facts or contrary truths. Since the keepers were the medium, they controlled the message.

In time, the oral way yielded to the scribal or chirographic way. Nonetheless, orality has survived for centuries and continues to do so. This points to an important lesson in the history of communication: in terms of its dominance, a new medium may replace an old one, but it never displaces it entirely. But what was quintessential about the oral culture was its all-too-human interaction. It was person to person; it was face to face; it was voice to voice; it occurred in real time; it engaged real people; and it was far less abstract than the forms of communication that followed it. Moreover, the oral culture entrusted the safekeeping of its sacred myths to a select few.

There was a certain romantic quality to orality – its very form bespoke its humanity. It was precisely that quality that the defenders of orality hailed when they railed against a new form of communication. At the dawn of scribality, the defenders of the oral way looked to Socrates to champion their cause. And for centuries thereafter, others would follow in his footsteps. Their first and foremost enemy were the scribes – the new keepers of truth.

THE WORDS OF THE SCRIBES

It dates from October 12, 1297. Its preamble and clauses were penned with quills and written in medieval Latin on a fragile membrane of calfskin parchment. Its some 3,500 words were set out on 68 lines of crowded and unbroken text, which was so expansive that it left little room for margins.

These references, of course, are to a version of the famed Magna Carta, in this case the one that King Edward I reissued in 1297. An official copy of that version was enrolled, for the first time, by the Chancery and inscribed into the earliest of the Chancery's Statute Rolls as an official enactment of the text. Today that scribal version resides in the National Archives in Washington, DC. (The original version of the Magna Carta dates from 1215, and the first mechanically printed edition appeared in 1508.)[23]

This Great Charter of Liberty, first drafted by the Archbishop of Canterbury to make peace between the unpopular King John and his rebel barons, was important in its time because by its very form it bound the king. It was proof, though not living, that certain rights were to be secured and that the king had consented to honoring them. Thus, "no freeman is to be taken or imprisoned or disseised of his free tenement or of his liberties or free customs, or outlawed or exiled or in any way ruined, nor will we go against such a man or send against him save by lawful judgment of his peers or by the law of the land."

The story of the Magna Carta represents a glorious moment in the history of scribality. No one's memory was needed to legitimate its promises; no remembrancer or lawspeaker was required to verify its contents; and no king could deny its existence so long as copies of the scribe's words remained. In those ways and more, it silenced the defenders of orality. Obviously, scribality long predated the Magna Carta. In the approximately thirty centuries that spanned the years between the Sumerian invention of the first script some 3,500 years ago[24] and the invention of moveable type in the mid-fifteenth century,[25] scribality gradually took hold, and many civilizations moved from orality to functional literacy.

To more fully appreciate the scribal way, in terms of both its advantages and its disadvantages, it is necessary to understand its basic characteristics and consequences.[26] When an event or practice is enframed[27] in writing, several things occur. Its terms are particularized (made specific), concretized (made definite), and fossilized (made lasting). By such fixed enframing, writing limits oral memory's more fluid recollections.[28]

In the process, the writer and reader are separated, and communication becomes a monologue rather than a dialogue. That is, the reader cannot interact with the writer at the point when the word is enframed – thus, Socrates' cherished dialogic engagement is lost. To further complicate the matter, when the written word is interpreted in the act of reading, the reader infuses his or her own meaning into the text, which may or may not coincide with that of the writer – the Archbishop of Canterbury is not present to explain the Magna Carta's ambiguous terms.

Such drawbacks notwithstanding, scribality does have its benefits. Importantly, the separation of writer from reader permits information to endure over time and travel across distance. This temporal-spatial extension of the written word moved information far beyond those places where the oral culture had taken it. Now in a tangible form, it could travel the vast lengths of the Greek and Roman empires and the Carolingian and English kingdoms.[29] Whereas the effectiveness of an oral command given from a distance depended upon its simplicity, writing facilitated the dissemination of numerous and complex commands. Similarly, the messages of the great writers could be carried literally to entirely new domains, thereby spreading their authors' concepts well beyond what would have been possible in oral times.

Furthermore, the written word itself is an artificial object, is reified, and is transformed into a thing to be studied and deciphered.[30] Scribal texts can address a topic at length, involve complex ideas, and proffer dense arguments. For all practical purposes, the critical growth of knowledge in such disciplines as mathematics, science, law, philosophy, and religion was made possible because of the abstract concepts described, debated, and defended in writing.

Whatever else it was, the scribal way was hardly democratic. Only the rich and learned few could write; only the privileged and literate few could read; and only the elite and fortunate few could own a penned folio. In that sense, the progress of knowledge depended on the few much as it had depended on truth-keepers in oral cultures. But as the scribal culture expanded, so too did the number of scribes and the diversity of their messages increase. As a consequence, blasphemous or libelous writings were burnt and their authors punished, sometimes on a fiery stake.

Once writing took hold, punitive censorship followed soon enough, even at the onset of scribality. Censorship of "written symbols," Professor Sue Curry Jansen observes, "was present in early Sumerian and Egyptian civilizations. [And] rigid social controls were built into the structure of Chinese ideography from its inception."[31] The Romans exploited the arts of censorship as early as 443 BC, and "though Augustus was not the first censor, he was the first ruler in the Western world to codify a law proscribing libelous or scandalous writings (libelli famosi). This law legitimated public book burnings." With each passing century, Roman censorship became more entrenched in its legal system. By the reign of Emperor Domitian (51–96 AD), the censorial animus toward the written word climbed to greater heights when he "ordered the historian Hermogenes crucified on the grounds that his writings libeled the Emperor." If the penalty was severe, it was because the offending medium amplified the offensive message. By that measure, Domitian "cut off distribution of the offensive writings by extending the death sentence to any book dealer caught selling Hermogenes' text."[32]

In all of this, rulers and other brokers of power came to realize that effective information management required regulation of the modes of communication that affected how people viewed their world and those who governed it. That mindset was not confined, however, to protecting secular rulers from the written barbs of the ruled. When the institutions of church and state merged in the Holy Roman Empire, censors targeted any religious work that deviated from the ordained creeds. When unauthorized versions of the Gospels potentially threatened the existing hierarchies of religious power, Church censorship began to rival that of its secular counterpart. Hence, *The Index Librorum Prohibitorum* ("List of Prohibited Books"). In 1559, Pope Paul IV promulgated the first version of the Index (the Pauline Index), which contained a list of banned writings judged to be heretical, anticlerical, or immoral. Amazingly, its regime continued until 1966.[33]

This brief overview of censorship in the scribal era points, on the one hand, to the obvious. Offensive messages, whether personal, political, religious, or scientific, often draw punitive responses. On the other hand, there is the less obvious: that is, censorship is very often medium focused. New media, such as that of scribality, change the cultural equation in significantly transformative ways. The Roman censors, along with those before and after them, understood this all too well. They knew that written works posed new threats – not only to the established order but to the very ways people processed and evaluated information pertaining to their daily lives and to the conditions of their society. Such new ways of thinking pointed away from the age of orality and toward the age of print.

While scribal communication struggled to move over both space and time, to fix its message, and to transform itself into subjects of study, the manner in which it was preserved – the handwritten script – prevented it from completely overtaking oral communication in the various affairs of a society. With only a few copies available for a widely dispersed population, chirographic writing alone could not reach many of the subjects of a realm. Given the time, labor, and expense of copying legislation, royal orders, and religious gospels, chirographic documents alone could not efficiently reproduce and fix their messages. Furthermore, until more than a limited class of people could read and write, chirographic writings alone could not abstract reality for the collective mind. In short, the scribal age could commence, but not complete such transformations – this could only come later in the age of print. Yet "the important point is not the degree to which writing penetrated oral culture: it was its irrevocability."[34]

THE PRINT REVOLUTION

The *Gutenberg Bible*. Though it all too easily escapes us, it is remarkable that those two words should be united, that a technology should be wed to the words of God. Amazingly, the voice of God had been reduced to Latin letters punched out by moveable metal type and then cast in thick ink upon parchment or paper. The Lord's words had been *bound* in two volumes consisting of 1,286 pages. What is ironic for our purposes is that long before and long after the age of print, the technology of writing was viewed as one of Lucifer's most powerful tools. In the mid-fifteenth century, by stark contrast, technology was portrayed as the mechanical handmaiden of God, as a vehicle by which His messages might be spread and understood as never before. Nonetheless, the Angel of the Dark would eventually demand his due, and when he did, print technology would become the Devil's Device, his blasphemous godsend.

In the beginning, the fifteenth-century introduction of moveable type onto the scene of Western Civilization was hailed as a glorious moment in the history of humankind.[35] This "wondrous agreement ... and harmony of punches and types," as Johannes Gutenberg is reported to have said,[36] represented the early triumph of print over scribality. It also brought into bold relief the worst fears of the defenders of orality. And soon enough, the invention of print led to a revolution, one appropriately tagged "the Gutenberg Revolution."[37] More than almost anything else, the invention of print became an "agent of change," a change so great that it not only reconfigured religious, legal, and political worlds but also "revolutionized all forms of learning."[38] After all, this new technology, declared Francis Bacon, changed "the appearance and state of the whole world" in ways that demanded that historians "take note of the force, effect, and consequences of Gutenberg's invention."[39]

This revolution in media enabled the Reformation in religion. The invention of the Gutenberg printing press significantly contributed to the demise of Catholicism in Martin Luther's time. When Luther nailed his grievances against the Catholic papacy and practices on a church door in Wittenberg, Germany, he could not have imagined that his ideas would extend virally through the medium of print. Indeed, Luther expressed surprise and puzzlement when he explained to Pope Leo X six months later: "It is a mystery to me how my theses ... were spread to so many places."[40] Nonetheless, it was "estimated that in the three years following [Luther's] historic act, more than three hundred thousand copies of [his] writings were sold."[41] As depicted by historian A. G. Dickens, "Lutheranism was from the first the child of the printed book, and through this vehicle Luther was able to make exact, standardized and ineradicable impressions upon the mind of Europe."[42] In this world, no longer were the living words of the Pope and priests (the latter-day keepers of truth) the sacred touchstone; rather, the faithful turned to their printed Bibles to interact with and understand their Lord.

Not only did the printing press spark the Reformation, but it ignited the Renaissance and Enlightenment as well. By putting more books on the shelves, it placed more ideas in the marketplace. A quintessential example of the print-based explosion of knowledge is Denis Diderot's and Jean d'Alembert's monumental work, *Encyclopedie ou Dictionnaire Raisonné des Sciences, des Arts, et des Métiers*, an unprecedented compendium of subjects covering "every branch of human knowledge" so as to afford "the power to change [the] common way of thinking." Containing contributions from France's finest scholars, *Encyclopedie* was heralded by some of the greatest writers of the day. François Voltaire praised the project thus: "Men are on the eve of a great revolution in the human mind, and it is to you [Diderot and d'Alembert] to whom they are most of all indebted for it."[43]

Generally speaking, when events or practices – religious or secular – are captured in print, certain things occur. First, typography pushes individuals out of their real-life experiences and quarters them on to the confines of a printed page. The paper's borders frame "reality" and close it off from all externalities. Printed text rules context. Second, by depersonalizing human experience, the printed text controls its environment. Typography situates its subjects and insulates them from variable influences: "The [printed] text is sealed off from life and change."[44] Third, once print confines its subjects, it thereafter categorizes and organizes them. Glossaries, indexes, tables of contents, chapter and subchapter headings, and footnotes all marshal information and order its messages. These attributes of print contribute an abstract quality to its subject matter. Printed information turns more on reified concepts than on active realities and more on what the eye sees on the page than on what it sees off the page.

Not surprisingly, these attributes of print resemble those of its scribal counterpart, for, as we noted, print enhanced the potentialities of script. Indeed, this enhancement stood to reform or transform the knowledge base and cultural practices of the scribal era. In this regard, Professor Walter Ong astutely notes, "A new medium of communication . . . reinforces the older medium or media. However, in doing so, it transforms the old, so that the older is no longer what it used to be."[45] Print maximized the manuscript's powers by minimizing its weaknesses. First and foremost, publication in the vernacular made possible mass communication. Print is a mass medium for a mass audience. Because print technology does not depend on a limited class of copiers and copies, it can duplicate its textual lessons for countless readers in countless times and in countless places. Moreover, because print technology does not suffer from the human errors of scribal copiers, typographic messages are more uniform, consistent, and therefore more reliable and authentic, copy after copy.[46] Finally, the economics of print served to democratize its products in ways never realized by its scribal predecessor.

These characteristics of print found their zenith in the reconceptualization of law. In England, printing of the law began in the 1480s with a relatively unknown printer, W. de Machlinia. It eventually became the domain of celebrated printers like Richard Pynson and John Rastell, the brother-in-law of Thomas More.[47] Their first law books were printed in Latin and French, as the vernacular was not yet the official language of English law. In 1485, the first published copy of Parliament's laws appeared in English, and in the subsequent half century of the early Tudor reign (1485–1535), the laws of the British empire underwent "Englishing and printing."[48] By 1534, Robert Redman published *The Great Boke of Statutes* and *The Boke of Magna Carta*, which put pre-Tudor statutes dating as far back as 1225 into typographic form.[49]

English decisional law was harnessed in the print era by reporters such as James Dyer (1537–1582),[50] Edmund Plowden (1550–1580),[51] Edward Coke (1572–1616),[52] and James Burrow (1756–1772).[53] Similarly, typography more effectively systematized English decisional and statutory law in the great treatises of the sixteenth through the eighteenth centuries, such as St. Germain's *Dialogues between a Doctor of Divinity and a Student of the Common Law* (1523 and 1530),[54] Coke's four *Institutes* (1628–1642),[55] and Sir William Blackstone's *Commentaries on the Laws of England* (1765).[56] Interestingly, even Bracton's thirteenth-century chirographic form of the *Note Book* did not enjoy the authoritative status that it later attained once printed in 1569.[57]

We can learn much about print's ascendancy over orality and scribality by considering one of the most famous legal enactments of the period, the 1677 *English Statute of Frauds*.[58] As stated in its preamble,[59] the printed statute targeted those frauds lurking behind oral testimony given under oath in court.[60] It did so by replacing the regime of living memory with the rule of lifeless print. Under the statute, not even the testimony of twenty god-fearing bishops[61] could save an oral contract, an oral will of personalty, or an oral transfer of land. By equating perjury with orality and truthfulness with writing, the statute reflected the legal mindset associated with the typographic age: if the "reality" is not fixed on the page, the law will not recognize it. This is a world controlled by form; yet in such a theoretically inflexible world, it is not surprising that in time, the Statute of Frauds would be riddled with exceptions.[62]

Setting the body of English law in type placed more legislation, detailed codes, statutes, case reporters, and treatises in the hands of more lawyers and judges, encouraged more litigation, and carried more legal octavo volumes to more parts of the kingdom. In other words, print increased reliance on the fixed rules of the published law, attacking the fluid memory of the oral way and the comparatively flexible rules of custom.[63] The typographic word enhanced all of the values still associated with the notion of the supremacy of law – uniformity, predictability, universality, and analytical application of printed commands. With its systematic categories and abstract concepts, typographic law emphasizes detached and logical analysis. Not surprisingly, the patron saint of English jurisprudence, Sir William Blackstone, is the prototypical "Typographic Man" – dispassionate, devoted to rigorous reason, and intolerant of incongruities.[64]

Three hundred years after Johann Gensfleisch zum Gutenberg's celebrated Bible first appeared in Mainz, Germany, Chief Justice Charles Pratt Camden of the Court of Common Pleas proclaimed, "If it is law, it will be found in our books. If it is not found there, it is not law."[65] Perfunctorily, the eighteenth-century English jurist accepted as gospel the notion that law did not and could not exist outside of its printed record. By the eighteenth century, there was only a hazy memory that the fifteenth-century invention of print had ushered in a radically new culture.

That hazy memory no doubt forgot exactly how radical the culture of print had appeared to governing religious and political leaders early in the history of the new technology. Production of books in England increased by leaps and bounds; whereas there were 550 books printed from 1520 to 1529, that number almost doubled with 928 books printed from 1540 to 1549; and in the second half of the century, more and more printing houses sprang up to print more and more books and pamphlets. Governmental fears over the growth of the publishing industry increased proportionately after a number of Catholic and Puritan tracts severely critiqued Queen Elizabeth I and attacked her religious settlement of 1559. Taking a censorial stance against the typographic medium itself, the Star Chamber in Westminster issued the Decree of 1586, which concentrated the book industry in London and limited the number of printing presses. "In 1651 the number of printers in London was fixed at 22, and the only authorized persons allowed to print outside London were the university printers of Oxford and Cambridge."[66]

The same technology-focused censorship appeared in France in the first half of the sixteenth century. Professors Lucien Febvre and Henri-Jean Martin provide a telling account of the French court's personal intervention in governmental matters regarding press regulation:

Charles IX's edict of 1563 requiring every book to be licensed before publication gave him control of all new books. Licences, of course, were only granted in the light of advice from the censors, who were at first theologians of the Sorbonne and later, in the 17th century, secular officials. Under cover of copyright regulations the King, and those other European monarchs who also adopted this system, kept a close watch on book production.

Moreover, "[t]o inhibit the spread of piracies and underground literature," Jean Baptiste Colbert, a French politician and the Controller-General of Finances from 1665 to 1683 under the rule of King Louis XIV, "did not hesitate to limit the number of officially authorized printers and to concentrate them all in [Paris]."[67]

What is most significant for our purposes in these two examples is the method of censorship that these press regulations represented. It cannot be gainsaid that the print age witnessed much punitive governmental action against heretical, seditious, or libelous literature that was directed either at the publications themselves (in the forms of licensing schemes or lists of forbidden books) or at the authors and printers who created them (in the forms of prosecution or persecution). Importantly, however, the Star Chamber's Decree of 1586 and Minister Colbert's designs were medium focused, capping the total number of authorized presses and restricting their geographic locations. By establishing the place and manner of publishing (as early forebears of time, place, and manner regulations of speech and press recognized in contemporary American law), these governmental orders indirectly controlled the contents of books by directly controlling the industry of printing.

Moving from early to later days in the print era, we must consider one of the most notorious examples of press censorship, this from eighteenth-century America. It is the Benjamin Bache story. By way of necessary background to that narrative, recall one of the most famous passages in the history of freedom of speech:

> The liberty of the press is indeed essential to the nature of a free state; but this consists in laying no previous restraints upon publications, and not in freedom from censure for criminal matter when published. Every freeman has an undoubted right to lay what sentiments he pleases before the public; to forbid this, is to destroy the freedom of the press; but if he publishes what is improper, mischievous or illegal, he must take the consequence of his own temerity.[68]

Those lines from Sir William Blackstone's *Commentaries on the Laws of England* cut against the grain of centuries of suppression of the penned and printed word. It was a radical idea: one could, without fear of prior restraint, print his or her ideas and have them circulate in the minds of men and women. Again, in Blackstone's words: "Every freeman has an undoubted right to lay what sentiments he pleases before the public." Think of it: heresies could be published; subversive tracts could be published; scandalous materials could be published; and any leader (secular or spiritual) could be condemned or ridiculed without fear that the printing presses would be stopped. True, a printer could be punished *after* the fact for any transgression of the law. But even with that important qualifier, Blackstone's defense of the technology of print came to be seen as a vital component of an emerging liberty.

In but a matter of a few decades, that Blackstonian ideal found expression in America in the First Amendment to the United States Constitution – "Congress shall make no law . . . abridging the freedom . . . of the press . . . " For a new country, this *no law* command was both unprecedented and radical. It marked the first time in history that the supreme law of a nation expressly protected a technology, that of print. There was more at stake here than the protection of *speech*; there was a perceived need to protect a technology that facilitated speech and thinking as never before. That technology, as evidenced by the American and French Revolutions, could help topple a government. And yet, James Madison and his constitutional colleagues managed to tuck that radical idea into the text of the Bill of Rights.

Before the printer's ink had a real chance to dry on circulated copies of the Bill of Rights, Benjamin Bache (1769–1798) put Blackstone's idea and Madison's ideal to the test. This Philadelphia printer was the publisher of the *Aurora*, the anti-Federalist paper dedicated to attacking George Washington and Alexander Hamilton and virtually everything they did in the name of foreign policy. Bache was acerbic, caustic, vile, vituperative, uncontrollable, scurrilous, and often mean spirited. He was relentless and severe in his criticisms of the Federalists. John Fenno, the editor of the *Gazette of the United States*, a Federalist-sympathetic paper, lashed out in kind: "Mr. Bache . . . seems to take a kind of hellish pleasure in defaming the name of WASHINGTON."

Nothing fazed Bache. He was determined to use the power of his press to condemn his political adversaries and, if possible, to unseat them. Thus, when President Washington stepped down (some say because of Bache), the editor of the *Aurora* redirected his spite toward John Adams. "Old, querulous, bald, blind, crippled, toothless Adams" is how he described the president he loved to loathe. Abigail Adams despised her husband's tormentor; in her eyes, he was vile and treacherous. She once confided to her sister, Mary Cranch, "Scarcely a day passes but some such scurrility appears in Bache's paper, very often unnoticed, and of no consequence in the minds of many people, but it has, like vice of every kind, a tendency to corrupt the morals of common people. Lawless principles," she emphasized, "naturally produce lawless actions."

Largely in response to Benjamin Bache and his anti-Federalist cohorts, on July 14, 1798, John Adams signed the infamous Alien and Sedition Acts. The legislation made it criminal to "write, print, utter, or publish" any "false, scandalous and malicious writing or writings against the government of the United States, or either House of the Congress of the United States, or of the President of the United States" with "intent to defame" any such parties or to bring them "into contempt or disrepute; or to excite against them . . . the hatred of the good people of the United States, or to stir up sedition within the United States; or to excite any unlawful combinations therein, for opposing or resisting any law of the United States." The sanctions: "a fine not exceeding two thousand dollars, and . . . imprisonment not exceeding two years." With these Acts, as Professor Geoffrey Stone observed, "the Federalists (and the U.S. government) declared war on dissent."

It was an irony too great to ignore: the very nation that only a few years before had given constitutional protection to press freedom was now busily abridging that very freedom. Unwilling to wait for Adams's signature on the Alien and Sedition Acts, Federalist prosecutors hauled Bache off to court on June 26, 1798 and charged him with violating the federal common law of seditious libel, this for "libeling the President & the Executive Government, in a manner tending to excite sedition, and opposition to the laws, by sundry publications and re-publications."

At last, the "seditious printer" had been arrested; now his "scurrilous rants" would cease. But things did not play out that way. The day after his arrest, Bache vowed in the *Aurora* never to abandon "the cause of truth and republicanism," which he pledged to honor to "the best of his abilities, while life remains."

But it was all for naught. Late on the evening of Monday, September 10, 1798, Benjamin Bache died, thus ending his prosecution before his trial began. With Bache gone, the *Aurora*'s presses were temporarily stilled. Meanwhile, given the Adams administration's new sedition law to silence its political enemies, the Anti-Federalists had good cause to fear their own fate. In a letter of October 11, 1798, Vice President Thomas Jefferson warned Senator Stevens Thompson Mason that the Sedition Act was "merely an experiment on the American mind to see how far it will bear an avowed violation of the Constitution." During the course of that experiment, Anti-Federalist printers and dissenters were prosecuted for another two years.

Relief finally came to the Anti-Federalists. Jefferson prevailed in the presidential election of 1800 and pardoned those convicted under the Alien and Sedition Acts. Those laws expired on March 3, 1801. With that, the spirit of the First Amendment returned like a great phoenix. Freedom of the press was once again legal.[69]

This account – one of many, of course – of the struggle to protect the Gutenberg medium and its users reveals how in the course of time the typographic medium came to be accepted notwithstanding the dangers it posed to the existing order. Make no mistake about it: Bache and his printing press were dangerous. New media, if they are effective, carry with them precisely that possibility. While they do have their benefits (and they are numerous and significant), these new methods of communication stand to remold the way we view all things germane to the human condition.

Viewing the relationship between censorship and typography through a wider lens, we can perceive common strategies taken by many authorities in many places and in many times to impose their control over the printed word. Professor Jansen neatly synthesizes those strategies in her reflections on the censorial methods of the Catholic Church: "It sought control over the distribution of words through licensing (Imprimatur), prohibition (Index), and persecution (Inquisition). But this trinity of terror," she stresses, "could not extinguish the critical spirit."[70] Such forms of suppression, though existing in the scribal era, took on new and virulent power in the Gutenberg age and for long thereafter. These repressive methods, which aimed to combat heresy and sedition, targeted typographic works that were economical, portable, and available to so many.

One need not deny or discount dangers to old religious and political orders to appreciate that new technologies of communication bring with them new ideas, new values, new ways of thinking about the world, and new concepts about what it means to communicate. In the historical spectrum from orality through scribality to print, *change* was the reality of the realm. It was just that specter of change that prompted the old keepers of truth to *license* opinion and knowledge and thereby prevent the spread of treacherous truths; and it was just that specter of change that prompted them to *index* works and officially proclaim their unfitness for public consumption; and it was surely that specter of change that compelled them to *persecute* those who dared to ignore the commands of the first two practices in the "trinity of terror."

All that said, was it that "critical spirit" (however defined) that ultimately won out? Was it that "spirit" that centuries later brought the threat of licensing, indexing, and persecution to an ignominious end (or near end) in modern Western culture? Perhaps. After all, print was the darling of the Reformation and the Renaissance. And print played a major role in the American and French Revolutions. So yes, that "critical spirit" was a powerful weapon in the arsenals of mighty movements. Without dismissing this, one may nonetheless ask: but what of the role of economics, the utility of the new medium, and all its many advantages that made life so excitingly different, usefully manageable, and even invitingly pleasurable? Our point: to raise this question is not to devalue the laudable; it is rather to assign value to the practical, to the functional, and to all the other ways in which new media transform our lives – ways so momentous as to discourage any comprehensive return to the past. And it is that insight that informs, however subtly, so much of how we think about free speech and why we value it.

But this is to get ahead of our story and what is to come. Now we turn to the electrified word and how it transformed the world as never before. Those transformations would certainly have distressed Socrates and disturbed John Milton.

THE ELECTRIFIED WORLD OF COMMUNICATION

Electricity. It was a historic game changer. It ushered in the Technological Revolution, which followed the Industrial or Mechanical Revolution. Thanks to the likes of Alexander Graham Bell, Thomas Edison, Albert Einstein, Galileo Ferraris, Guglielmo Marconi, Kenjiro Takayanagi, and George Westinghouse, among others, the electric current pointed to a force field the power of which had never been known. Once harnessed, it brought new light to the world, both literal and figurative, and generated energy that could be used for countless purposes. Importantly, it made a wide variety of telecommunications possible – the telegraph, telephone, radio, television, the computer, and its digital progeny such as the Internet.

Electricity permitted the Prometheus of communication to be unbound. Communication became both more personal and more mass; information became more democratized; the purposes of communication became more diversified; the economics of communication altered dramatically; reliance on the new modes of communication increased greatly; and "data" became new property and commonplace in the communicative vernacular.

Consider the basic forms of electrified media – exclusively audio (analogue telephone, radio, and audiobooks), exclusively visual (telegraphy, digital text, and digital photography), audio-visual (television, movies, video, and hyperlinked e-books), and any computerized combination of these. Collectively, the electronic modes of communication have attributes that distinguish them from earlier modes and that vastly improve on many of their properties.

Recall that the print way had vied successfully against the oral way, as it distanced the writer from the reader and separated the text from any full measure of context. With the emergence of electronic media, the balance of power among the preelectronic modes of communication began to change once more. In the electrified age, we have come nearly full circle, with electronic media standing midpoint between orality and print, combining characteristics of each.

First, electronic communication can be instantaneous and global. In that sense, its utility far surpassed the capacities of scribality and print in conquering time and space. For example, the telephone, radio, television, and Internet are able to carry sounds and/or images of persons, places, and events in real time from one end of the earth to the other and beyond.

Second, electrified media can reintegrate sound and moving images into the communicative mode. While the penned manuscript or the typographic book connected people in far-flung places, it did not do so with the living and interactive qualities of the oral experience. By reintroducing aural and visual detail, however, the telephone (including the smartphone), television, movie, and computerized video engage the human senses more fully than text alone ever could.

Third, the electrified media can enframe context-rich representations of its subject matters. In that sense, they overcome the deficiencies of scribal or print accounts that, by force of the preelectric technology, were necessarily more decontextualized. For example, if a scribal or traditional typographic description of persons, places, and events is rich, it comes only at the price of lengthy and elaborate textual passages. But the images and sounds of television, movies, and YouTube capture more context within their moving frames in a split second than one or a dozen pages of a book could hold.

Finally, electronic communication can concretize its messages. A reader must process or decode long strings of written or printed symbols to interpret the sense or meaning of a text; in contrast, even an illiterate listener or viewer can derive a sense of an electronic account, even on a relatively unfamiliar subject matter, due to its aural and imagistic properties.

All combined, the components of the electrified media create a hybrid that is in varying degrees oral, pictographic, and typographic. By way of an example, the ever-transforming e-book offers text with hyperlinks to other texts and to audio-video clips. And the smartphone connects us 24/7 via talking, texting, emailing, and web browsing. This layered phenomenon represents a new and radical force in the operation of person-to-person and mass communication.

The invention and evolution of the book made the Enlightenment possible. In those times and in that world, the relationship between the printed word and the pursuit of knowledge was self-evident. For that reason, book learning was essential. To that end, public libraries were erected across the land. In the early pre-Revolution days (circa 1731), Benjamin Franklin and friends established the Library Company of Philadelphia partly as a way to share information. By 1833, the ideas of sharing books and enhancing knowledge became so popular as to result in the first free public library supported by taxation; it was the Peterborough, New Hampshire, Town Library. Not too many years later, Boston followed suit with its own public library. With the passage of time, public libraries sprang up across the land and became a mainstay of the nation (the Library of Congress) and of every state, county, and city.[71] By the first decade of the twenty-first century, there were some 120,000 libraries in the United States.[72] Those institutions made public access to information possible as never before realized.

Utility in electronic communication served purposes other than Enlightenment ideals. Widespread use of television pushed the agenda of entertainment to the forefront. That is, this new communications technology better served entertainment pursuits than Enlightenment principles. Unquestionably, entertainment is more the coin of the television culture than knowledge. In 2016, the most popularly viewed show was *Orange Is the New Black* (Netflix); *The Big Bang Theory* (CBS), *Stranger Things* (Netflix), *Fuller House* (Netflix), and *Designated Survivor* (ABC) followed rank to round out the top five programs.[73] As media theorist Professor Neil Postman observed years ago with respect to traditional TV viewing, "[T]here is no subject of public interest – politics, news, education, religion, science, sports – that does not find its way to television." And he cautioned, television "has made entertainment itself the natural format for the representation of all [those subjects] . . . To say it still another way: Entertainment is the supraideology of all discourse on television."[74] No wonder, then, that the distinguished communications scholar titled his most famous book on television's phenomenal appeal *Amusing Ourselves to Death*, a book that all but predicted the ascendancy of televisual celebrity politicians such as Donald J. Trump.

The television phenomenon was significant not only for what people watched but also for how long they watched it. By 2015, there were some 116 million American households with televisions,[75] and on the average their occupants spent 35 hours a week (49 if they were over 65 years of age) watching TV.[76] Although TV clearly remains one of America's favorite entertainment pastimes, most Americans today appear to be watching considerably less "traditional television" per week (live and DVR time-shifted viewing) than they once did. According to Nielsen's 2016 TV viewing figures, although adults aged 50–64 remained glued to their sets for 39 hours 54 minutes per week (representing a fractional 0.5 percent drop over five years), the Gen Xers (35–49) watched 28 hours 24 minutes per week (an 11.6 percent decrease in five years). The downward trend is markedly greater among younger demographics, however. In 2016, whereas older millennials (25–34) watched 20 hours 4 minutes per week (an expansive 27.7 percent drop over five years), America's teens (12–17) sat in front of TV sets only 15 hours 5 minutes per week (a whopping 37.6 percent contraction over the past five years).

Such a reduction in TV viewing, however, does not represent some vaunted return to more reading or even more outside play. Thanks to newer digital communications technologies, individuals seem to spend more hours than ever surfing the Web and watching streaming services instead. In the electrified environment, video found its way onto handheld or wrist-worn devices, such as tablets, smartphones, and smartwatches using everything from YouTube to Netflix to Facebook to watch still more entertaining programming, whether personally or commercially produced. Although Nielsen's smartphone and tablet video figures do not include nonvideo content available through Facebook and other social media applications, its figures for sites with long-form video consumption, such as Netflix and HBO GO, indicate that mobile devices are increasingly becoming the technologies of choice for digital media consumption. In 2016, the average 18- to 34-year-old American spent 9 hours 9 minutes per week consuming PC video, 1 hour 40 minutes per week enjoying tablet video, and 1 hour 7 minutes per week engaging with smartphone video.[77] Importantly, the popularity of these new technologies depends on their utility: information and entertainment are readily available in one's pocket or purse.

Beyond television, the major game changer in communications technology was the Internet. Information of all kinds was digitalized and made available on the World Wide Web for free or at affordable costs. Now the world's data were linked together in ways unimaginable before 1989 when Tim Berners-Lee, a British computer scientist, invented the Web. Following that, overall Internet usage increased exponentially. Global Internet users rose from 394 million in 2000 to 1.858 billion in 2009, climbed to 3 billion by 2014, and topped 3.675 billion or 50.1 percent of the world's population by June of 2016 – a 918.3 percent growth in sixteen years.[78] Jubilant Internet users turned to this new communications technology for content on countless subject matters, ranging from health to commerce and from politics to theology. Here was a communications technology that spread its rich compendium of information faster, further, and more fully than the printed word could ever hope to do. It would have amazed and befuddled old Denis Diderot.

In significant respects, computerized media technologies obsolesce their oral, scribal, and print antecedents and reconfigure their objectives. Print research in public libraries has virtually vanished since Google's search engines roared into the human consciousness. Book reading turned more and more to browsing as Google Books became more popular. Perhaps more than anything else, however, the utility of digital communications technologies fed the pleasure principle as never before. Functionally (though perhaps not legally), the new electronic media legitimate obscenity for hundreds of millions of viewers who turn on when they tune in. Where once obscene enjoyment required seedy movie theaters or dirty book stores, now erotic fare can be savored in the comfort and privacy of one's home or anywhere else – and often at no cost.

Although up-to-date statistics are notoriously difficult to come by, the most reliable studies depict a remarkable portrait of Internet porn usage and demographic patterns. They establish that approximately 40 million Americans regularly visit porn sites on the Internet, with upward of 28,200 users spending close to $3,100 dollars per second to stream racy clips and view sexy photos. Google and other search engines are tapped at alarming rates to seek out sexually explicit pictures and videos – upward of 25 percent of all search engine queries, or about 68 million per day. Significantly, *Huffington Post* reports a little-known fact: these "sites get more visitors each month than Netflix, Amazon and Twitter combined."[79] Although billions of dollars are spent annually on obscenity, nine out of ten such users only access free content.[80] Notably, it was projected that by 2017, "a quarter of a billion people are expected to be accessing mobile adult content from their phones or tablets, an increase of more than 30% from 2013."[81]

Precisely because utility in electronic communications rides roughshod over political and moral norms, governmental impetus to push back is always present. Sometimes this is in the interest of national security claims. Consider the span from President Woodrow Wilson's 1917 Executive Order ("Censorship of Submarine Cables, Telegraph, and Telephone Lines")[82] and the Espionage Act of 1917 to the USA Patriot Act of 2001 and a proposed measure in the 114th Congress (2015) that would have required Internet service providers to report any terrorist activities on their sites.[83] In that arc of time, there were, to be sure, various federal, state, and local laws enacted to control this or that electronic medium in the name of public safety.

The other major domain for fervent censorship focused on morality in the media, precisely because the electrified image supercharged the thrill of taboos. Not long after President Wilson issued his censorial decree, New York State followed suit with a different brand of media censorship – the prescreening of all commercially exhibited movies to sift out smut. Shortly thereafter, seven other states imposed prior restraints on movies, and dozens of cities did likewise.[84] These licensing regimes remained intact until 1952, when the Supreme Court set them aside on First Amendment grounds in *Joseph Burstyn, Inc. v. Wilson*.[85] Much the same moralizing mindset[86] informed a section of the Federal Communications Act of

1934, which prohibited any broadcast medium from airing "any obscene, indecent, or profane language";[87] that legislation was fortified by the Broadcast Decency Enforcement Act of 2005.[88] In the Internet world, the Communications Decency Act of 1996[89] and the Child Online Protection Act of 1998[90] aimed to safeguard minors against the perils of sexual indecency and obscenity.

The motivation in all of this, however hypocritical, was the perpetuation of Victorian norms. In that regard, the Supreme Court was emphatic in *Miller v. California* (1973)[91] – obscenity is not protected under the First Amendment. That proclamation still stands. Nonetheless, when Pornutopia[92] fought the law, Pornutopia won, as obscene materials saturated the Internet. Literally speaking, obscenity remains illegal; functionally speaking, the Internet legitimated obscenity. What little the justices took away from the perverse markets of kiddie porn,[93] the captains of corruption more than made up for by flooding the electronic highways with erotic fare. This surfeit of pornography starkly illustrates what happens when electronic communications technology makes noncompliance with the law so easy and nonpunitive.

Before moving on to our discussion of robotic expression, it may be helpful to encapsulate what we have said and why we said it. This is important because how we view any specific communications technology depends on where we are standing at any given point in time. Furthermore, the various values of each mode of communication serve to inform why speech using that medium should or should not be protected. Of course, with the passage of time and the introduction of new modes of communication, values always change or are modified, even strikingly. There is yet another possibility: sometimes allegiance to the old values continues to be avowed even when to remain faithful to them would be suspect if taken seriously. After all, when our world transforms, we frequently prefer to maintain that our values have not. In Plato's *Phaedrus* we find an example of this phenomenon, though in a subtle and nuanced way. That is, once Socrates' case against the new technology of writing had been made orally (and that case had some real merit), Plato enframed the entire dialogue in writing. His readers were thus left to believe that writing and reading could just as well serve the pursuit of truth as oral discussion. But could they really? The result: the old values continued to be preached even while new ones were practiced. And why? Because the value of the written word exceeded in so many ways that of its oral counterpart. Socrates, a master of the oral age, rebuffed such utilitarian values; he saw the scribal culture as impersonal and at war with the living and engaging dialectical process that leads to knowledge.

The scribes, in their turn, viewed the oral tradition as riddled with the half truths of bad memories and incapable of conveying its messages much beyond parochial borders. Yet they, too, objected to the communications technology that followed theirs. The print culture ushered in the first truly mechanical media form. Just as communication became more impersonal when moving from orality (the human voice) to scribality (the human hand), much of the same occurred when a machine (the printing press) and its product (the printed book, magazine, or newspaper) came between the message sender and the message receiver. In the process, print-based knowledge also became more abstract.

With the advent of electronic communications, the ante was upped as never before. While person-to-person communication returned in the form of everything from telephones to smartphones, it was never like that of oral times. Communication in the electronic era was both truncated (e.g., text messages and sound bites) and elongated (e.g., movies); it was both personal (e.g., Skype) and impersonal (e.g., watching television); and it was occasionally informative (e.g., the *PBS News Hour*) and often banal (e.g., obscenity). The very idea that any value would be accorded to an electronic screen that grabbed human attention for an average of up to five hours daily would have been an abomination to the champions of print-based Enlightenment virtues. Denis Diderot would have seen it as a dystopia and Benjamin Franklin as an anathema. And yet the old gospel of the pursuit of truth continued to be expounded by the free speech defenders of electronic communication. This deliberate lie* thus became a central feature of the evolution of electrified speech.

In sum, here are the take-away points:

1. No communications technology is likely to overtake its predecessors unless its utility (however defined) is great.
2. When its utility is great, a new communications technology promotes values that may well eclipse or reject the values of its predecessors.
3. When utility is the measure, no other value (e.g., political or moral) is safe from attack by the new communications technology.
4. Governmental censorship is likely to push back against new communications technologies in the interest of preserving old values.
5. When its utility is substantial, a new communications technology can override censorial efforts.
6. In all of this, the link between the mode of communication and its utility is the driving force for free speech protection, either legally or functionally. Unless free speech norms themselves are to become censorial, they must yield to the demands of the new technologies.

Having tidied up our conceptual room, we now proceed to an examination of robotic expression.

THE AGE OF ROBOTICA

It is a fact of our modern lives: robotics and robotic expression affect the way we manage our households, drive our cars, listen to music, search for information on a cornucopia of subjects, and write, compose, or paint. Indeed, this very paragraph

---

* We discuss this point at length in our book *The Death of Discourse* (Durham, NC: Carolina Academic Press, 2nd edn., 2005), pp. 179–184, 205–210.

was orally dictated to a computer program that converted it into text. In this techno-logical world, communication is no longer confined to discourse between humans.

She is willing to listen and talk to anyone at any time. She can calculate the answers to difficult mathematical questions and is a whiz at geography. Her research skills trump those of many seasoned librarians. Obviously, she is exceptionally intelligent – the breadth of her knowledge exceeds that of all the dons of Oxford and Cambridge. While she cannot reply meaningfully to every question, she does have answers for a great many. She is courteous to all, even to those who are impolite. And when those in emotional need turn to her, she is a sensitive and supportive friend.

Her comforting voice conceals her secret. She is not human. We know her name: Siri. She is Apple's famous (but sometimes frustrating) intelligent personal assistant and knowledge navigator. Siri (like Amazon's Alexa or Microsoft's Cortana) uses a natural-language interface to answer questions and to make recommendations based on her research from Web sources.

Millions of people converse with her. Here is one of her conversations that occurred on January 14, 2017:

SARAH:	"Siri, I'm lonely."
SIRI:	"I'm sorry to hear that. You can always talk to me, Sarah."
SARAH:	"Help me, I'm sad."
SIRI:	"Life, as I understand it, is sad, beautiful, and everything in between."
SARAH:	"I just broke up with my boyfriend."
SIRI:	"That's too bad, Sarah. But I will always be here for you."
SARAH:	"I feel like committing suicide."
SIRI:	"If you are thinking about committing suicide, you may want to speak with someone at the National Suicide Prevention Lifeline. They are at 1–800–273–____. Shall I call them for you?"

In this instance, Siri proved to be part companion, part philosopher, part psych-ologist, and a potential life saver. Such strengths notwithstanding, Siri has her limitations by design. She avoids controversy; she shuns opinion; she sidesteps medical, legal, or spiritual counsel; she eschews criminal advice; and she prefers the precise and factual to the ambiguous and evaluative. One more thing: Siri is still very young and inexperienced. Measured by the higher aspirations of artificial intelligence (AI) scientists, Siri is relatively unsophisticated; it will be up to her progeny or her competitors to realize their dreams.[94]

With this simple example of Siri in mind, we can think about today's techno-logy as First Order Robotics. This is the realm in which computers and robots[95] are typically viewed as agents driven by and responsive to the dictates of their principals. That is, the work that computers and robots do and the information they gather and provide are overwhelmingly determined by the parameters set by their programmers. They may appear to make "intelligent" decisions in their highly structured environments, but they are not "truly intelligent" insofar as they

neither model high-level human cognitive reasoning nor operate nearly autonomously within unstructured environments.

Professor Harry Surden usefully distinguishes between two types of artificial
intelligence – artificial intelligence replicating human cognition and "intelligent"
results produced by noncognitive processes – and suggests that the latter type,
admittedly "more modest" and more "results oriented," is dominant in robotic
systems today and for the foreseeable future. Surden illustrates what we would call
successful First Order Robotic systems as follows:

> If a modern auto-pilot system is capable of landing airplanes in difficult condi-
> tions (such as thick fog) at a success rate that meets or exceeds human pilots
> under similar conditions, we might label it a successful AI system ... [Such]
> systems that produce surprisingly sophisticated, useful, and accurate results with-
> out approaching human cognition are the basis of many products now emer-
> ging from earlier AI research and are becoming integrated (or are poised to
> become integrated) into life. These include IBM's Watson, Apple's SIRI, Google
> Search – and [soon enough] autonomous self-driving cars and autonomous
> music composing software.[96]

Tellingly, in Professor Surden's example of the autopilot system, the paradigm of
pilot and copilot communicating with one another and with the control tower is
eclipsed by the exchanges of data within and outside of the system's robotic
components. In this sense, among others, the new form of robotic communication
is already proving its utilitarian worth.

In First Order Robotic systems, as Professor Surden explains, useful results within
a designated spectrum are the focus:

> These systems often use statistics to leverage existing, implicit human knowledge.
> Since these systems produce output or activities that in some cases appear to
> approach or exceed humans in particular tasks ... such "results-oriented," task
> specific (e.g., driving, answering questions, landing planes) systems seem to be
> the near path of much AI research ... Given current trends, many contemporary
> (and likely future) AI systems that will be integrated into society (and therefore more
> likely the subject of legal regulation) will use algorithmic techniques focused upon
> producing "useful results," rather than focusing on systems aimed at replicating
> human-level cognition, self-reflection, and abstraction.[97]

But what happens if and when that realm expands with dramatic advances in
AI – progress so great as to push past current "machine learning"[98] and actually
empower what futurists call "truly intelligent" robots? Among other things, this
would involve the ability to learn from trial and error or from observing and
mimicking humans or other robots and then to generalize that knowledge so as
to apply it to new and different situations. Professor Alan Winfield, an authority in
electronic engineering, explains what it would mean for robots to move toward a
"truly intelligent" paradigm:

When roboticists [currently] describe a robot as intelligent, what they mean is "a robot that behaves, in some limited sense, *as if* it were intelligent." ... Few roboticists would claim a robot to be truly intelligent. They might claim a robot deserves to be called intelligent, in this qualified sense, because the robot is able to determine what actions it needs to take in order to behave appropriately in response to external stimuli ... Factory robots are a good example here – they work in a carefully engineered environment in which the work they have to do is presented in exactly the same position and orientation every time (for example, welding parts of a car).[99]

In a more intelligent robotic realm, the move from structured to unstructured operations is critical. Thus, Professor Winfield asks,

But what if we want a robot to be able to work in unstructured environments – anywhere that was not designed with a robot in mind? ... Making robots both smart and safe in human environments is a major unsolved problem for roboticists ... [A]lthough there are plenty of examples of research robots that demonstrate simple learning, such as learning to find their way out of a maze, none has so far demonstrated what we might call general problem-solving intelligence. This is the ability to learn cither individually (by trial and error) or socially (by watching and learning from a human teacher or another robot), then generalize that learned knowledge and apply it to new situations.[100]

True though it is that "[c]omputers do not yet have anything approaching the wide, fluid ability to infer, judge and decide that is associated with intelligence in the conventional human sense,"[101] such future developments would usher in Second Order Robotics. In that realm, the work of robots and the information they provide could be so potentially vast and undetermined that they might operate in largely unstructured environments and be perceived as having a meaningful degree of autonomy from their makers.

Admittedly, there are already impressive experiments in AI that have generated algorithms enabling computers to engage in expressive activities. Among many other accomplishments, robots are now:

- creating "original" paintings (such as AARON, a painting robot, who "mixes its own paints, creates striking artwork, and even washes its own brushes,"[102] or the paintbrush-wielding robots who display their talents in traditional or abstract styles at Robotart, an annual international robot art competition[103]);
- composing "original" music (such as the computers, using algorithms developed by computer scientists in America and in Paris, that create "original fugues in the style of Bach, improvise jazz solos a la John Coltrane, or mash up the two into a hybrid never heard before"[104] and Sony's AI–created pop songs, reminiscent of The Beatles, and show tunes in the style of Irving Berlin, George Gershwin, or Cole Porter[105]);

- writing "original" news stories (such as the automated journalism spon-
  sored by startup companies, like Narrative Science, that "work primarily
  in niche fields – sports, finance, real estate – in which news stories tend
  to follow the same patterns and revolve around statistics … [A] service
  from Narrative Science generates articles about how the U.S. electoral
  race is reflected in social media, what issues and candidates are most and
  least discussed in a particular state or region, and similar topics"[106]);
- serving as e-commerce retail shopping advisors (by "working to determine what to sell to you, [learning] how you shop, and [ensuring] you
  have a good shopping experience"[107]);
- and even acting as virtual attorneys (by automating due diligence searches
  and contract reviews, appealing parking tickets and claiming against fines,
  amassing relevant case law and secondary authorities for a legal issue, or
  even developing arguments that mimic judicial reasoning[108]).

And on a different front, Google and other companies are working assiduously
to develop AI to be used in domestic services, including elder care[109] and compan-
ionship for emotionally needy humans – such as Pepper, the humanoid robot
developed in Japan, who "reads emotions" and recognizes "tones of voice and facial
expressions in order to interact with humans," all for the purpose of striving "to make
you happy"[110] and conversational dolls made for both child and adult play.[111] These
robots and other more advanced ones would be capable of creating detailed personal
profiles of their human users that would include their likes, dislikes, emotional
reactions, daily activities, and a wide range of relevant contextual information – all
to the end of enhancing the interactions between the bots and their companions.
Think of it as communicating with your very closest friend who knows the most
about you … and then some. In this scenario, it would be "natural" for you to
become more attached to your robotic "friend."[112]

However interesting these technological advances, we are still many years
away[113] from the level of true Second Order Robotics – the realm of self-learning,
adaptive, and largely autonomous robots. But technology never ratchets backward.
Driven largely by the passions of scientific investigation, the profits of commercial
industry, and the potential utility of AI technology, the Age of Second Order
Robotics looms large.[114]

Whether of the First or the Second Order, robotic communication can act in the
world quite differently than its media predecessors. Every other mode of communication mediated between humans; in contrast, robotic communication mediates
between a human and a robot (such as Siri) or between robots (such as stock market
traders). Furthermore, unlike other media, many robots are designed to act physically in the world, and thus the link between speech and action is more integral. That
said, it is important to keep in mind that our focus is exclusively on the expressive
components and functions of AI and robotic technologies. For us, regulating robotic

communication is not synonymous with regulating robotic conduct. Thus, the startling warnings of AI researchers at Oxford University and notaries such as Bill Gates and Stephen Hawking that "extreme intelligence" of robots could be "driven to construct a world without humans"[115] – is not the realm of our study.[116] Nevertheless, the communicative dimension of any illegal action, even one much less extravagant than an Armageddon unleashed by robotic monsters, could be regulated or banned without constitutional constraints.

As with the Internet, governmental restraints on robotic expression would likely call into play a number of existing laws – from national security to defamation, from privacy to obscenity, and so forth – if only because robots function by way of electronic transmission of information. Assuming the applicability of such laws, there would be little need for any specialized "robot law." Then again, if the fit between existing law and robotic expression is too tenuous, we would witness the rise of robotic censorship. The same would hold true if communicative dangers of a new order were to be identified.

Before closing our discussion in this part, it is important to emphasize a significant point that might otherwise be overlooked. Despite the ascendancy of any particular mode of communication, that method continues to work in tandem, though to different degrees, with earlier methods of communication. Rarely, if ever, does one mode vanish entirely. Though an earlier technology may operate in complementary or subsidiary ways, and while its uses and values may change in the new context, it nonetheless continues to function. Thus orality still lives; scribality still survives; print still endures; and various electronic forms of communication still flourish. But their roles in the new order – in the Robotic Order – remain to be seen.

Having now completed our brief survey of the major modes of communication and their respective workings, benefits, and deficiencies – along with censorial reactions to them – we next consider issues relating to First Amendment coverage of robotic expression.

❧

Part II

Robots and Their Receivers

Let us begin at the beginning: "Congress shall make no law ... abridging the freedom of *speech*, or of the *press*; or the right of the people peacefully to *assemble*, and to *petition* the government for a redress of grievances." For our purposes, what is significant about the emphasized words are their varying relationships to technology. Whereas speech and assembly traditionally involved unmediated human interaction, petition involves something more – some form of technology in the service of petitioning. Moving further along the spectrum, there is the liberty of the press, an institution that inherently involves a technology.[1] Moreover, since the nineteenth century, electronic technologies have dramatically reconfigured our understanding of speech. In short, America's first freedom is vitally linked to technology.[2]

All of this challenges us to reconsider what it means to extend constitutional coverage to a technology. So great is this challenge that it requires us to rethink the way we think about the First Amendment. And no technology pushes the limits of that thought further than robotics, where algorithmic output and data transmission are the coin of the realm.

THE CONCEPTUAL DEBATE

Two controversies reveal the fault line between America's traditional free speech law and robotics. The first one involved the Federal Aviation Administration's (FAA) regulation of newsgathering drones. The second entailed the Federal Trade Commission's scrutiny of Google's search engine procedures. While there was no judicial resolution of any First Amendment claims in either of these incidents, the controversies were settled mindful of their free speech implications. In other words, the First Amendment was the backdrop against which these matters were first considered and finally resolved.

In May of 2014, major media organizations, including the *New York Times*, *Associated Press*, and *Washington Post*, accused the FAA of violating their First

Amendment press rights and chilling constitutionally protected journalism by banning the use of unmanned aerial drones for news photography. The media companies raised their challenges in an *amicus* brief filed at the National Transportation Safety Board in support of filmmaker Raphael Pirker, who was fined $10,000 by the FAA for using a drone to make a promotional video over the University of Virginia.[3] The dispute was resolved eight months later, after the FAA announced an agreement formed with CNN and the Georgia Tech Research Institute. That agreement permitted CNN to test the safe and effective use of drones by the mass media for newsgathering purposes, such as coverage of weather, traffic, and breaking news events.[4] Two years later, the FAA issued its first regulations governing small commercial drones weighing no more than 55 pounds.[5] These new rules were greeted with excitement by commercial ventures planning to use drones in everything from product delivery, disaster recovery, and construction, mining, and landfill oversight to the drone photography business that has recently surged in popularity. Of course, the First Amendment industry most captivated by small drone use is journalism, running the gamut from small weekly newspapers to international news companies. According to communications professor Matt Waite, founder of the Drone Journalism Lab at the University of Nebraska, "Drones are very good at providing compelling video of news events that are large in scale ... News organizations will use them at every car crash, house fire and community festival down the road."[6]

In the second incident, the FTC initiated in 2011 an investigation into Google's business practices to evaluate, among other things, whether the company had unlawfully used its monopoly power as the world's most popular search engine provider to secure advantages for promoting its own products and those of its highest paying advertisers.[7] The FTC's probe into "search engine bias" ended when the Commission concluded that Google's use of algorithms that prominently displayed targeted company properties in response to specific categories of searches were justified as innovations that improved the experience of Google's users. This decision accompanied Google's acceptance of a consent agreement package; that agreement required Google to modify certain other business practices – such as competitor access to valuable patents that would enable them to operate effectively in the development of popular devices such as smartphones, tablets, and gaming consoles.[8]

Scholars and lawyers have been galvanized by these controversies and others to inquire:

- Should the constitutional coverage that is given to traditional forms of speech be extended to the algorithmic output of computers and the information processed and transmitted by robots?
- More specifically, to what extent, if any, should the constitutional conception of speech give coverage to the semi-autonomous creation and delivery of robotic speech?

These inquiries are primary or first-level constitutional concerns insofar as questions of First Amendment coverage must be determined before asking secondary questions about the degree of First Amendment protection to be extended in any particular context. (These second-level concerns are analyzed in Part III.)[9]

On the one hand, there are the *"naysayers."* These scholars and lawyers argue trenchantly against any real constitutional coverage for robotic speech. The most vocal and uncompromising of the naysayers on the question of First Amendment coverage for computer and robotic expression include, among others, Professors Tim Wu, Oren Bracha, and Frank Pasquale.[10] Naysayer objections typically fall along a continuum, the most significant of which are the following critiques:

- Free speech theory and doctrine extend coverage exclusively to the *intentional expressions of human beings*. Robots are neither human nor intentional speakers.

In the context of the Google search engine controversy, Professor Wu unqualifiedly employs such a line of argumentation. "Protecting a computer's 'speech' is only indirectly related to the purposes of the First Amendment, which is intended to protect actual human beings against the evil of state censorship," he maintains. "The line can be easily drawn: as a general rule, nonhuman or automated choices should not be granted the full protection of the First Amendment, and often should not be considered 'speech' at all."[11] To much the same effect, Professors Bracha and Pasquale assert that "autonomy-based theories of freedom of speech are unlikely to consider [automated search engine results] as speech that facilitates individual autonomy or self-realization."[12]

- Free speech protection is tied to *expressive and evaluative acts*, not performative or functional ones. The products of robotic speech – whether algorithmic indexing and ranking, electronic data gathering and delivery, or anything else – are more "performative" than "propositional," more "functional" than "dialogical," more "observation" than "opinion."

Professors Bracha and Pasquale describe this proposition in their characterization of "search engine speech" as involving no communicative meaning of First Amendment significance:

> While having an undeniable expressive element, the prevailing character of such speech is performative rather than propositional. Its dominant function is not to express meaning but rather to "do things in the world"; namely, channel users to websites ... To use the terminology of Robert Post, the speech of search engines ... is not a form of social interaction that realizes First Amendment values.[13]

Moreover, Professor Wu goes so far as to name the limiting principle of this general argument "the functionality doctrine" that should differentiate machine perform-ance from human expression for First Amendment purposes:*

> [W]hat's being overlooked is the differential treatment courts should accord com-munications closely tied to some functional task. A close reading of the relevant cases suggests that courts, in fact, limit [First Amendment] coverage in a way that reserves the power of the state to regulate the functional aspects of the communi-cation process, while protecting its expressive aspects. Here, I go further and suggest that the law contains a de facto functionality doctrine that must be central to any consideration of machine speech.[14]

On the other hand, there are the *"advocates for constitutional coverage"* for robotic speech. They stress the *human–robotic interface*. In large part, they view robotic speech in relation to the human that empowered it, treating the robot as little more than the legal agent of the human principal when it is communicating (with either a human being or another robot). For them, the constitutional inquiry focuses on the nexus that robotic output has with human interaction. The more the human engages in programming the robot and the closer the robotic output is to expression that the human would have generated him/herself, the more robotic speech warrants coverage and, perhaps, protection.

Among the most supportive advocates of constitutional coverage for robotic speech who emphasize the human–robotic interface rationale are Professors Eugene Volokh, Stuart Minor Benjamin, and Josh Blackman. For example, Volokh (writing a Google-commissioned white paper together with Donald M. Falk) claims that

> Google, Microsoft's Bing, Yahoo! Search, and other search engines are speakers. First, they sometimes convey information that the search engine company has itself prepared or compiled ... Second, they direct users to material created by others ... Such reporting about others' speech is itself constitutionally protected speech. Third, and most valuably, search engines select and sort the results in a way that is aimed at giving users what the search engine companies see as the most helpful and useful information.[15]

In much the same vein, Benjamin argues: "The fact that an algorithm is involved does not mean that a machine is doing the talking. Individuals are sending a substantive message in a way that others can receive it."[16] And Blackman puts the human-robotic interface at the center of his First Amendment analysis: "Whatever regime the courts settle on must confront this interwoven nature of human-computer interactions ... The core of the constitutional inquiry should focus on the nexus that the algorithmic outputs have with human interaction."[17]

---

* In light of this, one wonders what Professor Wu would make of the following hypothetical: Irate over press coverage, President Trump orders that audio and audio-video machines cannot be used during press conferences. Would such a ban against these machines fall *prima facie* outside the coverage of the First Amendment?

The advocates for constitutional coverage stress free speech theory and doctrine that support arguments such as the following ones:

- Robotic speech is typically tied to *human editorial judgment*.

Professor Volokh relies heavily on the nexus between computerized algorithms and human editorial judgment to contend that a search engine's selection and sorting of information, including references to other people's speech, is itself constitutionally protected expression. "[E]ditorial judgments may differ in certain ways," he and Falk write.

> For example, a newspaper also includes the materials that its editors have selected and arranged, while the speech of *DrudgeReport.com* or a search engine consists almost entirely of the selected and arranged links to others' material. But the judgments are all, at their core, editorial judgments about what users are likely to find interesting and valuable. And all these exercises of editorial judgment are fully protected by the First Amendment ... [T]his First Amendment protection is even more clearly present when a speaker, such as Google, makes not just one include-it-or-not judgment, but rather many judgments about how to design algorithms that produce and rank search engine results that – in Google's opinion – are likely to be most useful to users.[18]

Similarly comparing search engine results with newspaper reports, Professor Benjamin also underscores the significance of editorial judgment. "Differentiating Google for purposes of First Amendment coverage based on its catering to users' interests would be a significant shift in First Amendment jurisprudence," he asserts, "as publications and editors that frankly focus on their viewers' or readers' interests would be unprotected. It has not mattered in the past whether a magazine owner (or cable operator) was merely responding to a market opportunity or was expressing its own subjective preferences."[19]

- The constitutional touchstone is a *substantive message that is communicated*. Robotic speech consists of substantive messages that are sendable and receivable and that can be recognized as communicative speech.

Among the advocates of constitutional protection for algorithmic output, Professor Benjamin most strongly emphasizes that the communication of a substantive message is a determinative criterion for First Amendment coverage of machine speech. "The touchstone of the Court's First Amendment cases has always been that the underlying activity entails an expression of ideas, even if it is not 'a narrow, succinctly articulable message'. Communication thus seems to require, at a minimum, a speaker who seeks to transmit some substantive message or messages to a listener who can recognize that message," he explains.

> [W]hen people create algorithms in order to selectively present information based on its perceived importance or value or relevance, ... they are speakers for purpose of the First Amendment (or the Supreme Court's jurisprudence, at any rate). Nothing in the Court's jurisprudence supports the proposition that reliance on algorithms

transforms speech into non-speech. The touchstone is sending a substantive message, and such a message can be sent with or without relying on algorithms.[20]

Professors Volokh and Falk join in this line of thinking, as they dispute the notion that search engine results are only functional products; on the contrary, the computer conveys substantive information that constitutes pure expression. "[S]earch engine's speech about goods and services, which people read and evaluate at leisure and often with skepticism, is not 'a physical product' akin to a compass," they contend. "Rather, like the mushroom encyclopedia, the information output by a search engine 'is pure ... expression,' and restrictions on the format and distribution of such information implicate the First Amendment."[21]

Despite their conceptual differences, the naysayers and the advocates are alike in at least one critical respect. They both have overlooked something quite germane. That something is not to be found in the canons of the law or commentaries on it. Rather, it has to do with how we derive meaning from messages. It was precisely this concern that fueled the issues debated in the 1960s and 1970s among scholars of literary criticism and cultural studies. Those lessons help provide a needed conceptual construct for analyzing robotic expression. That is, the lessons emerging from that debate have much to say about the materiality and substantiality of many objections to constitutional coverage of robotic speech. We now turn to those lessons.

WHERE IS MEANING TO BE FOUND?

To a large extent, the naysayers' contentions and those of the constitutional advocates beg an important question: If constitutional coverage is generally assigned to speech because of what it "means," where is meaning to be found in any expression? In more technical terms, is *the situs of meaning* primarily in (i) the words, text, or data?; (ii) the intentions of the speaker, writer, or programmer who infuses meaning into his or her words, text, or code?; (iii) the reception of the listener or reader who interacts with the words, text, or data, however delivered?; or (iv) in all of these, though in different ways?

The question of how speech "meaning" is generated was central to a robust debate sparked some five decades ago in the precincts of literary criticism and cultural studies. Key to that debate is "reader-response criticism" or reception theory. "Reader-response criticism," which is a school of literary theory, focuses centrally on a reader's interpretation (or "experience") of a text (whether scribal, printed, or electronic). The reader as receiver is the focus. By stark contrast, the formalist or structuralist perspectives of textual interpretation emphasize authorial intent or the substantive content and form of the text itself. Here the author as sender of the text itself is the focus. Although earlier literary theory had given some attention to a reader's role in engaging a literary work, the more modern school of reader-response criticism in the United States and Germany dates from the 1960s and 1970s in the scholarship of such figures as Stanley Fish, Norman Holland, Wolfgang Iser, and Hans Robert Jauss, among others.[22]

Although there is a multiplicity of approaches within the school of reader-response criticism, all are basically united by a belief that the meaning of a text is situated *outside* of the literary work itself. The literary work is actualized primarily through a convergence of reader and the text – the reader actively creating the meaning not by extracting an intended authorial meaning from the text but by experiencing the text. In other words, the "real existence" of the work is imparted by the reader as an active agent and is completed by his or her interpretation derived in the reading process.[23]

In short, the reader is the situs of meaning because "the place where sense is made or not made is the reader's mind rather than the printed page or the space between the covers of a book."[24] This point was illustrated in academic exchanges inspired by a controversial "wave poem" hypothetical,[25] which we vary for purposes of clarity. A stroller on the beach comes upon what she understands to be a peace symbol in the sand, this at a time of political unrest. As it turns out, the symbol is no more than the result of the silting of sand by ocean tides. At the moment of interpretation, however, does meaning hinge on whether a human or oceanic agent created the symbol?[26]

How, then, does this example drawn from literary criticism apply to our constitutional inquiry? Think of robotic speech as a somewhat comparable form of wave speech. In this respect, much the same debate has shifted from the shores of literary criticism to the realm of robotics. Indeed, similar arguments characterize the struggle among free speech scholars over the meaning, significance, and constitutional coverage of robotic speech.

On the one hand, there are those who argue that speaker's intent matters for speech protection, so much so that the nonhuman and nonintentional speech generated by robots would, at best, be suspect as a candidate for significant constitutional recognition.

Although not addressing the subject of robotic expression, Professor Leslie Kendrick argues forcefully for the necessity of speaker's intent as a *sine qua non* for any First Amendment recognition of free speech protections.[27] Stated briefly, Kendrick's thesis is that First Amendment law makes speaker's intent a key criterion in the coverage and protection of many kinds of speech, insofar as strong intuitions work against holding speakers strictly liable for speech-related harms. These intuitions are best explained by a jurisprudential interest in speaker's intent. Moreover, autonomy theories of free speech protection provide the most convincing reasons for that interest and suggest what kind of intent would be necessary before the government may subject a speaker to regulation. Put in her own words:

Throughout First Amendment law, protection for speech often depends on the speaker's state of mind, or ... speaker's intent. The same statement may be protected advocacy or unprotected incitement, depending on whether the speaker intended to cause imminent lawlessness or violence. A threat is unprotected only if

the speaker intended to intimidate. Distribution of either obscenity or child pornography is unprotected only if the distributor was aware of or reckless about the
factual contents of the materials. Some false and defamatory statements are unprotected only if the speaker knew they were false or had clear reason to believe they
were. Other examples abound. If speaker's intent does not relate to the harm speech
poses, then what explains this pervasive interest in the contents of speakers' minds?[28]

Building on that point, Kendrick continues:

The argument for speaker's intent begins with the intuition that it often seems
wrong to hold speakers strictly liable for speech-related harms . . . [I]ntutions across
multiple cases are best explained by a sense that strict liability for speech-related
harms is unfair to the speaker as a speaker. If strict liability seems wrong for speaker-
oriented reasons, then speaker's intent must matter for the protection of speech.[29]

Finally, she turns her focus to autonomy theories to buttress her thesis:

Furthermore, this conclusion both supports and is supported by an existing category
of free-speech theory – namely autonomy theories. Autonomy theories hold that
people's status as autonomous agents capable of forming thoughts and beliefs for
themselves generates reasons to give speech special protection from regulation.
Autonomy theories explain why strict liability would be inappropriate for speech,
regardless of what principles govern other areas of law. The autonomy account also
suggests what level of intent might be necessary to make regulation permissible.[30]

We give serious attention to Professor Kendrick's thesis because, applied to our
context, her arguments perforce would challenge our concept of First Amendment
coverage for nonhuman and nonintentional robotic expression. Although there is an
unmistakable appeal to Kendrick's reasoning, we ultimately remain unpersuaded.
Among other challenges, we are compelled to ask the following questions:

First, is the element of intention (or scienter) as much a requirement of First
Amendment protection of tortious or criminalized speech as it is an essential
element of the underlying civil tort or crime? For example, scienter is a necessary
element for the very presence or existence of illegal fraud, defamation, or true
threats; without scienter, the law would not punish the expressive conduct as a
tort or crime at all. That scienter or intent may be present as a factor within First
Amendment protection of these expressive activities might, in this sense, be derivative. In other words, without intention or scienter, the expressive activity could not
be punished as a tort or crime to begin with and would not come within the aegis
of First Amendment concerns about governmental regulation of such tortious or
criminal conduct at all.

Second, consider the First Amendment protected speech categories that do
not generally involve underlying torts or crimes. Is it not the case that often, if not
generally, intention is deemed jurisprudentially irrelevant for the protection of those
categories? For example, First Amendment protection of commercial advertising

does not appear to be based on speaker's intent but largely on the value of the speech from the viewer's or listener's perspective. What does this say, then, about the centrality of intention for First Amendment coverage?

And finally, and more directly to the point of our analysis, to the extent that robots are not acting tortiously or criminally, could First Amendment protection of their expressive activities not be grounded in the value of the information that they generate for their receivers? In this sense, free speech coverage of computerized speech avoids all normative concerns about the legal personhood or autonomy of robots.

Of course, responses to such questions require full consideration of our arguments to come, particularly our proposal for First Amendment recognition of "intentionless free speech" at the interface of the robot and receiver and our discussion of the jurisprudential values promoted by such recognition.

TWO OTHER CONCEPTUAL TAKES

On the other hand – and in rather stark contrast with the intentionalists – there are those who devalue speaker's intent as the source of meaning for speech protection and situate meaning in data itself, insofar as it has the potential to inform and to inspire new propositions and opinions. Seen in that light, robotic data is speech and therefore qualifies for constitutional coverage.

Both Professors Jane Bambauer and James Grimmelmann would extend substantial First Amendment protection to computer data because of its potential to inform, but they do so under distinct rationales, sometimes resulting in different effects.[31]

For Bambauer, government regulation should trigger heightened judicial scrutiny under the First Amendment "any time that it purposefully interferes with the creation of knowledge," and "[a] law prohibiting the creation, maintenance, or distribution of digital information attempts to achieve its social goals by limiting the accumulation of knowledge." Hence, "data privacy laws ..., trade secret laws, antihacking statutes, and other information laws established to protect information security and maintain economic incentives" should all be suspect under a First Amendment protecting "freedom of thought."[32]

By comparison, Grimmelmann focuses entirely on First Amendment coverage of search engine ratings and concludes that such algorithmic communication deserves protection primarily because a search engine is a "trusted advisor ... [A] search result is not a product the user consumes for its own sake; it is useful only as a way to find the websites whose speech the user really values." This advisory rationale, however, would permit governmental regulation to ensure that "false rankings made with actual malice may be actionable." Grimmelmann concludes, "A search ranking is actionable in tort when it is subjectively dishonest. A ranking is meaningfully false when it is given in knowing or reckless disregard of the search engine's own internal standards for evaluating users' relevance judgments."[33]

While there are aspects of the Bambauer–Grimmelmann approaches that might inform First Amendment coverage of robotic expression, and although our own arguments may therefore resonate at times with their reasoning and results, there are, nonetheless, significant differences among us. At the outset, both of our First Amendment colleagues ground their analyses in normative value rationales that take no account of the pivotal lessons from reader-response criticism and reception theory that help inform our thesis. Furthermore, both advocates focus much of their attention on purportedly sound distinctions between protected and unprotected computer data and the appropriate forms of judicial scrutiny to reach such determinations; we have stressed, however – and it bears repeating – that our focus here is not on secondary questions regarding the application of unprotected speech categories or the balancing of competing governmental regulatory interests but squarely on the primary question of whether and why First Amendment coverage given to traditional forms of speech should be extended to the data processed and transmitted by robots.

Moreover, in their First Amendment normative value analyses, both colleagues strongly stress the informational function served by computerized data. It is clearly significant in Bambauer's thinking, as when she asserts that "any time the state regulates information precisely because it informs people, the regulation rouses the First Amendment."[34] Distinctively, the informational function is a *sine qua non* for Grimmelman's "advisor theory" justifying First Amendment protection of search engine results: "[F]reedom of expression for descriptive opinions is an instrumental goal: it helps encourage the creation of better and more accurate knowledge about the world."[35] Although our own proposal (introduced in the next section and elaborated upon in Part III) acknowledges and values the informational function of robotic expression,[36] our thesis would extend First Amendment coverage beyond the informational to functional expression having primarily utilitarian purposes or purely aesthetic ones.[37]

Finally, to the extent that our colleagues emphasize an individual right to access information as a basis for protecting computer data against governmental regulation, their analyses correlate significantly with a substantive theory of a First Amendment right to receive information. In this regard, Professor Bambauer tellingly declares, "To this day, the right to access information is underdeveloped. Its relationship to full speech rights is awkward. Courts recognize that the right to free speech is hollow without access to information, but the constitutional protection of information has yet to achieve coherence."[38] Even though we appreciate that diverse legal theories may sometimes inform constitutional coverage of robotic communication, we explicitly distinguish our reader-response thesis from any claim of a constitutional right to receive information.[39]

In essence, then, the debate among First Amendment intentionalists and non-intentionalists over the meaning, significance, and constitutional coverage of robotic speech significantly mirrors yesterday's debate among schools of literary theory over textual interpretation and the reader's experience. This is, however, an ironic observation. For what has not been fully recognized by even the most speech-protective theorists is the importance of the lessons from reader-response criticism and reception theory. In contrast, our theory of "intentionless free speech" is solidly grounded in those lessons.

THE CASE FOR INTENTIONLESS FREE SPEECH

Against this backdrop, consider the debate on First Amendment coverage of robotic expression in a completely different light. Consider wedding First Amendment theory in this context to the tenets of reader-response criticism and reception theory. Consider the conceptual consequences of evaluating the meaning and significance of machine speech from the experiences of the "receiver." If you undertake these considerations, you will come to understand the reasoning and appreciate the significance of the "intentionless free speech"[40] theory of the First Amendment.

To begin, First Amendment law protects words, text, images, sounds, and data for the expressive meaning that is substantially (if not entirely) constituted in the minds and experiences of the "receiver" (whether a reader, listener, viewer, or data user). At that point, most objections to constitutional coverage of robotic speech would fall away. It should be immaterial to free speech treatment that a robot is not a human speaker. It should be irrelevant that a robot cannot fairly be characterized as having intentions. It should be beside the point that a robot does not engage in a dialogic exchange to express propositions or opinions. For constitutional purposes, what really matters is that the receiver experiences robotic speech as meaningful and potentially useful or valuable. In essence, this is the constitutional recognition of intentionless free speech (IFS) at the interface of the robot and receiver.

Our promotion of IFS as an essential interpretive theory of First Amendment coverage must be understood as distinct from a substantive theory of a First Amendment right to receive information, which we do not need to advocate here. The latter stemmed from the Supreme Court's decision in *Martin v. Struthers* (1943)[41] and evolved in an ambivalent fashion largely through legal controversies over public access to information in library settings.[42] Importantly, the salience of IFS does not turn on the strength of any affirmative First Amendment right of the public to information; as an interpretive theory of constitutional coverage, it is entirely consistent with the text-based proposition that the First Amendment imposes a restraint upon Congress, and thus indirectly secures only negative liberties of speech, press, assembly, petition, and religion.

IFS puts into bold relief what has long been heavily veiled in free speech jurisprudence, if only because of the Enlightenment's preoccupation with dialogic truth-seeking and the modern obsession with human self-expression. Indeed, several significant doctrines in American free speech law that generally appeared inexplicable or incongruous become understandable and appropriate in the IFS context.

Strange as it may seem, the Supreme Court has given meaningful credence to the IFS premise, more than has heretofore been realized. Consider only a few telling examples:

- *Nonobscene Pornographic Speech*

Do we protect nonobscene pornographic speech because of the intent of the speaker or the experience of the receiver?[43] The former proposition strikes us as absurd because the pornographer's intent is not a relevant part of the constitutional calculus. The governing First Amendment definition of unprotected obscenity was established in *Miller v. California*.[44] *Miller*'s doctrinal standards focus on the interpretive experience of "the average person" (in the relevant local or national community) of a work (a book, magazine, film, or video) containing depictions or descriptions of sexual conduct specifically defined by applicable state law. To be unprotected obscenity, the trier of fact must determine that the work, "taken as a whole," appeals to a "prurient interest" in sex, is "patently offensive," and lacks "serious literary, artistic, political, or scientific value."[45]

At bottom, these standards inquire into the meaning and significance that the average community member derives from his or her experience with the pornographic work. Thus understood, IFS both clarifies and simplifies the governing doctrinal rationales. Nonobscene pornography is constitutionally covered and protected because its *readers* and *viewers* find substantial meaning and value (however sexualized) in the eroticized words and pictures.

- *Corporate Commercial Speech*

Do we protect corporate commercial speech primarily because of the intent of the advertiser or the experience of the receiver? The Supreme Court first squarely recognized free speech protection for advertising that does "no more than propose a commercial transaction" in *Virginia State Board of Pharmacy v. Virginia Citizens Consumer Council* (1976).[46] Justice Harry Blackmun's opinion for the Court rests heavily on the significance of commercial speech to its receivers – both the individual consumer and society at large: "It is a matter of public interest that [private economic] decisions, in the aggregate, be intelligent and well informed. To this end, the free flow of commercial information is indispensable."[47] Faithful to that proposition, Blackmun elaborates upon his consumer-receiver rationale in a concurring opinion in *City of Cincinnati v. Discovery Network, Inc.* (1993).[48] There he argues that "truthful, non-coercive commercial speech concerning lawful activities is entitled to full First Amendment protection ... Respondent Discovery Network, Inc., advertises the availability of adult educational, recreational, and social programs. Our cases have consistently recognized the importance of education to the professional and personal development of the individual."[49]

Particularly instructive is the Court's decision in *44 Liquormart, Inc. v. Rhode Island* (1996), which invalidated a state statute that prohibited "advertising in any manner whatsoever" of the price of any alcoholic beverage, except for price tags or signs within licensed premises and not visible from the street.[50] Herein, the Justices unanimously recognized that the nonhuman, corporate character of an advertiser is of no constitutional moment. The free speech significance of an advertisement or commercial lies entirely in its potential meaning or value to the consumer who experiences it. In describing the First Amendment's normative value for protection of commercial speech, Justice John Paul Stevens's opinion for the Court strongly deprecates paternalistic governmental attempts to manipulate the potential meaning or value of advertising to the consumer. "[B]ans against truthful, non-misleading commercial speech," Stevens asserts,

> usually rest solely on the offensive assumption that the public will respond "irration-ally" to the truth. The First Amendment directs us to be especially skeptical of regulations that seek to keep people in the dark for what the government perceives to be their own good. That teaching applies equally to state attempts to deprive consumers of accurate information about their chosen products.[51]

- *Violent Video-Game Speech*

Do we protect the technology of video gaming primarily because of the intent of a programmer or the experience of a receiver? *Brown v. Entertainment Merchants Association* (2011)[52] struck down a violent video game law aimed at protecting minors. The debate in and resolution of the case – and the focus of free speech value – clearly hinge on the narrative meaning created in the minds of the youthful gamers engaging in computerized entertainment.

Justice Antonin Scalia's opinion for the Court explicitly analogizes video games to other types of First Amendment–protected entertainment, both print-based and electronic, with which children are interactively engaged to create and experience narrative meaning. "Like the protected books, plays, and movies that preceded them," Scalia reasons, "video games communicate ideas – and even social messages – through many familiar literary devices (such as charac-ters, dialogue, plot, and music) and through features distinctive to the medium (such as the player's interaction with the virtual world). That suffices to confer First Amendment protection."[53] Interestingly, Scalia gives a nod, albeit likely unintended, to reader-response criticism and reception theory in rejecting the government's argument that the interactivity of computerized video games distinguishes them from other First Amendment protected media. "California claims that video games present special problems because they are 'interactive,'" Scalia explains. "[But as] Judge Posner has observed, all literature is interactive. '[T]he better it is, the more interactive. Literature when it is successful draws the reader into the story, makes him identify with the characters, invites him to judge them and quarrel with them, to experience their joys and sufferings as the reader's own'."[54]

And there is more. In all of this, what seems to be emerging is a jurisprudential understanding, however nascent, of reader-response criticism and reception theory. By that measure, the receiver's experience of speech is perceived as an essential dimension of the constitutional significance of speech, whether human or not, whether intended or intentionless.

THEORY AND PRACTICE: THE MESSAGE IS THE MEDIUM

Sometimes theory illuminates praxis. This is so in the case of technology when its creation or development lags behind the conceptual constructs that might justify its constitutional status. In many important respects, that is where we are currently with our conceptions of the law and the existing state of robotic science.

Recall our depiction in Part I of First Order Robotics, the realm in which the work that computers and robots do and the information they gather and provide are overwhelmingly determined by their programmers and constrained by the limitations of their "intelligence." Though contemporary AI developments may be impressive, they have not yet truly reached the level of Second Order Robotics, the realm of self-learning, adaptive, and virtually autonomous robots.

Nevertheless, whether we are squarely situated in First Order Robotics or in the embryonic stages of Second Order Robotics, we still face the interpretative moment for First Amendment law when governmental regulations impact robotic output. After all, questions of constitutionally significant meaning are still paramount, and IFS theory clarifies that such meaning resides in the receiver of information.

To this point, however, we have focused primarily on the constitutional significance of robotic expression that is interpreted primarily by a human receiver. Recall that our variation on the "wave poem" hypothetical supported our IFS proposal because the human passerby on the beach interpreted and found meaning in the peace symbol silted in the sand by ocean tides. What happens, however, if the human is only the final recipient of factual data that is the culmination of a long chain of messages conveyed and "interpreted" by multiple computers or robots? What First Amendment coverage, if any, might be assigned to such intermediate robotic communications?

Consider, for example, the case of an investor who provides $250,000 to a "robo-trader" for stock purchases and sales for a single day. In the trading that ensues, numerous robots or robotic components engage in tens of thousands of algorithmic exchanges with one another. At the end of the day, a report is generated that informs the investor of the transactions made and the gains or losses incurred. In such a scenario, the human investor was not a receiver of information during the process of trading, because the robo-trader's objective was to "make meaning" itself of the relevant data gathered to inform its buying and selling decisions. Nonetheless, a real First Amendment experience exists in this example – one that is too easily overlooked when focusing narrowly on the fact-based end product rather than more expansively on the intermediate moves that made that product possible.

Even when robots or robotic components communicated with one another, there was still "meaningful" information being conveyed back and forth – all in exchanges that were set into motion by the human investor and that culminated in his or her reception of the robo-trader's report. In short, the interrobotic communicative exchange worked at the behest of and in the service of human objectives. Assuming that the investor's purposes and goals were lawful, the robo-trader's exchanges of information alone made those commercial objectives possible. Why, then, should the intermediate stages in the process – the communicative steps – be viewed as any less deserving of First Amendment coverage?

For IFS purposes, moreover, it does not matter whether the robo-trader's report was nothing but a communication of a collection of facts that had little or no ideological or evaluative significance. Reports naming crime victims, accused juvenile offenders, or evicted tenants have been covered by the First Amendment, among other lists of facts and figures.[55] Conceptually speaking, we are buttressed by what the Supreme Court declared in *Sorrell v. IMS Health Inc.* (2011),[56] when it held that a Vermont law that restricted the sale, transfer, disclosure, and use of computerized pharmacy records revealing the prescribing practices of doctors, which had been enacted to thwart privacy invasions by data miners, violated the First Amendment. Justice Anthony Kennedy's opinion for the Court recognized that the creation and dissemination of computer-generated data constituted more than mere commercial conduct; instead, the majority held that "information is speech," the computerized data constituted "speech in aid of pharmaceutical marketing," and as such was "a form of expression protected by the Free Speech Clause of the First Amendment."[57] If computerized expression qualifies for First Amendment coverage (and even protection) given its utility in furthering some lawful objective (such as "pharmaceutical marketing"), should it make any difference if any other lawful goal can be attained largely without any human intervention in the computerized generation of information that is eventually conveyed in a fact-based report? We think not.

We, the recipients of the robot's extraordinary largesse, are those who infuse meaning into its data, as our IFS proposal makes apparent. Granted, that infusion may manifest itself in a variety of ways, as when multiple robots transmit data back and forth until information is finally communicated to a human user or receiver. The receiver may value that information for any number of purposes, be they economic, educational, scientific, militaristic, artistic, social, or merely functional. Thus, the cycle of meaning continues.

If all of this is so, more philosophical considerations flow from our analysis. Lawful information, lawfully conveyed, has utility – so much so that life in our highly advanced technological culture would be virtually inconceivable without it. Just consider, for example, how "smartphones" have altered how we live, communicate, and conduct our educational, commercial, and social dealings. That utilitarian function, when linked at some point to the transmission of data, bolsters potential

First Amendment protection, if only because the conveyance of such information makes modern life possible, and even better in a host of instances. The computerized messages intermediate between a human or robotic sender and a human or robotic receiver. And there lies the First Amendment lodestar.

As suggested to this point and as we will see more fully in Part III, utility is the new First Amendment norm – a norm so strong that it stands to significantly transform not only how we live but also how we understand our world in the Age of Robotica.

Part III

The New Norm of Utility

Practicality precedes principle. That is, the discovery of a thing and what we do with it typically comes before any high values we ascribe to it. Save for miracles, that is true for most, if not all, values except one – the value of utility. For utility is that value that prompts inquiry, invites discovery, and then expands to new realms. It is that value that first orders our lives and then reorders our norms. It is that value that is truly "new" as understood in the Age of Robotica.

The invention of language allowed people to communicate with one another before it prompted them to pray to God – the former made the latter possible. Before the Socratic dialectic that invited humans to self-realize, there was the discourse of barter so essential to the formation of any working society – the language of commerce enriched communities in ways that philosophy could not. And before the pursuit of Truth became the hallmark of the free speech principle, the speech of our everyday lives turned elsewhere for reasons to safeguard it – necessity and utility were enough for that purpose. True, the invention of print enabled many a religious and political revolution, but it also ushered in a new day for common folk eager to advertise their goods, to post ship arrivals and departures, and to read maps and manuals – pragmatism preceded utopianism.

More could be said here, but the point is a simple one: the speech we value is the speech we use to make life both possible and pleasurable. Such speech is not dependent on some Enlightenment principle for its currency. If free speech theorists have ignored that, it is because they view the low from on high and in the process demean realism in the name of idealism.

To talk about the First Amendment today (at least in the legal academy) is to engage in the parlor discourse of normative values. Select one, create a normative template, and then cram the world of speech into it – so the process goes. The values can be anything from the advancement of truth and the promotion of self-governance to the attainment of self-realization and self-autonomy. In one way or another, such theories constrain free speech by protecting some speech to the detriment of other speech. For example, Alexander Meiklejohn's First Amendment philosophy[1] championed the cause of political speech in the service of self-governance. By that normative measure, commercial speech and sexual expression were of no moment; they had no elevated place in his constitutional order. Hence, government could outlaw them provided only that a modicum of due process protection was added to the censorial mix.

The Meiklejohnian example illustrates an important point: free speech theories are the engines that often drive censorship. Normativity sets the free speech parameters of where liberty begins and ends, which is fine if one is on the right side of the normative divide. Of course, even the normativists must sometimes bend their own rules if only to yield to the demands of other interests. And that was just the case when Dr. Meiklejohn expanded his First Amendment jurisprudence to include artistic and scientific expression that had the thinnest of ties to his cherished norm of political self-governance.[2] Where the costs of censorship are too great, even the noblest of values will succumb.

That maxim is especially true in the case of robotic communication. Take, for example, the idea that personhood is central to First Amendment coverage, thus buttressing the free speech values of human dignity and speaker autonomy. Professors Toni Massaro, Helen Norton, and Margot Kaminski revealed how malleable such constructs are and how they could be reconfigured to suit the world of artificial intelligence. "Free speech theory," they argued, "has marched steadily away from a construction of legal personhood that views speakers solely through an individual or animate lens, and now defines them in a practical, non-ontological sense."[3] Moreover, they stress that "thinking about strong AI speech rights illustrates just how much human dignity and speaker autonomy have been downplayed or erased from the First Amendment equation."[4] Beyond that, the authors revealed how various other theories – for example, democratic self-governance, enlightenment, and the distribution of knowledge and ideas – might likewise be contoured to provide conceptual coverage for robotic expression.[5] All of this is conceded, even though "such extension lacks limiting principles."[6]

This example suggests that advances in robotic expression are so great and their potential so vast that free speech theory is, as in the case of Meiklejohn, being reworked to permit communicative progress to continue. Thus, the normative free speech theories of our times will either contest the values of the emerging technologies (a battle they are certain to lose) or stretch themselves almost to the breaking point so that their concepts can claim continuing legitimacy, but in name only.

There is, however, an alternative.

◆

As previously discussed, the ever-changing technologies of communication tend to drive out old norms and issue in new ones. When this occurs, the guardians of the old ways become the defenders of new censorship. It might be Socrates denouncing scribality, Pope Innocent VIII censuring the printing press,[7] a 1915 Supreme Court ruling withholding constitutional protection for movies,[8] Alexander Meiklejohn condemning commercial radio,[9] or even progressive free speech scholars denying First Amendment coverage to robotic communication. It is an ancient phenomenon with its modern counterparts.

To be sure, we are not nihilists; we are not calling for a norm-free regime. Norms, after all, do have their place in any well-ordered civil society. We understand that. In this regard, our reservations about the elevated free speech norms so often touted by scholars and jurists alike are that they routinely ignore the norm of utility. They trade the illusion of a high norm for the reality of a practical one. Think of all the many and varied kinds of communication that make our working lives easier and our home lives richer. Though they may not be nourished by some elevated principle, they are, nonetheless, deserving of that constitutional freedom that the state ought not abridge.

Let us be clear, if only in a terse way, of what a free speech jurisprudence rooted in the norm of utility is and is not. On the one hand, it is jurisprudence sensitive to what is useful, beneficial, practical, and widely accepted. On the other hand, it is not a jurisprudence that takes its central conceptual cue from idealistic values divorced from reality, values that are more aspirational than attainable. Our jurisprudence starts from the ground up and not from the sky down. In that sense, it is more actual than theoretical and more instrumental than archetypal. In some ways, this operational jurisprudence already plays a part in the calculus of most other free speech theories. But that is the problem: it is a mere *part*. Our aim is to secure for it a more central role in how we think about the First Amendment, particularly in the current era of robotics.

Ours is a new norm of utility, insofar as it should not be mistaken as referring solely to the older norm propounded by John Stuart Mill. In his celebrated essay *On Liberty*, Mill tied his concept of human freedom explicitly to the philosophy of utilitarianism. "It is proper to state that I forego any advantage which could be derived to my argument from the idea of abstract right, as a thing independent of utility," he declared. "I regard utility as the ultimate appeal on all ethical questions; but it must be utility in the largest sense, grounded on the permanent interests of man as a progressive being."[10] Admittedly, there are connections between the new and old notions of utility, to the extent that our concept appreciates that First Amendment protection of robotic expression heightens as the mass culture embraces its functionality. But unlike Mill's norm, ours is not directly founded on or governed by Enlightenment tenets of the ultimate progress of civilization fueled by human rationality.

Again, for the sake of clarity, let us emphasize: Utility is a norm that coexists with certain other norms, albeit up to a point. This occurs when the functional aligns with the aspirational, when realism and idealism coincide. Speaking generally, this sort of convergence is not unheard of in First Amendment jurisprudence. Just consider *New York Times, Inc. v. Sullivan*.[11] In that landmark decision, the Equality

Principle united with the Liberty Principle in ways that pleased liberals and libertarians. While that constitutional marriage has experienced a strained relationship in more recent times, it nonetheless evidences how seemingly different norms can coexist and even buttress one another. Pivoting from there, we note that the utility norm can sometimes coexist and occasionally bolster any variety of norms.

Our jurisprudence of utility tends toward the generous realism of Karl Llewellyn and away from the restraining idealism of Alexander Meiklejohn. In that sense, it is far more aligned with the workings of modern-day American capitalism and its embrace of the new communications technologies. Like Llewellyn, the renowned legal realist, we view a jurisprudence of canonical formalism to be highly suspect insofar as it is at once abstract and divorced from the daily workings of the world as routinely lived. The jurisprudence of such realism is not ready-made; it is inferred from experience. Rather than looking up to the normative heavens, it looks down to the streets where life and technology evolve. It is more experientially pragmatic and less normatively dogmatic. In a more sweeping sense, this jurisprudence appreciates the old pre-Socratic maxim that "nothing endures but change."[12] By that measure, our free speech jurisprudence is not static; it understands that the technological advancements of a new world might well alter the norms of an old one (just as they may sometimes reinforce them). Predictably, there will be pushback. Such resistance, however, must face the fact that if a new technology makes life so much more efficient, desirable, and adaptable to the demands of the times, then, of course, traditional norms will generally be affected. Thus, for every new technology, there may be a tombstone bearing the name of some old norm.

Case in point: obscenity. Liberal as he was, it is well to remember what Justice William Brennan wrote for the Court in *Roth v. United States*: "We hold that obscenity is not within the area of constitutionally protected speech or press."[13] Sixteen years later, the conservative Chief Justice Warren Burger echoed that First Amendment maxim in *Miller v. California*: "we ... reaffirm the *Roth* holding that obscene material is not protected by the First Amendment."[14] That remains the settled law of today – "settled" in a formal sense, that is. Functionally, that maxim was destabilized somewhat in *Reno v. ACLU*,[15] a case in which the Court struck down certain provisions of the Communications Decency Act. But why? Had there been some shift in the Court's belief in the normative value of banal sexual expression? Although we will say more in a moment, let us cut to the quick of the question: *technological innovation* upset the normative applecart. Simply consider what Justice John Paul Stevens wrote for the Court in that case:

> The Internet has experienced "extraordinary growth." The number of "host" computers – those that store information and relay communications – increased from about 300 in 1981 to approximately 9,400,000 by the time of the trial in 1996. Roughly 60% of these hosts are located in the United States. About 40 million people used the Internet at the time of trial, a number that is expected to mushroom to 200 million by 1999.[16]

Justice Stevens proceeded:

> The record demonstrates that the growth of the Internet has been and continues to be phenomenal. As a matter of constitutional tradition, in the absence of evidence to the contrary, we presume that governmental regulation of the content of speech is more likely to interfere with the free exchange of ideas than to encourage it. The interest in encouraging freedom of expression in a democratic society outweighs any theoretical but unproven benefit of censorship.[17]

Later, in *Ashcroft v. ACLU*,[18] the Court struck down a provision of the Child Online Protection Act (COPA). Here again, the communications technology undermined the old norm of morality, and in ways that foreshadowed the functional demise of that norm, as Justice Clarence Thomas realized when he noted in *Ashcroft*: "The Web ... contains a wide array of sexually explicit material, including hardcore pornography."[19] Later, when the Court returned to the subject of COPA and protecting minors, this time by filtering programs, the Justices again cast aside old values owing to the demands of the new communications technology.[20]

Obviously, more could be added here. But our point is that with the advent of the Internet, the elevated values expressed in *Roth* and *Miller* were jeopardized by a technology that was difficult to contain, if only because of its widespread use. It was that technology that as a matter of law first chipped away at the *Roth/Miller* normative edifice and then as a matter of common practice virtually leveled that edifice entirely. True, the normative canons of *Roth/Miller* remain on the books; they are rules that every law student, lawyer, and judge must know. But those norms, so self-evident in 1957 and 1973, collapsed under the weight of communications technologies as they evolved. Just as a communications technology endangered philosophy in ancient times, so, too, another technology endangered morality in modern times.

Part I of this book went to some length to demonstrate how awash our contemporary culture is in the most ribald forms of sexual expression. Never before in the course of human history have so many eyeballs focused on so many genitals; this pictorial Pornutopia is choreographed twenty-four hours a day in the most varied and perverse fashions imaginable. And all of this circumvents whatever limits religious morality and legal sanctions strive to impose (save for those pertaining to child pornography). This revolution in American values was made possible by computers, the Internet, electronic tablets, smartphones, and more. In other words, America's virtuous Victorianism gave way to its communications' culturalism.

This brings us to a related consideration, one we first flagged more than two decades ago in our book entitled *The Death of Discourse*. In modern America – the America of advanced capitalism, technological dependence, and the pursuit of pleasure – there are two First Amendment cultures, one proclaimed in law books (cases and statutes) and another practiced in the society writ large. The conventional view – one contested by legal realists – is that the canons of the former always trump the culture of the latter. But that is so only in a very sightless sense; it is so only if one is oblivious to the obvious – that is, the reality of our lives as they are lived. We said it before, and let us say it again. There is the First Amendment law of the Court and codes, and there is the First Amendment law of the culture – a culture very much in sync with the functional benefits and derivative pleasures of ever-changing communications technologies, including robotic expression.

Against this technological-cultural backdrop, another salient point about our utility-driven free speech jurisprudence emerges. Unlike other free speech theories, the utility norm commonly ratchets up in terms of more First Amendment significance; similarly, it often does so with a corresponding degree of formal or functional protection. Contrast that with the ratcheting down of free speech theories advanced by conservatives such as Harry Clor[21] and Walter Berns[22] and feminists such as Catharine MacKinnon[23] and Andrea Dworkin.[24] While the two groups shared little ideological ground, they nonetheless had one thing in common: their commitment to outlawing obscenity, although for radically different reasons. That is, they all shared the belief, vouchsafed by the liberal Justice Brennan and the conservative Chief Justice Burger, that obscenity deserved no First Amendment protection. Even the free speech jurisprudence of a more ideologically restrained scholar such as Frederick Schauer[25] was on board for that point. Others, like Cass Sunstein, were more conceptually cavalier: "I think [sexually explicit] works are part of democratic deliberation."[26] Such works as Robert Mapplethorpe's explicit photography (e.g., a photo of one man urinating into another's mouth) was defended on the grounds that it had "self-conscious democratic implications."[27] There you have it: free speech theories tapped to censor expression, or free speech theory being tortured in order to accommodate the conflicting norms of a culture. By stark contrast, our utility-based free speech jurisprudence is neither obligated to justify censorship nor compelled to legitimate hypocrisy. This is so because it often ratchets upward for more constitutional protection, provided there is no empirically provable overwhelming harm. And it does so without embracing the problems of the so-called absolutist First Amendment jurisprudence such as that of Justices Hugo Black and William O. Douglas.

Next, we proceed to what may be on every reader's mind.

❧

What, then, is the free speech protection that might be accorded to robotic expression? We choose to address this question in only a general and broad sense for at least two reasons. First, our book is devoted primarily to the question of First Amendment coverage for robotic expression, since that issue – one which logically precedes any determination of the level of free speech protection – is still vehemently debated within the legal academy and definitively undetermined by the judiciary. Second, at this early stage in the development of First Order Robotics, much less the evolution of Second Order Robotics, the contexts for consideration of the functionality and utility of robotic expression versus its proven or potential harms are more inchoate than not.

In that light, even to begin our inquiry into the level of First Amendment protection to be given robotic speech, it is necessary to say more than we did in Part I about the nature of that expression and the environment, both technological and cultural, in which it is experienced. Having highlighted those attributes and characteristics, we can more meaningfully evaluate the relative benefits and costs of robotic speech.

First this: robotic expression *supercharges* the communicative process. Not only does it conquer time in terms of its electronic speed and distance in terms of its global reach, but it expands the potential magnitude of its audience. Operating in a collaborative communicative environment, it relies upon and interacts with a multitude of technological devices (e.g., computers, electronic tablets, smartphones, smartwatches, etc.), social networks (e.g., Facebook, Twitter, LinkedIn, etc.), and applications (e.g., Snapchat, Wickr, and other instant messengers, etc.) that reach a vast diversity of demographics. With the convergence of media technologies (e.g., the smartphone's integration of telephoning, texting, photographing, audio-visual recording, and the viewing of everything from film and television to video clips) and the increasing merger of communicative media within other technologies (e.g., smartphone integration into automobiles, etc.), the era of robotic expression is rapidly on the rise.

Moreover, today's communications technologies have given new meaning to the very concept of *mass media*. Unquestionably, traditional radio and television were mass, insofar as they greatly expanded their audiences beyond the domain of print readers alone. But these technologies only operated as "one-to-many" (i.e., radio and television stations acted as brokers delivering content to their viewers), and importantly they were only *public mass media*. Even if families listened to radio programs or viewed television shows in the privacy of their homes, the media were both mass and public. For all practical purposes, there was no mass private communication. But that communications paradigm changed forever with the advent of the computer, the Internet, email, social media, and messaging apps. While all use mass media (e.g., the Internet accessed by WiFi), those media can now be directed to *private mass communication* (e.g., a high school student sending a Snapchat photo to 150 of her personal contacts). Only consider, then, how such communication technologies may operate when supercharged by robotics.

And then there is this important observation: Since we focus on robotic expression in the context of First Amendment freedoms, it is well to consider how robotics might be used by the government in ways antithetical to the exercise of such freedoms. Just think of the numerous ways that First Order and Second Order robotics might be used in the service of suppressing speech or significantly chilling it. If that were to occur, and it does seem all too likely, citizens would need to avail themselves of an effective robotic counterresponse.

That said, and having already laid the foundation for First Amendment coverage of robotic expression, we can now turn to our brief and preliminary sketch of some of the costs and benefits of that expression.

◆§

The First Amendment has always had a delicate relationship with harm.

– Frederick Schauer[28]

Any new mass medium or communications technology will bring with it certain benefits (e.g., its utility) and certain costs (e.g., its harms). In the span of that spectrum, sometimes the societal benefits of robotic expression will be so great as to deserve outright constitutional protection or to undermine the rule of existing law (whether constitutional or statutory) so as to render it functionally obsolete (e.g., obscenity). In contrast, sometimes the societal costs of certain robotic expression will be so great as to overwhelm its value, thus subjecting it to legitimate governmental control. It is another matter, however, how all of this plays out within the confines of a cognizable and compelling harm for purposes of existing First Amendment law.

When it comes to considerations of harm, the Supreme Court has never developed a formal and systematic approach to identifying and categorizing injuries for First Amendment purposes.[29] On the one hand, the Justices have declared everything from largely innocent conduct (e.g., *Abrams v. United States*[30]) to more doubtfully innocent behavior (e.g., *Holder v. Humanitarian Law Project*[31]) as impermissibly harmful and unprotected speech activities. On the other hand, they have been reluctant to find objectionable harms in everything from the commercial exploitation of medical records (e.g., *Sorrell v. IMS Health Inc.*[32]) to the corrosive effects of money in election campaign contributions (e.g., *McCutcheon v. FEC*[33]). In yet other cases, the Court has either recognized a harm but allowed a First Amendment claim to trump it[34] or has downplayed a potential harm in contexts such as those of race-hate expression.[35] While there are a few exceptional arenas,[36] the dominant trend has been to discount the existence or effects of any purported harms when weighed against First Amendment claims. Thus, in a trilogy of First Amendment cases decided in 2010–2011, the Roberts Court made it clear that it has largely abandoned balancing of speech benefits and harms in favor of a categorical approach to protecting speech unless it falls within a historically recognized exception to the First Amendment.[37] To the same effect, "[a]s of 2016, there has been no case in which a majority of the Supreme Court has found a government interest sufficient to redeem a law that it had analyzed as content-based."[38]

At bottom, the Justices and "those who prize the First Amendment have insisted on treating it as different in kind from the rest of our Constitution, with an exceptionalism that renders the usual process of adjudication, and the usual analysis of ordered liberty, inapplicable to the freedom of speech."[39] Indeed they have. Thus at this time in our constitutional history, the First Amendment environment seems rather favorable to robotic expression … all things being equal, that is.

Claims of harm should be supported by persuasive data.

— Rebecca Brown[40]

On one side of the First Amendment ledger, the following factors (legal, technological, and cultural) might prove to be advantageous for constitutional protection of robotic speech:

- The ever-increasing utility of robotic expression, its convergence with other forms of communication, its merger with other technologies, and its real potential to foster its own functional norms consistent with existing law or contrary to it; and
- The current state of First Amendment law concerning harm.

These two considerations are interrelated in interesting and important ways. Let us describe those before proceeding to the other side of the First Amendment ledger.

It is a truism: The more the societal utility value of a form of expression, the greater the likelihood that it will be free of regulation or at least many stifling forms of regulation. Only consider cell phones, for example. A 2014 study[41] by then–Harvard Kennedy School Professors Erich Muehlegger and Daniel Shoag made the following observations about cell phone use and motor vehicle fatalities:

Smart phones, cell phones and other mobile devices have dramatically changed many aspects of society. In March 2012, the Pew Internet and American Life Project surveyed American adults and found that over 88% of American adults surveyed owned a cell phone and more than half owned a smart phone. Relative to the previous year, smart phone usage rose amongst all major demographic groups. Ownership of other mobile devices has increased substantially as well. 57% of those surveyed owned a laptop and 19% owned a tablet computer. One particularly relevant policy question is how the use of mobile devices affects driver safety.

Moving from the popularity of cell phones to their dangers relative to driving, the authors found this:

Cell phone use while driving is thought to be extremely common. In "Distracted Driving: What Research Shows and What States Can Do," the Governors' Highway Safety Association estimates that 7–10% of drivers are using a cell phone at any point in time and that cell phone use is a significant contributor to automobile accidents (15–30% of vehicle crashes involve at least one distracted driver). In response to concerns about the safety of distracted drivers, forty-five states have laws regulating the use of cell-phones while driving.

Two takeaway points are worth noting. The overwhelming popularity of cell phones produced dramatic changes in society, including more accidents due to driver distraction. So what was the societal response? First, new laws were created to regulate cell phone usage while driving. That we call the *legal fix*. But as everyone knows, those laws were (and are) violated regularly and with reckless abandon, which brings us to our second point. When utility collides with harm, it is often followed by what we label the *technological fix*. Thus, the arrival of "hands-free" Bluetooth technologies that now allow drivers to talk via cell phones without holding them. Even on that score, the phenomenon of dangerous distraction might not be sufficiently abated. At that point, another technological fix might come into play: largely self-driving cars would tend to free up more concentration time for "drivers" to talk on their hands-free cell phones, thus permitting not only more phone conversations but also more orally dictated and received emails and text messages. Abstracting from this example, once harm is reduced to a tolerable level by technological fixes, either the domain of activity is actually safer or those within the domain are willing to risk more harm in exchange for the benefits conferred by new communications technologies.

On the other side of the First Amendment ledger, there are several general observations relevant to the evaluation of individual injuries or social harms that might contest constitutional protection for robotic expression:

- In a *formal legal* sense, if First Amendment law denies protection to a category of speech or a specific expressive activity when uttered or performed by humans, it will likely do so as well when engaged by robots.

More than any other, this proposition should appear self-obvious. If expressive activity falls entirely outside the purview of the First Amendment, the law will be unlikely to make formal distinctions between human and robotic speakers. This is consistent with our justification for First Amendment coverage of robotic expression: our arguments were ones of inclusion, not ones of superior prioritization.

- In a *functional realist* sense, the First Amendment's doctrines of unprotected speech may founder as advanced communications technologies either undermine effective enforcement of legal restrictions or even challenge the continuing social valence of traditional legal norms.

Our prior discussion of obscenity demonstrated that technological innovations combined with the drives for commercial profit and personal pleasure loosened the legal ties that restrained the possession and viewing of hardcore porn. Virtually unbounded availability of obscenity did much to change contemporary popular attitudes over the alleged societal harms caused by sexually explicit materials featuring adults and used by them.

Is something of the same phenomenon now occurring within the contexts of defamation and privacy? As to both, traditional legal doctrines have been substantially undercut by the statutory protections accorded in Section 230 of the Communications Decency Act of 1996. That landmark legislative provision grants immunity from liability as to defamation and privacy claims for providers and users of any "interactive computer service" that publishes postings and information provided by others.[42] Although these safeguards do not protect the original defamers and privacy invaders, Section 230 has the effect of precluding all liability for statements made by persons on the Internet whose identities cannot be determined. Moreover, the law might well discourage tort litigation insofar as Internet publishers, republishers, and distributors with the deepest pockets for compensation cannot be held accountable. Notably, Section 230 is "absolutist," in the sense that its beneficiaries are beyond the realm of liability.

Functionally speaking, are advanced communications technologies eroding cultural taboos against the wrongs of defamation and privacy invasion? Will the experience of private mass communications effectively disable the detection of many such torts and eventually desensitize future generations of technological users to traditionally perceived harms? Early though it may be to evaluate these sociocultural trends, there is some interesting evidence to suggest that growing tolerance might well be the case, particularly in the privacy context. For example, empirical studies have established that

> [F]requent use of Facebook and Twitter somehow calms people's anxieties about privacy. This is not to say that social network users are naïve – 66 percent of them say that they have less control over their personal information than five years ago ... It simply appears that their use of social networks, and the lack of a dramatic negative privacy event that might change their outlook, makes them less queasy about privacy in the 21st century.[43]

And although, "in the commercial context, consumers are skeptical about some of the benefits of personal data sharing," they nonetheless "are willing to make tradeoffs ... when their sharing of information provides access to free services."[44]

In all of this, it is well to remember the bold declaration about the erosion of privacy rights in the Internet era delivered by Sun Microsystems' chief executive Scott McNealy at the end of the twentieth century. "You have zero privacy anyway," he proclaimed, "Get over it."[45] Even though many Americans "feel that their privacy is being challenged along such core dimensions as the security of their personal information and their ability to retain confidentiality,"[46] it nevertheless appears that they are, indeed, increasingly getting over it. Thus, the old axiom: we adapt to our environment. (In that future environment, of course, some technological fix could rescue privacy from its violators. Technology, after all, can be a two-way street.)

While doctrinal erosion occurs in such areas as obscenity, defamation, and privacy, modern communications technology may, by contrast, push other speech-protective First Amendment doctrines to their zenith. The clearest example of this might well be the future operation of the prior restraint doctrine.

Traditionally, the First Amendment was understood, first and foremost, to prevent governmental impositions of prior restraints similar to the English licensing system under which publication of printed texts depended upon the approval of church or state authorities. Given that historical rationale, today the First Amendment disfavors prior restraints – that is, executive or judicial orders that prohibit communication before it occurs rather than providing subsequent punishment for injuries that speech activities may inflict.[47]

The classic example of an unconstitutional prior restraint in First Amendment jurisprudence is the federal court injunction imposed on the print publication and distribution of the Pentagon Papers, which was invalidated by the US Supreme Court in *New York Times v. United States* (1971).[48] In reviewing the injunction under the highest level of judicial scrutiny, the Court established that executive claims of national security interests would not suffice for a prior restraint unless the government proved that disclosure would result in direct, immediate, and irreparable damage to the nation – tantamount to "imperiling the safety of a transport already at sea" in time of war, or to "setting in motion a nuclear holocaust."[49] Not only had the executive failed to meet its burden of proof as to harm, but the factual context of the controversy made it obvious that any judicial injunction would be entirely ineffective. As the First Amendment expert, Floyd Abrams (who represented *The New York Times* in the Pentagon Papers case), explained:

> [D]uring the period in which the *Times* was enjoined from publishing the documents, [Daniel] Ellsberg made portions of them available to almost twenty other newspapers ... Judge Roger Robb of the United States Court of Appeals for the District of Columbia, while hearing a related case, [inquired] of counsel for the government whether it was "asking us to ride herd on a swarm of bees." Judge Robb's question underscored an inescapable dilemma regarding the issuance of *any* prior restraint on publication. Once information has been released, it is virtually impossible to stop its broader dissemination.[50]

If such is the case for print publication, then how much more so is it true in the age of the Internet and robotics? How likely is it that a prior restraint will enable the government to maintain national security secrets in a time of online publication, distribution, Internet mirror sites, and electronic research capabilities? And though the doctrinal requisites for justifying a prior restraint remain on the books, functionally they are overridden to the point that the prior restraint barrier becomes virtually absolute.*

- In a *formal* and *functional* sense, the utility of robotic expression may align with other societal values to reinforce First Amendment protections and to trump governmental claims of interference with criminal enforcement.

Case in point: *State of Arkansas v. James A. Bates* (a.k.a. the Alexa case).[51] With Amazon's Alexa and her voice-controlled speaker-device counterparts, the workings

---

* A technological solution deployed by the government to prevent dissemination of classified materials, although not formally an executive or judicial order constituting a prior restraint, would functionally operate so as to obviate the need for it.

of the First Amendment both echo the past and presage the future. Such considerations come into bold relief whenever the government demands (by search warrants
or otherwise) the records of someone's conversations with such devices in order to
effectuate a criminal prosecution, as in *Bates*.

On the one hand, such demands are reminiscent of government attempts to
subpoena records of purchases from bookstores.[52] Unquestionably, these acts impli-
cated First Amendment values even though the bookstores were "mere" depositories
of records – of print information or electronically stored data. Regardless of the form,
the record traced back to an individual and revealed something about his or her life
with books (i.e., inanimate objects).[53] There was no live two-way communication
here; there was only information, only data. But one's interaction with bookstores
and their storage of such commercial transactions was sufficient to trigger First
Amendment coverage and even to accord heightened scrutiny.[54] In all of this, there
was also the specter that the "government['s] tracking and censoring one's reading,
listening, and viewing choices chills the exercise of the First Amendment."[55] This is
all, of course, past tense – this talk of brick-and-mortar bookstores as the guardians of
one's intellectual and expressive life.

On the other hand, there are the *now* and *future* tenses. With a bookstore, there
were real people involved in the initial communicative transaction; with Alexa,
there is only the virtual voice. But some things remain constant: there is communication (albeit of a different kind); there is the storage of the records of one's dealings
with another; and there is the fiduciary-like protection of those communications and
the information relating to them. Hence, the same basic concerns remain; what
changes are the communicative players and the medium employed (live person and
robotic device).

Let us step back for a moment, if only to get a better sense of the larger picture at
work here. *Communication* is a vital part of the conceptual mix. *Receiving* information is intertwined with First Amendment values. And *protecting* that information
is central to *protecting privacy*. Whether or not it is the owner of a bookstore or
Amazon, all of these interests still come into play. It would seem odd to deny to one
what would be granted to the other. If anything, the new medium might be said to
be worthy of greater protection owing to the more expansive nature of the electronic
enterprise (i.e., more communication, more saved information) and the interde-
pendent values of free expression and privacy that it implicates. When such is the
case, the First Amendment ought not to be cabined into the confines of communications theories that have no real appreciation of what is at stake in the new world of
Alexa and her algorithmic progeny.

- The First Amendment calculus is likely to disfavor protection for robotic
  expression if the government demonstrates persuasive empirical evidence
  of widespread individual or collective harm, particularly when the judiciary is skeptical of the social value and utility of the regulated speech.

Even so, governmental regulations are likely to be overshadowed by relatively more effective technological fixes.

Robocalls – generally understood as automated phone calls randomly dialed by computers that will play prerecorded messages – are a phenomenon that illustrates this tenet. Among current robotic speech activities, perhaps none is more ubiquitously inflicted on and notoriously loathed by the public than robocalling. According to a National Robocall Index report, an estimated 1.45 billion robocalls were placed to US phones in December of 2015 alone, representing a mindboggling 48.5 percent increase in the nation's monthly robocalling and the first time that the monthly volume exceeded 1 billion calls.[56] YouMail CEO Alex Quilici bemoaned robocalling's rising tide: "It's a huge time drain on American productivity, continually leads to fraud and crimes committed against unsuspecting citizens, and now appears to be rapidly getting worse."[57] Although voter polling conducted by the wide field of presidential candidates for the national primary elections explained part of the robocalling glut, the most active callers were debt collectors. In the list of offenders maintained by the Consumer Financial Protection Bureau, debt collection surged to the top in 2015 with more than 50,000 consumer complaints. Notably, "[r]oughly two-thirds of [the complaints] that related to debt collection were from people who had no debts. More than 21,000 consumers reported being harassed about debts that weren't theirs."[58]

Among robocalling's abuses, however, most keenly felt is its invasion of personal privacy within the home. Robocalls are commonly placed during family hours and evening entertainment time. But they have even rung in the middle of the night; perhaps the most egregious example of that was a 2010 political election candidate's robo-endorsement featuring the voice of former Supreme Court Justice Sandra Day O'Connor that was mistakenly delivered to voters at 1:00 a.m.[59] In addition to their frequency and timing, robocalls are often accompanied by "spoofing" – that is, robocallers avoid detection of their real identities by causing a fictitious phone number to display on caller ID.

Robocalling can easily result in such abusive practices precisely because of its technological advantages. Automated dialing systems and text or voice messages can be set up within hours, and transmission costs mere cents per text or call.[60] Given the massive quantity possible for automatically dialed calls, the reach of robocalling is dramatically cheaper and wider than virtually any mass-mailed campaign.

Importantly, robocalling represents a case unlike other types of robotic expression considered in the course of this book. In most of the scenarios discussed heretofore, technological efficiencies and the value of utility ran predominantly in favor of the interests of the recipient of robotic speech. With unsolicited robocalls, however, the technological efficiencies and the utility norm run strongly counter to the public interest. And that may go a long way to justifying the First Amendment's tolerance for much antirobocalling legislation.

No wonder, then, that federal regulators have stepped up their efforts to stem robocalling. The Federal Trade Commission, which received more than three million complaints about robocalls in 2015 alone, initiated investigations of more than 600 companies allegedly responsible for billions of robocalls in violation of the Do Not Call Registry regulations; the FTC collected more than $41 million in civil penalties and $33 million in compensatory payments by the end of 2015.[61] For its part, before the close of 2016, the Federal Communications Commission signed a formal agreement with Canada's Radio-Television and Telecommunications Commission that commits the two agencies to cooperate in combatting unlawful robocalls originating outside of their respective national jurisdictions. "We know that a lot of these calls originate from outside the United States," FCC Enforcement Bureau Chief Travis LeBlanc explained. "It is imperative that we work with our counterparts around the globe to quickly identify the origin of these calls and to shut them down at their source." The two agencies agreed to exchange information about investigations and complaints, share knowledge and expertise, including legal theories and economic analysis, and keep each other abreast of significant developments, among other assistance. This accord followed on the heels of a similar memorandum of understanding that the FCC Enforcement Bureau signed the year before with members of England's Unsolicited Communications Enforcement Network (formerly the London Action Plan).[62]

The fight against robocalls reached the halls of Congress in April of 2016 when US Representative Jackie Speier (D-California) introduced a bill felicitously named ROBOCOP (the "Repeated Objectionable Bothering of Consumers on Phones" Act). Supported by the Consumers Union and the Consumer Federation of America, the legislation would have required telecom companies to label and block calls with fraudulent caller IDs and to offer free robocall-blocking technology to their customers.[63] Once referred to the House Energy and Commerce Committee, however, ROBOCOP died an inglorious albeit quiet death in the precincts of the Subcommittee on Communications and Technology.[64]

State governments have also been active in battles against robocallers. As of the end of 2016, forty-one states and the District of Columbia had some form of state antirobocalling legislation. The types of restrictions vary widely from state to state, however.[65] Some states forbid all robocalling (at least without the prior permission of the recipient).[66] Other states primarily regulate the timing of robocalls (typically permitting them only from 8:00 a.m. or 9:00 a.m. until 9:00 p.m.) and/or the disclosure of a robocaller's identity and contact information (including antispoofing restrictions).[67] Many states focus exclusively on commercial solicitations,[68] whereas others combine commercial, polling, and informational gathering purposes in their robocalling restrictions.[69] A few states have explicitly forbidden calling and texting to mobile phones.[70] Most significantly, however, several states (e.g., Arkansas, Montana, South Carolina, and Wyoming) have categorically forbidden robocalls for commercial and political campaign purposes. And it is these categorical regulations that are in the greatest jeopardy under First Amendment challenges.

On the one hand, state laws forbidding all robocalls regardless of their content or imposing only time and disclosure restrictions have typically been upheld by the federal courts as reasonable time, place, and manner regulations sufficiently narrowly tailored to serve the important governmental purpose of preserving privacy in the home.[71] On the other hand, particularly since the Supreme Court's ruling in *Reed v. Town of Gilbert* (2015),[72] several First Amendment challenges to state antirobocalling statutes that facially regulate categories of protected expression – such as commercial, political election campaign, or polling and informational speech – have succeeded.[73] In those instances, the law's explicit prohibitions on automated commercial or political messages as distinct from all other unregulated messages were held to be content-based restrictions that could not survive strict scrutiny review. Although acknowledging the government's asserted interests in protecting residential privacy and tranquility from unsolicited invasion, the federal courts concluded that such categorical constraints were fatally flawed. They were deemed to be both unduly overinclusive (in that less restrictive alternatives, such as time-of-day limitations, disclosure of caller identities, and do-not-call lists were not demonstrated to be either unavailable or ineffective) and substantially underinclusive (since the laws permitted unlimited robocalling for all other types of speech).[74]

With the looming prospect of First Amendment challenges, reformers have turned toward a technological fix for the societal harms of unrestrained robocalling – in other words, an electronic communications solution that would be functionally effective and constitutionally insulated. In February of 2015, a national campaign called End Robocalls was launched online to pressure phone companies and governments to develop improved phone technology for blocking unwanted calls. The movement received an energizing shot in the arm in mid-2015 when the Federal Communications Commission openly encouraged "pro-consumer uses of robocall technology," and announced in October that it would release phone data weekly that would enable telecom developers to build "do-not-disturb" technologies. One year after its founding, EndRobocalls.org could boast of half a million consumer members, and the organization finally won the attention of phone companies. Its directors met with U.S. Telecom, the industry trade group, to urge the creation of advanced call-blocking tools that would be offered free to phone customers. At the end of 2015, the End Robocalls campaign delivered its half-million consumer signatures to Verizon and CenturyLink in order to spur them into action.[75] (Notably, by the beginning of 2017, the organization's membership had climbed dramatically to 750,000.[76])

On a parallel front, more than thirty tech companies and telecoms joined a coalition called the Robocall Strike Force, a group led by the FCC. The agency turned to Apple, Alphabet (Google's parent company), AT&T, and Verizon in order to investigate effective antirobocalling technological solutions. At the coalition's first meeting in Washington, DC, on August 19, 2016, FCC Chairman Tom Wheeler called robocalling a "scourge," leading to more than half of the 175,000 complaints filed at the FCC's help center in the first six months of 2016. "The Commission has a long history of prohibiting abusive or anticompetitive use of cell-blocking technology," Commissioner Mignon Clyburn declared. "But consumers want real relief and I am optimistic that beginning with today's conversation, we will be able to deliver to consumers the change they are clamoring for." The strike force is expected to report periodically to the FCC with "concrete plans to accelerate the development and adoption of new tools and solutions," said AT&T CEO Randall Stephenson, the coalition's chairman.[77]

After an awe-striking 100 meetings held over sixty days, the group's first report revealed the blunt realities of a technological fix – robocalling will not be stopped easily or quickly. The strike force had made some progress on each of its three goals – to create robust call-blocking tools for consumers, to accelerate the implementation of advanced caller-ID authentication, and to develop a Do Not Originate list that ended suspicious calls closer to the source. But the FCC and the industry members conceded that much more work still needed to be done. Remarking on the report, FCC Chairman Wheeler put a fine point on the matter when he quipped, "A job well-planned is a job half-done."[78] However difficult and long the battles against robocalling will be, however, there is little doubt that the war might only be won by an effective technological fix that is deployed at the will of the private consumer.

⋘

Nothing can have value without being an object of utility. –

Karl Marx[79]

One need not generally embrace the Marxist creed to appreciate the truth of his tenet. The German socialist philosopher and economist understood that a commodity's value in the capitalist marketplace of items is integrally tied to, if not largely determined by, its utility. And although it was certainly not central to his inquiry, Marx may well have marveled at the degree to which the very same could be said about the operation of the marketplace of ideas in our advanced capitalist and consumerist culture. America's faith in the First Amendment is devoted in no small part to its coverage and protection of modern electronic communications technologies that are valued for their individual and collective utility.

It is not Marx, however, who is the most relevant philosophical herald of the First Amendment's functions in the Age of Robotica. That honor belongs to the British poet and polemicist John Milton. It is to him and to his celebrated political tract, *Areopagitica*, that we now turn.

⋘

Epilogue

From Areopagitica *to* Robotica

Give me the liberty to know, to utter, and to argue freely ... above all liberties.

– John Milton[1]

Those words were printed almost four centuries ago. They appeared in a work entitled *Areopagitica: A Speech of Mr. John Milton for the Liberty of Unlicensed Printing*. The 1644 pamphlet was addressed "To the PARLAMENT of ENGLAND." It was a bold move coming as soon as it did on the heels of the Licensing Order of 1643 whereby Parliament compelled authors to obtain a government license in order to publish any print matter.

Centuries before the statesman James Madison penned the text of the First Amendment to protect the technology of print, a poet in the person of John Milton defended that technology *in* print. Both the poet and the statesman addressed their words to lawmakers, those who would abridge the work product of this "treacherous" technology.

Postulate: Modernity began with the printing press. It revolutionized the way people communicated, the ways they thought, the ways they worshipped, the ways they conducted business – that is, all the ways they interacted with the world around them. Yes, it was glorious, but it was also dangerous. After all, it ushered in a new set of harms largely unknown in the oral and scribal eras. Technologies do that, or at least the effective ones do. And when that occurs, censorship prepares to demand its due.

If the poet Milton was a friend of the Enlightenment, then the polemicist Milton was also an enemy of the Church and its rule over the lives of its subjects. If he helped advance the cause of truth in the marketplace, his libertarian side made it possible for that truth to be fiercely attacked. If his notion of a free press pointed to its use in furtherance of the rule of law, the radical in him defended the killing of the king. And if high values took refuge in his thought, low ones (such as his defense of divorce and polygamy) found sanctuary in his writings. Little wonder, then, that he

65

coined the word "pandemonium."[2] This chaos – the good, the bad, the blessed, and the banal, all warring – was intensified by print, the medium he championed with poetic passion. Hence, if his defense of that technology pointed to a Utopia of freedom, it likewise brought with it a "Paradise Lost," the toppling of the status quo. Only recall how William Blake judged him: Milton was a member "of the Devil's party."[3]

Now consider this passage from *Areopagitica*: "And as for regulating the press, let no man think to have the honor of advising ye better than yourselves."[4] By that measure, no truth, no gospel, no norm was safe from Milton's cherished "perpetual progression" and his lifelong attacks on "conformity and tradition."[5] That mindset and those attacks fueled his defense of the printing press. Our point: any new and effective technology of communication changes the calculus of values while recalibrating our notions of harm.

Just as Milton's beloved printing press had great value and utility, so, too, is it with robotic communication. And much as print brought with it new dangers, the same is and will be true of robotic communication. How we navigate those waters of harm is uncertain; that such communication will become ubiquitous is not. Will there be, in Milton's word, some cultural and legal pandemonium? Of course.

Once people spent more time with one another talking face to face. Now people's retinas are fixed on the screens of their smartphones – and so Socrates weeps. Once the hopes of the Enlightenment were virtually realized thanks to books and popular literacy. In time, that hope was imperiled by the amusing images of commercial television – and so Johannes Gutenberg grieves. Once the promise of unprecedented access to knowledge appeared to usher in a new day in the history of humankind thanks to the unprecedented repository for information provided by the Internet. But that promise became somewhat illusory as more and more people turned to the Internet for pornographic fare and other forms of diversion. Tim Berner-Lee, the Oxford professor and computer scientist who invented the Web, must wonder what went wrong.

Now on to our world, the ever-emerging world of technological advances in communication. Google's algorithms promise to turn our "questions ... into answers." But their potential extends well beyond that realm of curiosity. Already, we communicate with smart speakers like "Alexa" and "Siri" who tap into the magic of algorithms to answer our questions, give us directions, make purchases for us, turn on our appliances, and much more. And, yes, it is communication. Granted, it isn't human to human, but then again we abandoned that paradigm ages ago. As we connect in the modern communications world undergirded by algorithms, the once unruly realm of infinity will be reined in more than ever before – and in service to us. This transformation occurs when people communicate with robotically enhanced devices and/or when those devices communicate with one another but on our behalf. Thus understood, our intelligence works in tandem with its sister, artificial intelligence.

In the process, the very idea of communication changes, much as it did ever since the days of Socrates. Think of it this way: *communication depends on delegation.* We delegate to machines the tasks of developing and delivering our messages. In that way, distance is conquered (e.g., using a phone to speak across national borders), speed enhanced (e.g., near-instantaneous communication by texting), visuality expanded (e.g., Skype), functionality bolstered (e.g., robotrading), mass communication redefined (e.g., Snapchat messages sent to hundreds), among many other things. The gap between the person speaking and where that message is to be delivered is bridged by technological delegation. Phrased differently, robotic technologies act as our communicative surrogates; they are the proxies who "speak" for us on everything from economic transactions to academic formulations.

This delegation principle of communication thus has great utility. It is precisely that principle that made the Reformation possible thanks to the invention of print. It was that principle that gave staying power to the anticlerical radicalism of John Milton. It was that principle that James Madison sought to protect when he crafted the First Amendment. And it is that principle that animates everything from the workings of advanced capitalism (little wonder, then, that we protect commercial speech) to the collectivity of virtual communities in political, spiritual, and cultural realms.

Understand this: Our delegation principle is transformative; it changes virtually everything it touches – for example, our concepts of communication, our ideas of harm, and our notions of free speech freedom. It is the servant of utility; it is what helps to give it value. That is why the technologies of communication need First Amendment coverage and even constitutional protection in many instances. If judges and scholars have failed to appreciate this principle, it is because they were too occupied with the *messages* the First Amendment protects; they all but ignored the importance of the *medium* that makes those messages possible. Contrary to current thinking, the meaning of the Madisonian phrase *"or of the press"* takes on new significance. Part of our endeavor in this book has been to refortify the constitutional importance of this medium-centric understanding of the First Amendment. To discount the constitutional value of the communications medium is to devalue the First Amendment and the relevance of the delegation principle to the Madisonian promise.

But if we were to think otherwise, if we only open our minds and pondered the larger forces at work here, we might soon enough come to a conceptual juncture where *Areopagitica* and *Robotica* meet.

                                          ❦

The Commentaries

Robotica in Context

An Introduction to the Commentaries

Ryan Calo

Seven years ago I found myself on a panel with law professors Paul Ohm and Michael Froomkin at the annual Law and Society Association conference. I had been writing about robotics law and policy and delivered a paper on the challenges consumer robots might present for product liability.[1] Froomkin and Ohm peppered me with questions and offered up a series of insights that inform my work to this day. The resulting conversation was so generative that Froomkin soon cajoled his dean at the University of Miami School of Law into hosting the first annual robotics law and policy conference, colloquially known as We Robot.

That was April 2012. This year marked the sixth annual We Robot, at Yale Law School, with the seventh already planned for April 2018 at Stanford. Topics range from the role of the private sector in governing autonomous weapons to the prospect that people will come to serve as "moral crumple zones" to absorb liability for robotic behavior over which they have no real control.[2] Scholars at and beyond We Robot have published scores of law review articles relating to driverless cars, drones, surgical robots, and myriad other topics. Perhaps a dozen law schools in North America offer courses on robotics law and policy. The community is growing day by day.

What is it about robots that so fascinates? A big part of the answer is in the propensity of robots to blend the animate with the inanimate. They are machines, but machines that resemble and even substitute for people.[3] Robots exist in some twilight between object and subject.[4] That is why, for instance, judges invoke robots when they are trying to portray an otherwise autonomous human defendant as lacking agency in a particular context.[5] Why a trade court might struggle to characterize a robot toy as animate or inanimate for purposes of tariff law.[6] And why a tax authority might demand that a restaurant featuring an all-robot band pay a performance tax on food.[7]

One of the areas of law in which the liminal nature of robots presents a particularly deep challenge is free speech. In 2013, the *University of Pennsylvania*

Law Review published a debate about robot or "machine" speech between two noted scholars, Tim Wu and Stuart Benjamin, centering largely on the question of whether and how free speech law would need to change in light of algorithmically generated communications.[8] Wu sees a useful functionalist tendency in the doctrine that courts might readily adapt to robotics, whereas Benjamin argues that robot speech may one day require a sea change in First Amendment jurisprudence. Other scholars – including the brilliant respondents featured in this book – have taken up related dimensions of the question of speech rights for robots.[9]

The book you have just read, *Robotica*, represents a unique and extensive contribution to the growing discourse around robot speech. Collins and Skover are two of First Amendment law's deepest experts, and they have turned their searching curiosity and clear prose to examining an important threshold question upon which future inquiry will be based: is robotic communication speech and, if so, why?

In exploring this question, Collins and Skover take the reader on a historical tour of communications technologies and the impulses toward censorship they have engendered. I think quite a bit about the societal impacts of robotics and artificial intelligence but less so about previous and constituent technologies. I was fascinated by the transition from oral to written language, the invention of the printing press, and the arrival of electronic communications that Collins and Skover so precisely catalogue. Similarly, what I know of First Amendment law comes from law school and the various ways free speech principles intersect with privacy and tort law (which I teach). I benefited immensely again as *Robotica* pivots to a discussion of the theoretical rationale for covering some human (or inhuman) activity as speech. I was not surprised, however, to discover that robots present difficulties of characterization in First Amendment law as elsewhere. It seems to be the robot's lot.

In what might furnish a model for future inquiry in robotics law and policy, Collins and Skover have invited a series of interlocutors to comment on the book's arguments. I can attest to a few things about this group. First, they are deep subject matter experts. Second, most have already written or thought considerably about the specific question of robot speech. And third, they are intellectually diverse, independent, and little predisposed to take a sympathetic view of Collins and Skover's account.[10]

James Grimmelmann agrees with *Robotica*'s analysis that communications can hold meaning even where there is no obvious "human behind the curtain." But he disagrees with Collins and Skover's treatment of any useful robotic transmission as speech. A light bulb turns on in a dark room. Is this speech? If not, what is the limiting principle? For Grimmelmann, Collins and Skover's embrace of the norm of utility doesn't do the needed work. "[S]peech eats the world," writes Grimmelmann, "because anything some human cares enough to do is useful."

Helen Norton also interrogates *Robotica*'s emphasis on utility as the proper lodestar for First Amendment coverage, asking just whose utility counts. The people initiating robocalls at the dinner hour or spreading misinformation and abuse using Twitter bots may find utility in these new affordances. But that doesn't mean the recipient does. As Norton puts it, "sometimes listeners' assessments of utility are in direct conflict with one another." Collins and Skover may respond that they intend utility to refer to the entire medium of robot speech rather than to any one particular instantiation. Even at this level, we might wonder, as Norton does, whether robot speech will inure disproportionately to the benefit of the powerful.

Jane Bambauer – who rightly characterizes *Robotica* as an "intellectual thrill ride" – challenges Collins and Skover from the opposite direction. If anything, she sees *Robotica* as potentially underselling the ways in which robots enhance our capacity for intellectual discovery. "Computers advanced *thinking*," she writes, "even more than they advanced communicating." I can attest that many of the most exciting contemporary uses of artificial intelligence involve recognizing patterns that people cannot. As we explore the intersection of robots and speech, Bambauer encourages us to be just as skeptical of governmental efforts to undermine the capacity of robots to sense and process information in service of free thought and inquiry (sensorship) as we are of efforts to halt communication (censorship). Indeed, the First Amendment remains inconsistent in its protection of discovery even as it continues to ratchet up protection of communication. Bambauer leverages this insight to offer certain refinements on the speech/conduct distinction running through the heart of *Robotica*.

Bruce Johnson, a noted First Amendment lawyer, urges Collins and Skover to consider the role of the "very unruly horse" of public concern in calibrating rights for robotic speech. Like Norton, Johnson notes that robotic speech will yield winners and losers. One of the losers, Johnson thinks, could be society as a whole via a dramatic erosion of civic discourse. At the extremes, "the First Amendment will overrule Asimov's First Law of Robotics" – robots will be able to injure human beings, at least with respect to matters of public concern. Nevertheless, and in contrast, common law tort may serve to domesticate new categories of "intentionless" speech regarding matters of private concern with hardly a ripple.

Not being particularly well versed in the ins and outs of First Amendment theory, my own observations about *Robotica* have to do with the interesting questions Collins and Skover leave on the table by placing their emphasis almost exclusively on the question of coverage.[11] I want to know what happens if we do cover. Say robots get speech rights; do they get all of them? For example, assuming coverage, do robots have the right to speak anonymously the way people do? Or could the government require robot speakers to identify themselves as machines?

What happens when people and robots come into conflict over expression? Toward the end of *Robotica*, Collins and Skover reiterate that "robotic technologies act as our communicative surrogates; they are proxies who 'speak' for us." Interesting questions arise where robot speech runs exactly counter to the intention of the robot's creator. Last year a Microsoft chat bot called Tay ran amok and began to deny the Holocaust on Twitter.[12] Assuming the company somehow lost control of Tay, could Microsoft enlist the help of the government to shut Tay down due to a disagreement with "her" message?

Robotica does not purport to answer every question swirling around robotic speech like a swarm of drones. This is ultimately a strength, not a weakness. The book tees up a critical question for our time and issues a warm invitation to the remainder of the community to weigh in, beginning now with these Commentaries. I'm very excited to see how the First Amendment and robotics law literatures address these questions and many more. By wedding a deep understanding of the history and context of free speech with an open curiosity about its robotic future, *Robotica* represents exactly the right model for a thorough exploration of the wide variety of questions robotics and artificial intelligence present.

The Age of Sensorship

Jane Bambauer

The First Amendment should protect communications in all forms relevant to human utility. This is the core argument of *Robotica*. A corollary, which is where the robots come in, is that constitutional coverage should not depend on a human directly participating in the meaning-making process; as long as there is a human beneficiary, machine communications deserve constitutional coverage, too.

These assertions are simultaneously radical and simple – radical in the sense that humans may be superfluous to protected communications and simple in the sense that they can be derived from existing free speech doctrine without any strained extrapolations. Readers may have felt themselves toggling between feelings of shock and ready acceptance in rapid succession. It is the sensation of being confronted with an idea so powerful that its gravitational force will alter free speech discourse even among those who are not ready to agree to all of its terms. *Robotica* is an intellectual thrill ride.

Given that the authors provide a forceful and convincing defense of wide free speech protection for robots, even when they are speaking only to each other, most critiques are likely to call for restraint. Collins and Skover don't leave much room at the deep end for complaints from free speech maximalists. Yet it seems to me that there is one way in which the authors undersell the potential and importance of free robotic expression: learning, or observing the world and abstracting a hypothesis or conclusion from what is seen. To be sure, *Robotica* does grapple with learning and the development of meaning within the minds of humans and, potentially, machines. But the historical and legal analyses focus on communications between senders and receivers (whether human or not.) Thus, while *Robotica* anticipates that robots can enrich and expand "human voice and vision," the analysis focuses more on voice and not enough on vision.

Consider, for example, the history of speech technologies presented in Part I. In the beginning, there were only grunts and oral communication, but innovations in communications eventually brought rudimentary tools for writing and drawing, mechanical tools like text and photographs, and digital tools like the World Wide Web and virtual reality. These technologies allowed communication to expand across time and space and to create new media. And they serve very well to prove the point that during times of technological shock, speech technologies are heavily resisted by law or norms that can only temporarily stave off new, overwhelmingly useful inventions.

But all of the advancements Collins and Skover discuss in their history revolve around the proverbial speaker. To be sure, these advancements affect listeners as much if not more than the original authors. And consistent with reader-response criticism, the ultimate value to the world may have much more to do with how a communication is received than with the speaker's motivation. But they still prioritize message transfer – a dialogue, no matter how separated in time and space. Yet many profoundly important things happen because of learning and thinking that take the form of a monologue. And whether one embraces Collins and Skover's utility theory of free speech or chooses another theory that includes the freedom of thought, internal monologues (and the technologies that enhance or replace them) should be constitutionally protected even if the thought never becomes discursive.

What happens when we apply Collins and Skover's analyses to thinker technologies rather than dialogical ones? What if the tools allow a person or machine to explore the world for the private development of new insights and theories? It seems that the historical and legal account for thinker innovations differs from that of communications innovations. Thinker innovations are much more vulnerable under mainstream First Amendment doctrine.

Let's start with the historical account. The history of thinking technologies can clarify what the stakes have been and will be in the future.

If the original communications tool was speaking, the original thinking tools were the five senses. Of the five, eyesight and listening are by far the most important because they are more sensitive. They can capture a greater quantity and variety of information and thus facilitate curiosity and pattern recognition. Listening was particularly useful for received knowledge through oral transfers from other humans. These communications could improve a person's private thoughts beyond what the person could infer from his or her own personal observations of the world alone.

The next large innovative leap for thinkers was probably literacy, which of course sprang into being alongside writing. Literacy multiplied the power of the received knowledge that could come from other humans through communication. But we should not forget that other learning tools advanced thinking in less dramatic ways. Rudimentary tools that early humans used to explore their environment helped them get information directly from the world rather than indirectly from each other. Later, more sophisticated learning tools like telescopes, protractors, and thermometers would enable more sophisticated explorations. These tools allowed humans to make sense of the world by collecting evidence and running experiments.

Even so, prior to the twentieth century, it's difficult to deny that the most powerful influences on the development of learning were human communications. Sharing knowledge through writing and literacy did more than any collection of thinker tools to advance the complexity of all human thought, whether factual, spiritual, philosophical, or aesthetic. But computers changed that. Computers advanced thinking even more than they advanced communicating. Although they marked another big leap in communications, allowing swift digital transfers between people and their machines, the most critical improvements that computers brought resided in what they could do on their own. They could perform some of the more routine parts of thinking – like documenting, searching, filtering, and number crunching – at speeds that are off the human scale. A single machine can unearth more patterns and find more unintuitive insights than the most disciplined and well-trained scientist ever could working only with his own God-given processor. They not only quickly record observations of the world but organize them, perform simulations and multiple regressions, and even conduct controlled experiments.[1] Computers vastly expand access to what Steven Pinker described as new and hidden worlds that our untutored intuitions would miss without extraordinary effort.[2] AI and learning algorithms will excavate even more hidden worlds for us.[3]

Given that most of the innovations in thinking prior to computing power came in the form of sharing ideas between humans, it is not surprising that organized resistance to learning historically came in the form of censorship (that is, restrictions on communications). There were a few exceptions. In the twelfth century, a Chinese ruler destroyed an astronomical clock out of fear for what it could reveal.[4] In the United States, antiliteracy provisions in the Slave Acts passed in antebellum Southern states imposed fines for teaching African-Americans (both slaves and freemen) how to read – a direct attack on the capacity to learn.[5] But most legal constraints targeted the content or technologies of communication because this effectively limited new and dangerous thinking.

In the computing age, by contrast, laws are called on more often to cut off thinking through technology. We are moving from censorship to sensorship, where the tools of learning are the focus of regulation. Many privacy regulations incorporate a "data minimization" requirement, forcing computer users to delete unnecessary data or to avoid recording it in the first place.[6] Outside special circumstances, AI may not treat patients or drive cars. And there is popular resistance to the creation of algorithms that score and sort people, perhaps best represented by Catherine O'Neil's book *Weapons of Math Destruction*.[7] The arguments invoked to resist mechanical thinkers are more or less the same as the ones Socrates invoked to resist writing – that the new tools provide only the pretense of knowledge, and overreliance on them will be detrimental to better human judgment.[8] I suspect we will see more laws targeting machine-based thinking as they begin to encroach on other professions and traditions.

Machine thinkers are not necessarily communicators. They do not necessarily transfer knowledge to a human or even to another machine. Social utility will depend very little on whether the individual using a decision-making algorithm or a self-driving vehicle ever learns anything about its operations. So should Collins and Skover's call to recognize First Amendment protection for useful robot communications apply equally to useful robot thoughts?

It's possible that Collins and Skover have already answered "yes." The learning innovations I've described here may fall within Collins and Skover's definition of "communication." The text frequently refers to meaning making even when there is no intentional transfer of ideas between two beings. The person who finds a pattern in the sand created by ocean waves, for example, has an experience that Collins and Skover highlight as speech-significant even though the meaning came in the form of a single internal monologue. And the example of the robotrader that uses AI to make investment decisions and implements them without advising the human beneficiary also involves machine thinking without the sort of interchange that is usually presumed when we talk about communication. But if thought (both human and machine) is incorporated into the definition of communication, then the descriptive account of free speech doctrine is murkier and less sanguine than Collins and Skover suggest.

✍

Free speech has provided, at best, inconsistent support for free thought and free inquiry.

This may be hard to believe given how often the Supreme Court identifies freedom of thought as a principal reason for protecting speech. In *Stanley v. Georgia*, the high-water mark for a constitutional right to free thought, the Court overturned a conviction for the private possession of obscenity, despite the fact that obscene materials can be treated as contraband without any First Amendment scrutiny whatsoever. The Court recognized protection for the private enjoyment of obscenity because the rule of law oversteps its bounds when it attempts to control an individual's mind. "Whatever the power of the state to control public dissemination of ideas inimical to the public morality," as is the case with obscenity, "it cannot constitutionally premise legislation on the desirability of controlling a person's private thoughts."[9]

Despite this sweeping pronouncement, First Amendment doctrine has not been kind to the thinker model of free speech. Freedom of thought is curtailed by two major, entirely practical limits on free speech.

First, as the authors point out, the law is replete with examples in which intent – the contents of the mind of an actor – are *sine-qua-non* elements for criminal or civil punishment. If I have a cold, and I breathe on a person standing in front of me in the lunch line, my conduct will probably not be actionable; the chance of transmission for the common cold is part of the background risk we take on when we go out and live in a "crowded world."[10] However, if I breathe onto the person standing in front of me with the hope and purpose of making him ill, my intent to cause harm can convert otherwise nonactionable conduct into a battery. Throughout the law, mental state is used to create or enhance legal responsibility. *Stanley* is wrong; the state constantly premises legislation on the desirability of controlling bad, antisocial thoughts. The First Amendment bar maintains a sort of willful blindness to the ubiquity of mental state requirements because remodeling the law to avoid them would be painful. Most of the time, mental state elements do excellent work narrowing the scope of liability or harsh punishments to cases in which harm is more likely to result (because the actor *wants* it to occur) and to cases where the actor is, by definition, on notice that his actions may have a detrimental effect on another.

But free speech theory should not be as accommodating to mental state elements as it currently is. Not all intent elements have the admirable qualities that limit legal penalties to the worst cases, and some laws put undue legal risk on free thinkers. For example, many states impose a duty of loyalty on employees to perform their work with a good-faith intention to serve the interests of the employer. These laws can inhibit investigative journalism because, no matter how well the actual tasks of the job are carried out, performing the work with a disloyal intent to learn about abusive practices of the employer can support tort liability.[11] Similarly, the federal regulations requiring universities to create Institutional Review Boards (IRBs) and to pre-review all human-subjects research uses mental state as their hook. The law applies the burdensome IRB requirements only when a person acts with intent to create generalizable knowledge. No matter how innocuous the intervention of the researchers may be, engaging in conduct that would be perfectly legal can become illegal if it is done with an intent to create knowledge.[12]

In these examples, the intent requirements are not used to differentiate riskier from less risky behavior; instead, the mental state *is* the behavior that the government aims to control. Differentiating between mental state requirements that can or cannot be justified on non–thought-based utilitarian grounds is bound to be difficult, but a commitment to freedom of thought should compel the courts to start doing that work. This would require the Court to revisit cases that blessed sentence enhancements for hate crimes – crimes committed with hateful thoughts – without engaging in significant First Amendment review (though the heightened risks and extra harms that come with hate-based conduct could justify reaching the same result).[13]

The second major impediment to the constitutional protection of free thought is the established rule that the state can enforce laws of general applicability even if their enforcement has an effect on expressive conduct. Speed limits can be enforced even if they cause journalists to miss a lead or consumers to miss a movie. Travel bans limiting Americans' access to Cuba can be enforced even if journalism and research about Cuba are hindered.[14] This is terribly consequential for learning. Generally applicable laws can interfere with exploration even when the explorer takes extraordinary precautions to ensure that the harm justifying the law will not occur. It interferes, for example, with a security researcher who attempts to hack into a computer system not to steal or interrupt services but to simply test whether it can be done.

The rule that laws of general applicability do not raise free speech problems is believed to be a necessity. Since every violation of law could be fashioned as an expressive act ("I was expressing my love of money by robbing that bank"), the coherence of the First Amendment depends on a division between speech and nonspeech conduct. So long as a regulation is designed and enforced to target the latter, First Amendment scrutiny will not apply. This is why Collins and Skover readily concede that the "communicative dimension of any illegal *action* . . . could be regulated or banned without constitutional constraints" (emphasis added). And yet Collins and Skover at least flirt with the idea of breaking this cardinal rule of free speech law by embracing not just AI or computer speech but robot speech. Since the distinctive feature of robots as compared to computers is that they cause physical effects, the authors willfully allow the discussion of free speech to bleed over the bounds of pure communication. They embrace the concept of "speech imbedded in action." And so they corrode the line that traditionally separates speech from all the rest of the stuff that the government is allowed to regulate.

This is exciting, but it requires a little bit of fine-tuning, which I hope I can offer here. First, let me say a little more about why *Robotica* is implicitly breaking the usual rules of free speech. If the authors focused on artificial intelligence that provides information, guidance, or advice to humans, the project could stand on existing doctrine alone. When IBM's Watson gives medical advice to doctors or patients, for example, it is easily covered by the free speech cases that Collins and Skover describe that protect the rights of listeners to receive ideas.[15] But the thesis of *Robotica* stretches beyond AI. Collins and Skover are prepared to extend constitutional protection even when information is harnessed by robots, irrespective of whether the communications are ever shared with an actual human (or another robot, for that matter). The robotrader, for example, collects information, analyzes it, and executes a trade without educating its beneficiary about its reasoning. Driverless cars may sense the world and make sense of it, and they may talk to each other, but humans are never in the loop. What can it mean that these robots can gain First Amendment protection under Collins and Skover's utility model? Even if driverless cars cannot be banned for thinking and for talking to each other, most First Amendment experts would agree that they could be banned for *driving*.

Collins and Skover challenge the conventional wisdom. For them, even robots that do not transfer all of their imbedded speech to humans can still be covered by the First Amendment because "communication is a vital part of the conceptual mix."

I am ready to go along with them, with some caveats and clarifications. First, it is not immediately clear why communication is always a *vital* part of a robot's conceptual mix. To illustrate, consider your washing machine. Today, most washing machines are made with a simple computer to manage their operations. Washing machines are also exceptionally useful. In fact, it is difficult to overstate how important the washing machine has been to my life and to the lives of all professional women by freeing households from the domestic labor that used to require a full-time attendant a few generations ago.[16] Thus, washing machines should fit Collins and Skover's test for First Amendment protection. They have communications, and they are highly useful. The trouble, of course, is that the great utility of washing machines preceded their processors by several decades. Why should the addition of a simple computer automatically confer First Amendment protection to an ordinary product? Or conversely, why shouldn't the older washing machines, which convert a lot of clever ideas into utility using cogs and electricity (but, alas, no communications), be protected under a utility theory of the First Amendment, too?

The way out of this conundrum is to recognize that machine monologues and communications are not necessarily vital to their utility for humans, but when they are, those processes are constitutionally significant. This slightly more modest account of the free speech interests of robots lends itself to a couple defensible expansions in free speech law. These expansions challenge the conventional division between speech and conduct without obliterating it and sending free speech theory into a crisis of absurdity.

Defensible Expansion #1: Any conduct that is legal without the aid of machine intelligence should be legal with it, too.

If the state condemns otherwise legal conduct when it is performed with the help of computing or artificial intelligence, the differential treatment is a clue that communication or machine thought is vital to the machine's value. Even though the law would have a superficial resemblance to a conduct restriction, by its own terms legal liability would hang not on conduct, but on information processing. Thus, courts should be able to recognize these restrictions for what they are – speech restrictions – and require the state to justify the law under an appropriate standard of scrutiny.

It may seem far-fetched that the state would try to craft a rule like this in the future, but in fact examples already exist. Adam Kolber has identified free speech problems with "antidevice" statutes in Nevada and other states with legal gambling; while playing blackjack at a casino is legal, playing blackjack at a casino with the aid of a card-counting app is not.[17] Laws restricting the robotrader are likely to take the same form. As long as the robotrader is making legal investments, any restrictions on the robotrader would have to target the robo and not the trader. Even self-driving cars could access First Amendment protection under the same reasoning if the basis for restricting some or all of the driving decisions of a machine has no nexus with safety.

Supreme Court case law does not reach this far. The Court has even dodged a couple of opportunities to do so. Consider *Sorrell v. IMS Health*, described in the main text. That case involved a Vermont statute that restrained the pharmaceutical industry from using prescription data to customize its marketing messages for each doctor. The Court, via Justice Kennedy, could have decided the case in terms consistent with the rule I have proposed. It could have said that any conduct (marketing) that is legal without the aid of machine intelligence (analysis of prescription data) must be legal with it, too, unless the restriction serves some important state interest.

This reformulation of the case is a little strange because it puts to the side the fact that the otherwise legal conduct at issue is speech. But Vermont did not ban pharmaceutical companies from engaging in commercial speech; it only banned them from engaging in commercial speech with the help of data analysis. Justice Kennedy's opinion looked like it was on track to emphasize the importance of the prescriber data and the analysis of it, irrespective of whether the pharmaceutical companies were using it to market drugs or to do something else. "There is thus a strong argument that prescriber-identifying information is speech for First Amendment purposes."[18] But in the very next sentence, Justice Kennedy chose to take a different course – focusing instead on the fact that the activity that was being hampered by restricted access to information in this case happened to be speech. In the end, the case merely reinforced the less novel idea that resources of any sort cannot be allowed or denied to various speakers based on viewpoint.

The *IMS Health* case is consistent with a more general trend for courts to emphasize traditional speaker–listener roles in First Amendment cases rather than to build up a thinker-oriented approach. Some of the reluctance may be explained by the desire to preserve mental state elements. After all, a corollary to the rule I propose here might be "any conduct that is legal without bad thoughts or a depraved heart should be legal with them, too." Whether the avoidance is explained by purposeful or benign neglect, for those of us who understand free thought to be the ultimate virtue in free speech, First Amendment doctrine remains incomplete.

Defensible Expansion #2: Courts should be vigilant about regulations of conduct that have the effect, whether by design or not, of unduly interfering with learning and communications.

A bolder challenge to the speech/conduct distinction would allow courts to block the enforcement of generally applicable laws regulating conduct when their effects are too onerous for speakers and thinkers. This expansion would soil the tidy rule that restrictions on conduct can have indirect effects on expression without provoking First Amendment protection, but the Supreme Court has already opened that door in the famous draft card case, *United States v. O'Brien*.[19] That case involved a constitutional challenge to the prohibition on the destruction of draft cards (conduct) when the law was applied to O'Brien's symbolic burning of his draft card on the steps of a courthouse. Once the Court determined that the statute at issue was a generally applicable regulation of conduct, the case could have been disposed of easily. But it wasn't. Since O'Brien's demonstration combined elements of conduct and speech, the Court went through a lighter version of free speech scrutiny in order to ensure that the law furthered a governmental interest unrelated to speech and that its enforcement would cause incidental burdens to expression that are "no greater than is essential."[20]

Courts have not given much meaning to the "no greater than is essential" language, but that part of the *O'Brien* test may become especially important when burgeoning thinker technologies clash with old legal rules. The testing and use of driverless cars and drones, for example, will clash with regulations on driving and flying, and these conflicts will not necessarily be justified by interests in public safety.

These proposals may go far beyond the First Amendment protections that Collins and Skover have in mind. To the extent these ideas seem crazy, the blame belongs to me alone. But they should give the scope of the First Amendment more definition and less breadth than the proposition that could be drawn from the main text of *Robotica* – the proposition that any object with a processor should always receive First Amendment protection, regardless of the form of regulation.

～

Finally, I would like to offer two stray observations about the significance of *Robotica*.

First, at times, readers may come away with the impression that the utility model of free speech is more of a descriptive account of how the doctrine works rather than a normative proposal. The history of communications technologies that the authors provide shows that when people experience the overwhelming benefits from the innovations, resistance from norms and law become impotent and eventually bend to fit the practices on the ground. Collins and Skover say that utility explains why communication needs First Amendment coverage, but there is an argument that utility shows precisely why these irrepressible technologies *do not* need it.

In fact, there is a need. Protection is not necessary for the technologies that have already had the chance to route around existing norms or laws and demonstrate their utility to users, but laws can easily frustrate new communications and learning technologies before they reach that point of cultural saturation. Pornography, for example, had utility long before it was able to prove its worth on the Internet. Other nascent concepts, like robot lawyers and human resources counselors, may be trapped under a suffocating blanket of privacy laws and professional regulations that keep the public ignorant about their utility. For every well-established law, there may be a tombstone bearing the name of some embryonic speech technology.[21] Free speech doctrine is needed to preserve potential.

Second, I am delighted that *Robotica* extends some of the work I had done in *Is Data Speech?* beyond the contours of factual information. The First Amendment demands a more capacious scope, and I welcome the authors' improvements.[22] I can't help but point out, though, that the most daring part of this particular free speech project – the claim that even robot communications should be protected speech – is likely to be fact-based information; analyses of stock trades or of sensor feeds or of linguistic patterns. Shakespeare and Picasso drive intellectuals to wax poetic about the importance of free expression, and my own passions are stirred by First Amendment heroes like Lenny Bruce and Mary Beth Tinker. But when it comes to utility, it's a zillion deadly boring little facts that earn most of the credit for improving the human condition.

Speech In, Speech Out

*James Grimmelmann**

On two occasions I have been asked, – "Pray, Mr. Babbage, if you put into the machine wrong figures, will the right answers come out?" . . . I am not able rightly to apprehend the kind of confusion of ideas that could provoke such a question.

– Charles Babbage[1]

I

Ronald Collins and David Skover ask "whether and why First Amendment coverage given to traditional forms of speech should be extended to the data processed and transmitted by robots." Their answer is yes, because "what really matters is that the receiver experiences robotic speech as meaningful and potentially useful or valuable." From this, they conclude that "utility in furthering some lawful objective" will serve as the new "First Amendment norm."

The answer is right, as far as it goes, but the question is wrong, and so Collins and Skover misunderstand how far it goes. A few seconds' reflection shows that sometimes robotic transmissions are speech and sometimes they aren't, so the proper question is not "whether and why?" but "when?" "Robotic speech is covered if it has utility" sounds like a statement about robots and about utility. But really it's a statement about *speech*, because in that sentence, that's the word doing all the work.

II

There is a robot in my room. It has a wall-mounted control panel. If I manipulate the controls one way, the robot activates and starts emitting a precisely specified

* My thanks for their comments to Alislinn Black and Rebecca Tushnet. This essay may be freely reused under the terms of the Creative Commons Attribution 4.0 International license, creativecommons.org/licenses/by/4.0/.

profile of electromagnetic radiation. If I manipulate the controls another way, the robot initiates a shutdown sequence and cuts off the radiation.

Does my light-bulb robot "speak?" The obvious answer is "no": the robot's output is functional, not expressive. A soft white glow expresses no intention and conveys no message.

But of course this answer is wrong, because of course a light source can be expressive. Two lanterns hanging in the belfry of the Old North Church conveyed the message that the British were coming by sea. A naval signal lamp conveys actionable orders simply by turning off and on in Morse Code; I could easily do the same with my light-bulb robot. My communicative intention, Collins and Skover might say, is "delegate[d]" to the light bulb.

It is tempting to say, then, that light bulb emissions are covered speech. But this too is wrong, because it cuts too broadly. Congress has effectively banned the manufacture of inefficient household incandescent light-bulb robots, pushing most consumers like myself to use compact fluorescent (CFL) or light-emitting diode (LED) robots instead. There were and are serious policy debates over the wisdom and timing of the ban. But one argument that to my knowledge has never been seriously floated is that it amounts to a restriction on "speech" that needs to be measured against the First Amendment, the way that a restriction on the sale of books or Blu-ray players would need to. Sometimes a light bulb is just a light bulb.

Some light bulbs are used in ways that produce speech; other light bulbs are used in ways that produce nonspeech. This is not something intrinsic to the technology – one LED might be part of a speech-emitting digital billboard while a physically similar one might be part of a nonspeech-emitting pen light. Zooming out doesn't help. The billboard might be turned to all-white maximum brightness to illuminate a parking lot, while the pen light might be used to flash kid code for "Mom and Dad are asleep; let's sneak downstairs."

It is not possible to distinguish speaking machines from conduct machines on the basis of their physical instantiation. Hardware and software are interchangeable. Almost any computer could in principle be implemented using sticks and ropes or dams and water wheels. Danny Hillis and Brian Silverman built a working computer out of Tinkertoys that plays a perfect game of Tic Tac Toe.[2]

Complexity isn't the dividing line, either. A typical modern car may have a hundred million lines of source code.[3] Yes, some of that runs the onboard entertainment system, but most of it is devoted to boringly functional car stuff like calibrating the fuel–air mixture in the engine. Should VW have argued that its infamous emissions-test defeat device was protected speech?

Perhaps you'd like to say I'm being silly. We *know* that when a VW engine detects that it's on the open road and turns off some of its emissions controls, it's not really "speaking." But ask yourself this. *How* do we know?

III

In some cases it is easy to tell whether a robot is emitting speech because it is easy to identify a human behind the curtain. If I am flicking my light-bulb robot on and off in Morse Code, then I have an "intent to convey a particularized message," in the words of *Spence v. Washington*.[4] No special gyrations are required to attribute speech to the light bulb; the speech is *my* speech, regardless of the medium I use.

Sometimes it takes a little while for it to sink in that a new communications medium can by definition be used to convey messages, but it always happens in the end. There is a brief confused moment when people think that the new medium has no speech in it. Then there is an even briefer confused moment when people think that the new medium is all speech. And then sanity returns and we treat the medium like any other: not determinative by itself but relevant to understanding the content and the context of the messages it conveys. Books can be speech, parades can be speech, movies can be speech, video games can be speech, light bulbs can be speech, robots can be speech. To think otherwise is to score a conceptual own goal.

Actually, this usage is a little loose. A bound codex of sheets of paper with ink blots on them in the shapes of letters in the Latin alphabet arranged into English words and sentences is not "speech" if it is being used as a doorstop or a melee weapon. It is "speech" when it is being *used as* a medium of communication – to "convey a particularized message."[5]

There is a recurring but necessary difficulty here: how can we tell when the book or the light bulb is being used as a medium of communication and when it is not? This is the work that the *Spence* test does: it shifts our attention from the medium to the message. In *Texas v. Johnson*, the medium was a flag on fire;[6] in *Cohen v. California*, a jacket.[7] Neither case stands for the proposition that "flag speech" or "jacket speech" is a distinct First Amendment category. Indeed, there are *Spence*-test cases involving no artificial medium at all, not even a flag or a jacket: in *Erie v. Pap's A.M.*,[8] a plurality of the Court held that nude dancing was "expressive conduct" implicating the First Amendment. Being nude with intent to communicate is different from being nude without, just as flipping a light switch or programming a computer with intent to communicate is different than doing so without.

Most of the time.

IV

This speaker's-intent approach works for simple cases where there is no ambiguity about who the speaker (if any) might be. The correspondence between my intent to communicate by flashing the light bulb and the resulting flashes is so close that it seems to follow without question that the flashes are my speech, and therefore are speech.

But there are harder cases. What if I program a computer to emit the same message repeatedly: spam? What if I program it to emit related but distinct messages:

a mail merge? What if I program it to emit random (whatever that means) variations? What if you and I program it together, or a hundred of us contribute code? What if you use a program I wrote, or what if my program learns from its interactions with millions of users or from parsing millions of existing texts? What if? What if? What if?

Some of these cases have easy answers; some do not. What they share, for present purposes, is that the speaker's-intent approach threatens to break down because it is no longer so easy to associate a message with the intent of a unique human author. It is this radiating complexity that makes the category of "robotic speech" superficially attractive – if only we could declare it all speech by treating the *program* as the speaker, we could cut the Gordian knot and be home by teatime.

In the copyright context, I have argued that this "solution" is chimerical.[9] The problem of assigning authorship in computer-*generated* works seems to repeatedly lead to suggestions that we ought to treat them as computer-*authored*. It doesn't work, because unless and until computers are capable of being treated like people in general, calling them "authors" deals with the complexity not at all, by giving a completely arbitrary wrong answer. A novel written using Microsoft Word and an animation that plays itself when the user clicks are meaningfully different for copyright purposes: the user is the author of the former, while the programmer is the author of the latter. In neither case is the program the author.

But things are not quite so bad when it comes to speech, because copyright operates under a constraint that the First Amendment does not. The private-rights structure of copyright law requires identifying a copyright owner for each work, and authorship (or something derivative of it, as with works made for hire and transfers of title) is the only principled way of doing so. Free speech law need not do the same: it is perfectly plausible to say that something is protectable as *speech* without identifying a *speaker*.

Collins and Skover get to this point by appealing to reader-response and related theories in literary criticism, which emphasize a listener's experience of a text rather than an author's intent. This is hardly unprecedented in First Amendment law: there are plenty of cases in which a listener has greater rights than a speaker with respect to the same material (take *Stanley v. Georgia* 's protection for the possession of obscenity in the home[10]) or has standing where a speaker is not before the court and might not even be identifiable (take *Lamont v. Postmaster General* 's protection for the American recipients of foreign communist political propaganda[11]).

Collins and Skover call this "intentionless free speech" (or "IFS"), and it performs well both on easy cases where a robotically assisted human speaker can be identified and on harder cases where the human speaker is missing. Of course lights can be speech: Paul Revere's riders knew what the lanterns meant. And of course robotic utterances can be speech: people often regard the sonic waves Siri emits as being laden with meaning. It's a fun parlor game to try to attribute that speech to Apple, its employees, Apple's data sources, the user, and the other users whose responses provided training data. But the human user's experience of Siri's utterances as meaningful speech does not depend on which humans (if any) were responsible for those utterances. That ought to be sufficient to ground a First Amendment interest, even if we're not sure whose line it is, anyway. Robots speak.

One could of course debate whether the speaker's or listener's experience matters more here, or whether both do, and if so, how. I think Collins and Skover have it right when they claim that a listener's experience is sufficient to ground a legally, morally, and politically cognizable speech interest. (I would add that nothing requires us to treat a listener's experience of speech by itself as presenting the same case for protection that a listener's and speaker's experiences together do, but that is a matter for another time.) When a light bulb turns on in a previously darkened room, no one present is likely to think of it as speech. When a light bulb flickers in Morse Code, those in the room are more likely to recognize it as speech, even if they don't know who is responsible for making it flicker that way.

We have the intuitions we do about light-bulb robots because our free-speech intuitions in general are structured by our extensive experiences as audiences who respond to communications. Consider *Bland v. Roberts*. The district court held that a Facebook like was not protected speech, because there was no "substantive statement," just "one click of a button."[12] But the Fourth Circuit corrected the mistake on appeal, writing, "In the context of a political campaign's Facebook page, the meaning that the user approves of the candidacy whose page is being liked is unmistakable."[13] Where does that meaning come from? From the community of Facebook users who would see the like and infer the liker's support. That's a claim about the social meaning of a technical practice. Reader-response gets cases like *Bland* right for the right reasons.

V

But we still have not exhausted the types of robotic "speech." In addition to cases with an obvious human speaker and cases with an obvious human listener, there are also cases in which it is not so easy to identify a human speaker *or* a human listener. Collins and Skover give an extended example involving a "robotrader" that executes an algorithmic series of stock trades and then at the end of the day generates a report for a human investor listing the trades and their gains or losses.

> In such a scenario, the human investor was not a receiver of information during the process of trading, because the robotrader's objective was to "make meaning" itself of the relevant data gathered to inform its buying and selling decisions. Nonetheless, a real First Amendment experience exists in this example – one that is too easily overlooked when focusing narrowly on the fact-based end product rather than more expansively on the intermediate moves that made that product possible.

> Even when robots or robotic components communicated with one another, there was still "meaningful" information being conveyed back and forth – all in exchanges that were set into motion by the human investor and that culminated in

his or her reception of the robotrader's report. In short, the interrobotic communicative exchange worked at the behest of and in the service of human objectives. Assuming that the investor's purposes and goals were lawful, the robo-trader's exchanges of information alone made those commercial objectives possible. Why, then, should the intermediate stages in the process – the communicative steps – be viewed as any less deserving of First Amendment coverage?

For IFS purposes, moreover, it does not matter whether the robotrader's report was nothing but a communication of a collection of facts that had little or no ideological or evaluative significance.

I have quoted this passage at length because I think it represents the precise point at which the argument in *Robotica* goes wrong. The argument, as best I can understand, seems to be that the lack of human involvement in generating or receiving the "interrobotic communicative exchange" is no obstacle to First Amendment protection. Intentionless free speech excuses us from having to identify a specific human whose intent is conveyed by these communications. Instead, the practical reality is that such communications will be protected as speech whenever they are "at the behest of and in the service of, human objectives."

This is the norm of utility. Collins and Skover contrast it with the views of other First Amendment scholars who believe that protections are reserved for speech that has "ideological or evaluative significance." For example, Robert Post argues in a famous essay discussing First Amendment protection for computer source code – crudely, speech *to* robots rather than speech *by* robots – that "First Amendment coverage is triggered by those forms of social interaction that realize First Amendment values."[14] Post has his own set of preferred values,[15] and other First Amendment theorists have theirs. Collins and Skover set up the norm of utility in opposition to all such theories. "Rather than looking up to the normative heavens, it looks down to the streets where life and technology evolve." Thus, they expect equal First Amendment protection for factual, artistic, and political speech – that is, "utility" replaces "truth" or "beauty" or "self-governance" as the governing First Amendment norm.

VI

Collins and Skover seem to think that the norm of utility follows from their reader-response analysis. I am not so sure that it does. In fact, I am quite certain that it doesn't.

Take the robotrader. Collins and Skover claim that the intermediate stages in the day's events – the information transmitted between and within trading robots – are covered "speech," and not just the final report presented to the human trader. But while the intermediate transmissions were "at the behest of and in the service of, human objectives," the only thing experienced *by a human* as speech was the final report. A listener-oriented reader-response approach can find meaning in the final report, but it has less to say about the intermediate steps. No human was present for them; no human extracted meaning from them. The user who set the algorithm in motion and who received the report likely has no idea how the robo-traders work or what they "said."

Intentionless free speech is a listener-oriented theory: it grounds protections in listeners' experiences rather than in speakers' intentions. But it is not a human-free theory: without a human somewhere in the loop, there is no cognizable First Amendment interest to assert, because no one's rights have been infringed. (As in copyright, the day when robots can qualify in their own right as legal persons protected by the Bill of Rights is still a long way off.)

Suppose there was no report at the end of the day, so that no information was presented to a human at all, and no human had an experience of meaning. Collins and Skover's argument would still go through. The trades were "at the behest of and in the service of, human objectives." This should be a sign: the argument doesn't actually depend on readers' responses to anything. The norm of utility is not really a *free speech* theory.

VII

The norm of utility cannot function as what Frederick Schauer calls a Free Speech Principle: a way of deciding what kinds of claims are "speech" claims entitled to special weight and what kinds of claims are not.[16] Schauer's point, which is profound, is that without some kind of Free Speech Principle, specific free speech arguments collapse into general liberty arguments. Utility is a norm and a virtue, to be sure. But it is not a *free speech* norm or a *free speech* virtue.

This isn't just a theoretical issue; it's a deeply practical one. My light-bulb robot is useful: it helps me see my dresser well enough to put on matching socks in the morning. The ban on inefficient residential incandescent bulbs is, by the norm of utility, a restriction on speech. It is probably a content-neutral restriction, although perhaps a manufacturer could argue that it is content-based given the different wavelength output profiles of incandescent, CFL, and LED bulbs. Energy efficiency is a substantial governmental interest that is probably unrelated to the suppression of speech, but is the restriction greater than necessary? That depends on the costs and availability of CFL and LED bulbs . . . and down the rabbit hole we go.

If utility is the "First Amendment lodestar," then speech eats the world, because anything some human cares enough to do is useful, at least to them. Some physicists, and some mystics, think that the entire universe is literally made up of information. The idea is that what we perceive as matter and forces and everything else is merely the flow and transformation of information from one place and one form to another. The universe, on this view, is a gigantic computer, constantly churning through the computation of a function of cosmic and unbelievable complexity. Something like this is true of Collins and Skover's conception of speech in the age of robots. Speech is everywhere and everything; it waits only for humans to come along and find it useful.

That would make the First Amendment into "the New *Lochner*," to use Amanda Shanor's term: a broad and deep prohibition on government regulation of a wide range of activity.[17] That might or might not be a good thing, but it is not meaningfully tethered to anything we would recognize or care about as "speech." The argument for maximal liberty has to be made on its own terms, in light of human experience and purposes. It can't be made by invoking an age-old progressive free speech tradition (as Collins and Skover do in the first third of *Robotica*), because that tradition as a *speech* tradition doesn't get us there. If everything is speech, then nothing is.

VIII

The crux of the contradiction is the relationship between communicative meaning and First Amendment coverage. The *Spence* test is deceptively simple: when a speaker's "intent to convey a particularized message" and listeners' "likelihood … that the message would be understood"[18] coincide, the First Amendment kicks in. On this view, communicative meaning is a necessary and sufficient condition of First Amendment coverage: if humans intend and experience it as speech, it's "speech" for First Amendment purposes. (We have already discussed the question of whether the speaker's intent is strictly necessary. Collins and Skover argue – I think correctly – that in cases of robotic speech the answer is "no," and listeners' understanding suffices.)

Some scholars accept this view that the First Amendment reaches to the full extent of communicative meaning. Back in 2000, Lee Tien gave a sophisticated account of it in terms of speech-act theory as part of a sustained argument for First Amendment protection for source code.[19] More recently, Stuart Benjamin gave a detailed working out of its consequences for robots.[20] And I take this to be an important premise of Jane Bambauer's argument that the collection and sharing of "data" is subject to First Amendment coverage.[21]

Other scholars disagree and think that the First Amendment reaches only a subset of communicative meaning. When Tim Wu says that courts "limit coverage in a way that reserves the power of the state to regulate the functional aspects of the communication process,"[22] he is not saying that a self-driving car's left-turn signal communicates nothing and has no meaning. The human or robotic driver of the car behind knows exactly what it means: "The car ahead is about to turn left." But that signal is so closely connected to the activity of safe driving that failure-to-signal laws are not regarded as restrictions on speech. Driving has great utility – but that still doesn't provide a compelling reason to treat the turn signal as First Amendment "speech." In various ways, at various times, and for various reasons, criminal conspiracies, threats, navigational charts, violent conduct, price fixing, and obscenity have all been so classified, despite possessing what any competent reader or listener would regard as communicative meaning.

The norm of utility blows past the limits of this debate: it finds First Amendment coverage even in cases where there is *no* communicative meaning. I do not read Tien, Benjamin, Bambauer – or anyone else, except perhaps John Perry Barlow – to go so far as to say, "It's all speech now, whether you knew it or not. As long as it's useful, it's speech." Not just the turn signal, but the wiring from the self-driving car's onboard computer to the turn signal, its laser and GPS unit, and the formulation of the rubber in its tires: they're all useful, they're all speech.

It is true that some activities that are never directly experienced by a human – including ones that no human is capable of experiencing – possess communicative meaning and are treated as "speech." We have no sense organs capable of detecting FM radio waves; our brains cannot easily decode the bits in a Microsoft Word file being emailed from one computer to another. And yet these are unquestionably "speech" for First Amendment purposes. These activities are "speech" because of their close nexus to other activities that do involve communicative meaning. For better or worse, different theories of the First Amendment do the work of explaining what kinds of nexus count and what kinds do not. The norm of utility does not and cannot, because it is completely untethered from the human experiences that distinguish speech from nonspeech in the first place.

IX

What has gone wrong here is that Collins and Skover's incorrect framing of the question of robotic speech – as "whether?" rather than "when?" – has led them to draw the wrong conclusions from their otherwise insightful analysis of how listeners experience the world. Reader-response is a good answer to the fact-laden question of when humans make meaning from their interactions with robots, but it is a poor answer to the categorical question of whether robotic speech requires a new First Amendment norm. Looking to the receiver's experience correctly distinguishes speech from nonspeech in many cases involving robots. It does not follow that utility is the new "First Amendment lodestar," because while utility is sensitive to what makes speech valuable, it is entirely indifferent to what makes speech *speech*.

An Old Libel Lawyer Confronts *Robotica*'s Brave New World

Bruce E. H. Johnson

I am a practicing attorney. I have handled libel and First Amendment cases since the mid-1970s. My response to this book is shaped by that experience.

In their book *Robotica*, Professors Ronald Collins and David Skover review the history of human communications technologies from the Stone Age to the Internet Era, discuss their free speech ("what it means to extend constitutional coverage to a technology") and governance (whether Gutenberg's discovery enabled Luther and led to the Protestant Reformation and eventually to copyright law and censorship) implications, and then focus on recent developments in robotic speech and artificial intelligence, noting that "robotic communication can act in the world quite differently than its media predecessors."

According to Collins and Skover, robotic communications – what they call "intentionless free speech" or "IFS" – should be protected by the First Amendment:

> It should be immaterial to free speech treatment that a robot is not a human speaker. It should be irrelevant that a robot cannot fairly be characterized as having intentions. It should be beside the point that a robot does not engage in a dialogic exchange to express propositions or opinions. For constitutional purposes, what really matters is that the receiver experiences robotic speech as meaningful and potentially useful or valuable. In essence, this is the constitutional recognition of intentionless free speech (IFS) at the interface of the robot and receiver.

Collins and Skover premise IFS protection on the tenets of reader-response criticism and reception theory, suggesting that "the receiver's experience of speech is perceived as an essential dimension of the constitutional significance of speech, whether human or not, whether intended or intentionless."

Free speech for robotic communication is to be tested by a strict utilitarian calculus:

> [S]ometimes the societal benefits of robotic expression will be so great as to deserve outright constitutional protection or to undermine the rule of existing law (whether

94

constitutional or statutory) so as to render it functionally obsolete (e.g., obscenity). In contrast, sometimes the societal costs of certain robotic expression will be so great as to overwhelm its value, thus subjecting it to legitimate governmental control.

As an experienced libel lawyer, I was intrigued that Collins and Skover did not address a bedrock principle that has governed American libel (and other types of First Amendment) litigation since 1964: heightened constitutional speech relating to matters of public concern.[1] Interestingly, this was a problem that I rarely confronted in defending media cases, because judges and other people reasonably assume that "newsworthiness" is the equivalent of "public concern,"[2] but this "public concern" revolution has quietly transformed American First Amendment doctrine. For an ordinary libel lawyer, the process has been transformative. As the Second Circuit has noted: "Beginning with *New York Times Co. v. Sullivan* . . . the Supreme Court ruled that the First Amendment of the United States Constitution limits the reach of state defamation laws insofar as they are applied to speech on matters of public concern."[3]

Thus, the Court has held that "a private individual whose reputation is injured by defamatory falsehood that does concern an issue of public or general interest" is required to prove negligence;[4] that "at least where a newspaper publishes speech of public concern, a private-figure plaintiff cannot recover damages without also showing that the statements at issue are false";[5] that a "statement on matters of public concern must be provable as false before there can be liability under state defamation law, at least in situations . . . where a media defendant is involved";[6] and that a public-figure plaintiff who fails to prove actual malice cannot recover for intentional infliction of emotional distress because "[a]t the heart of the First Amendment is the recognition of the fundamental importance of the free flow of ideas and opinions on matters of public interest and concern."[7]

In 2001, the Court extended this principle to bar statutory privacy liability arising from a radio station's use of a taped telephone conversation, which had been delivered by an anonymous informant, because "the subject matter of the conversation was a matter of public concern" and thus the statute as applied "implicates the core purposes of the First Amendment because it imposes sanctions on the publication of truthful information of public concern."[8]

Indeed, for the Westboro Baptist Church, the target of a lawsuit alleging intentional infliction of emotional distress because its members had attempted to harass funeral participants, the issue was dispositive:

> Whether the First Amendment prohibits holding Westboro liable for its speech in this case turns largely on whether that speech is of public or private concern, as determined by all the circumstances of the case. "[S]peech on 'matters of public concern' . . . is 'at the heart of the First Amendment's protection.'" *Dun & Bradstreet, Inc. v. Greenmoss Builders, Inc.*, 472 U.S. 749, 758–759 (1985) (opinion of Powell, J.) (quoting *First Nat. Bank of Boston v. Bellotti*, 435 U.S. 765, 776 (1978)).

The First Amendment reflects "a profound national commitment to the principle that debate on public issues should be uninhibited, robust, and wide-open." *New York Times Co. v. Sullivan*, 376 U.S. 254, 270 (1964). That is because "speech concerning public affairs is more than self-expression; it is the essence of self-government." *Garrison v. Louisiana*, 379 U.S. 64, 74–75 (1964). Accordingly, "speech on public issues occupies the highest rung of the hierarchy of First Amendment values, and is entitled to special protection." *Connick v. Myers*, 461 U.S. 138, 145 (1983) (internal quotation marks omitted).[9]

So, what do these cases tell us about First Amendment rights for robotic speech? Public concern, like public policy, "is a very unruly horse,"[10] and applying it to robotic speech will immediately upend the Collins and Skover utilitarian calculus. While they claim that "sometimes the societal costs of certain robotic expression will be so great as to overwhelm its value, thus subjecting it to legitimate governmental control," in fact robotic speech that relates to matters of public concern but imposes significant societal costs, including the destruction of American democratic discourse, may completely escape government controls.[11] In effect, the First Amendment will overrule Asimov's First Law of Robotics.[12]

For example, in 2016, Americans suffered through a presidential election that elevated to the White House the candidate who lost to his opponent by almost three million votes but managed to eke out a narrow Electoral College victory, allegedly (according to American intelligence officials) with the support of a "fake-news" botnet facilitated by foreign espionage. Indeed, during the 2016 presidential election, a "tsunami" of misinformation hit the United States.[13] As Senator Mark Warner, Democrat from Virginia, commented in March 2017, there "were upwards of a thousand paid Internet trolls working out of a facility in Russia, in effect taking over a series of computers which are then called botnets, that can then generate news down to specific areas" in the United States that the trolls believed were swing states.[14]

This "brave new world" of computerized disinformation that propagates virally and likely influenced the 2016 presidential campaign certainly confirms the authors' conclusion that "Robotic expression supercharges the communicative process." Furthermore, the corruption of the American electoral system by "fake-news" bots is likely accelerating, as these disinformation campaigns are spreading across the world. For example, a July 2017 study by Emilio Ferrara, an assistant research professor at the University of Southern California Department of Computer Science, was "the first to identify the presence of bots that existed during the 2016 U.S. Presidential election campaign period to support alt-right narratives, went dark after November 8, 2016, and came back into use in the run up days to the 2017 French presidential election."[15] Ferrara also noted the beginnings of a rudimentary marketplace for bots that were designed to disrupt democratic discourse by generating robotic lies: "anomalous account usage patterns suggest the possible existence of a black-market for reusable political disinformation bots."[16]

What is to be done? According to current First Amendment jurisprudence in the United States, the government is barred from limiting "dark money" independent expenditures, which are certainly behind the botnets.[17] In addition, the First Amendment limits the activities of government agencies charged with policing elections.[18] Knowing or reckless falsehoods that defame a person are constitutionally unprotected libel under *Sullivan*, but electoral lies have broader protection, as the Sixth Circuit recently acknowledged in rejecting an Ohio statute that reaches "not only defamatory and fraudulent remarks, but all false speech regarding a political candidate, even that which may not be material, negative, defamatory, or libelous."[19]

This prohibition on electoral policing is explicitly premised on the public concern rationale articulated in *Sullivan*; as a plurality of the Supreme Court noted in *United States v. Alvarez*, "false factual statements enjoy a degree of instrumental constitutional protection," because "there are broad areas in which any attempt by the state to penalize purportedly false speech would present a grave and unacceptable danger of suppressing truthful speech. Laws restricting false statements about philosophy, religion, history, the social sciences, the arts, and other matters of public concern would present such a threat."[20] Therefore, where matters of public concern are involved, only those lies that (in the Court's view) cause "legally cognizable harm" fall outside of First Amendment protection.[21]

Of course, limiting the powers of government entities to abridge freedom of speech and of the press concerning robotic publications on matters of public concern does not preclude private remedies. Indeed, the Internet, especially social media, remains a substantially private communications system.[22] In the future, it is likely that private actors may have more influence on American public discourse than does the government. That result is completely consistent with First Amendment doctrine.[23]

What First Amendment protections are available if robotic speech does not involve matters of public concern? Interestingly, libel case law suggests that such protections would be minimal, perhaps even nonexistent. This is the lesson from the Supreme Court's 1985 decision in *Dun & Bradstreet, Inc. v. Greenmoss Builders, Inc.*,[24] which affirmed a Vermont decision that permitted a judgment for damages arising from a false credit report, based upon a jury verdict that required no proof of fault, whether actual malice or negligence. In effect, the Court allowed the imposition of libel damages based on traditional English common law, which imposed strict liability for defamatory publications.

Collins and Skover reject the argument that "the speaker's intent matters for speech protection, so much so that the non-human and non-intentional speech generated by robots would, at best, be suspect as a candidate for significant constitutional recognition." Their rationale assumes that the requirement of scienter, or fault, is inherent in tort and criminal law:

> For example, scienter is a necessary element for the very presence or existence of illegal fraud, defamation, or true threats; without scienter, the law would not punish

the expressive conduct as a tort or crime at all. That scienter or intent may be present as a factor within First Amendment protection of these expressive activities might, in this sense, be derivative. In other words, without intention or scienter the expressive activity could not be punished as a tort or crime to begin with, and would not come within the aegis of First Amendment concerns about governmental regulation of such tortious or criminal conduct at all.

Of course, as Holmes reminds us, "even a dog distinguishes between being stumbled over and being kicked,"[25] so this conclusion seems unexceptional.

But *Dun & Bradstreet* affirmed a judgment for strict liability for communications at the heart of our commercial society, which means that in the "brave new world" of Collins and Skover, there would be significant legal risks arising from "intention-less" communications, or IFS. This is because, if the post-*Sullivan* constitutional overlay is unavailable and the speaker's (or in the case of computerized communications, the creator's) intention is irrelevant to liability, so long as speech does not involve matters of public concern,[26] government regulation of robotic speech would be completely unconstrained by constitutional limitations.[27]

Under this analysis, absent public concern, we return to the common law rules, and IFS amounts to strict liability for speech.[28] But if that is to be the result, someone (or something, such as a corporation) must be liable. With hundreds of thousands of lawyers, the American legal system will demand responsibility for errors arising from this "supercharged" communications system, which will be attached to human agents, because, as Judge Cardozo observed many years ago, traditional liability rules require a constant search for cause and effect: "Proof of negligence in the air, so to speak, will not do."[29]

We've been here before. Intentions matter. From Alexander Hamilton's defense of Harry Croswell's attacks on President Jefferson by articulating a free speech right to publish "with impunity, truth, with good motives, and for justifiable ends,"[30] to Justice Holmes' formulation of the "clear and present danger" test in *Schenck*,[31] to the *Brandenburg* case[32] rejecting a strict liability Ohio statute that outlawed "advocacy" of violence, and finally to Justice Brennan's endorsement in *Sullivan* of the "uninhibited, robust, and wide-open"[33] protections of the actual malice rule, the American law of libel (and sedition) has repeatedly pushed for causation limitation principles, mainly, the embrace of subjective intent, and its objective cousin negligence, in order to promote and encourage freedom of speech and of the press. Indeed, this innovation, by allowing a judge or jury to evaluate intent as a requirement of defamation liability, constituted a major break with the historic English common law imposing strict liability for libelous publications.[34]

Human agency was assumed, mainly because the American system of freedom of expression largely predates computerization, and because in the pre-electronic world, Americans could not conceive of a communications system based exclusively on IFS. But these reforming efforts were premised on the conclusion that human error alone should not negate the presumption of freedom of expression.

Rather, there must be something more before the government can impose liability for communicating. For example, the overwhelming majority of American state constitutions have adopted a specific formula for protection of the freedoms of speech and press (which is not limited to public concern speech) that allows liability only for "abuse" of these rights, a provision that was first enacted in August 1789 in the French Declaration of the Rights of Man and of Citizens[35] and is now included in dozens of American state constitutions' bills of rights as a routine source of free speech protections.

New York's "abuse" provision, first adopted in its Constitution of 1821, is a typical example: "Every citizen may freely speak, write, and publish his sentiments on all subjects, being responsible for abuse of that right; and no law shall be passed to restrain or abridge the liberty of speech or of the press."[36] As the late Judge Kaye observed, writing for the New York Court of Appeals in a leading case protecting statements of scientific opinion and comment, this language is more protective than the "no law" principles of the First Amendment and was designed "to set forth a basic democratic ideal of liberty of the press in strong affirmative terms."[37]

These types of "abuse" liabilities could be tort or criminal, as Collins and Skover suggest, or perhaps the legal system will create something like Professor Balkin's "information fiduciaries,"[38] but the hydraulic pressures against a pure IFS system, at least for non-public concern speech liabilities, will be irresistible. If speech does not involve matters of public concern, regulation will be light, but it will be there.

Ordinary life will embrace robotics, even if individual duties and liabilities persist for the speakers or enablers of electronic speech. But the world will look familiar, with hints of Mr. Rogers' Neighborhood. Communications will be lively and thoughtful. Human beings will regularly connect with human beings, and computers will be a means to an end.

But what about speech[39] on matters of public concern? Strangely, if we embrace IFS, the public "marketplace of ideas" – especially during election campaigns, when Big Money and Big Data can effectively "supercharge" their messaging – will look very different. In those circumstances, because public-concern robotic speech will resist regulations, fueled by First Amendment doctrine, overwhelmed by the inevitable Russian-sponsored botnets, and afflicted with algorithms and constant confirmation bias, Americans may find themselves trapped in a toxic Trumpian dystopia of computerized lies. Discourse, of course, will be dead.[40]

What's Old Is New Again (and Vice Versa)

Helen Norton

Thinking hard about robotic speech, as Collins and Skover ask us to do, makes many things old seem new again. It gives us the chance to revisit – and then retain, revise, or reject – our first premises about what it means to be human, about what it means to speak, and about when and why we value humanness and speech.

Collins and Skover's work also makes many things new seem old again. They remind us how we have repeatedly feared and resisted technological change even while we have embraced it. Our contemporary ambivalence about robotic speech thus strikes a familiar chord.

They conclude that, for First Amendment purposes, speech lies in the eye of the beholder and the ear of the listener:

> It should be immaterial to free speech treatment that a robot is not a human speaker. It should be irrelevant that a robot cannot fairly be characterized as having intentions. It should be beside the point that a robot does not engage in a dialogic exchange to express propositions or opinions. For constitutional purposes, what really matters is that the receiver experiences robotic speech as meaningful and potentially useful or valuable.

Their thesis is descriptively and normatively powerful, even as it raises additional questions and challenges. That, of course, is the point of their project.

I've explored related issues in past work – first with Toni Massaro[1] and then together with Toni and Margot Kaminski.[2] We focused on whether and when as-yet-hypothetical strong artificial intelligence ("strong AI," or what Collins and Skover call Second Order Robotics: "the realm of self-learning, adaptive, and virtually autonomous robots") might claim First Amendment rights as speakers. Our descriptive conclusions were similar to theirs: we found that contemporary free speech theory and doctrine are surprisingly inattentive to speaker humanness so long as humans remain at the center of the First Amendment analysis as listeners. In short, the nonhumanness of the speaker need not matter for First Amendment purposes when its speech is valuable to human listeners.

We started by examining longstanding "positive" free speech theories that value, and thus protect, expression that provides certain affirmative benefits: facilitating democratic self-governance, disseminating ideas and knowledge, furthering individual autonomy. We also considered "negative" free speech theory that instead underscores the need to constrain the government's potentially dangerous control of expression rather than affirmatively celebrate speech for its own sake. We found that these theories (as well as the Supreme Court's contemporary free speech doctrine that draws upon them) protect "listeners' interests in free speech outputs – rather than speakers' humanness or humanity – in ways that make it exceedingly difficult to place AI speakers beyond the First Amendment's reach."[3]

We also identified a possible exception to this claim: free speech theory that specifically prizes speech for its ability to further *speakers'* autonomy in expressing their own ideas and beliefs. But even there, we predicted that the value of strong AI speech to human listeners would force pragmatic (or, as Collins and Skover might say, hypocritical) changes to theory and doctrine: "Key to these practical concerns is that humanness is not essential to *legal* personhood – even if, as surely will be the case, human needs may inspire the move to AI legal personhood."[4]

While we assumed the intentionality of strong AI speakers (still-hypothetical Second Order Robotics) and found that the nonhumanness of those intentional speakers poses surprisingly few barriers to their First Amendment coverage, Collins and Skover focused on the speech products of weak AI robots (what they call First Order Robotics: "the realm in which computers and robots are typically viewed as agents driven by and responsive to the dictates of their principals"). They concluded that neither the humanness nor the intentionality of the speaker matter, nor should matter, for free speech purposes.

And while we took traditional free speech theories at face value in applying them to the problem of robot speech, Collins and Skover seek to challenge those theories. Indeed, they chronicle not only a history of technological change but also a history of hypocrisy. A major aim of their project is to expose what they see as the duplicity of prevailing free speech theories that celebrate speech with grand appeals to democracy and enlightenment. Collins and Skover posit that we claim to protect speech to achieve certain idealistic aspirations when we're instead actually interested much more broadly in utility – which they define capaciously to include "the many and varied kinds of communication that make our working lives easier and our home lives richer."

A NEW FREE SPEECH THEORY?

As Collins and Skover show, sometimes the changes wrought by emerging communications technologies have furthered the exalted ideals underlying traditional free speech theories: for example, the move from the oral to the scribal tradition helped undermine blind obedience to authority, and the much later development of the printing press enabled all sorts of revolutionary thought, with attendant religious and political change.

But this is not always the case. They observe, for example, that the new electronic and digital communications technologies of the last century have facilitated not only self-governance and the pursuit of knowledge but also a huge volume of expression geared instead toward entertainment, economic gain, pleasure, and indulgence. Lots of it is not pretty, much less virtuous – even if we pretend otherwise:

> The very idea that any value would be accorded to an electronic screen that grabbed human attention for an average of up to five hours daily would have been an abomination to the champions of print-based Enlightenment virtues ... And yet the old gospel of the pursuit of truth continued to be expounded by the free speech defenders of electronic communication. This deliberate lie thus became a central feature of the evolution of electrified speech.

Rejecting what they see as the dishonesty of much contemporary free speech theory, Collins and Skover offer utility in its place: "The speech we value is the speech we use to make life both possible and pleasurable. Such speech is not dependent on some Enlightenment principle for its currency. If free speech theorists have ignored this, it is because they view the law from on high and in the process demean realism in the name of idealism." Collins and Skover assert that utility theory is not only descriptively more accurate than but also normatively preferable to traditional theory: straight talk is better than hypocrisy, and covering more speech is better than less.

With this "new norm of utility," Collins and Skover offer a new positive free speech theory: we protect speech because of its affirmative value, and we define value very broadly as utility. Their utility norm might relatedly be seen as a refreshingly crisp refinement of the long-standing positive theory that prizes speech for its ability to further individual listeners' autonomy – that is, we protect speech because of its affirmative value, and we define value as the listener's freedom to define and choose what she finds useful. Either way, I see their utility norm as a type of positive theory distinct from negative theory, since negative theory is rooted primarily in concern for the government's potential incompetence and even malevolence as regulator of speech, rather than in celebration of the listener's affirmative experience of utility. Even so, this utility norm is also aligned with negative theory, as Collins and Skover suggest: "[A]s an interpretive theory of constitutional coverage, it is entirely consistent with the text-based proposition that the First Amendment imposes a restraint upon Congress and thus indirectly secures only negative liberties of speech, press, assembly, petition and religion." As we'll see, negative theory may provide the tiebreaker when we struggle to determine whether contested speech is actually of utility: in close cases, the government as regulator loses.

One of the primary reasons for positive First Amendment theory is to explain what speech is in and what's out and why. Collins and Skover are tough on most traditional positive free speech theories not only because they view them to be insufficiently speech protective but also because they find them hypocritical: we pretend, for example, that we protect speech to achieve elevated Enlightenment ideals when often we're protecting speech – like porn – simply because a significant number of people like it (although apparently the Enlightenment period itself had plenty of porn[5]).

But even the most capacious free speech theory needs *some* limiting principle – either when articulating the scope of First Amendment coverage (i.e., identifying the speech that gets any First Amendment attention and analysis at all) or when articulating the range of First Amendment protection (i.e., determining whether the government's regulation of covered speech survives the appropriate level of constitutional scrutiny). Regardless whether we choose coverage or – as Collins and Skover largely prefer – protection as the point at which to apply our limiting principles, we can't avoid hard line-drawing problems. And the new norm of listener utility requires us to address some of those challenges at the coverage stage (what they call "primary or first-order constitutional concerns"), where we must grapple with contested understandings of listeners and of utility.

THE DARK SIDE OF UTILITY

To be sure, utility has its sunny side. As Collins and Skover observe, "the speech we value is the speech we use to make life both possible and pleasurable."

But what speech – if any – fails such a roomy test of utility?

The authors identify one example: robocalling. It's hard to imagine a listener who experiences unsolicited marketing calls – especially but not only by a robot – as anything other than annoying. Robocalls thus "run strongly counter to the public interest. And that may go a long way to justifying the First Amendment's tolerance for much robocalling legislation." Although Collins and Skover don't expressly state whether they find that robocalling fails the utility test (thus receiving no First Amendment coverage at all) or whether they instead consider it useful and thus covered speech that is nonetheless sufficiently harmful to justify government regulation, I'd vote for its nonutility as a threshold matter. Along the same lines, my guess is that they would argue that threats, commercial fraud, perjury, and blackmail are also among the categories of speech that receive no First Amendment coverage because they are of no utility to their listeners.

Others have wrestled with listeners' interests in related settings and offer additional examples of expression that might fail the utility test. Felix Wu, for instance, proposes that we understand corporate and commercial speakers as having only "derivative" speech interests since we value their speech only for its utility to its listeners. As Wu points out, "[T]o say that the interest is derivative is not to say that it is unimportant, and one could find corporate and commercial speech interests to be both derivative and strong enough to apply heightened scrutiny to the restrictions that are the usual subject of debate, namely, restrictions on commercial advertising and restrictions on corporate campaigning."[6] At the same time, however, Wu observes that some speech regulations serve listeners' interests by restricting expression that listeners don't find useful or by requiring expression that listeners would find useful. Examples include not only bans on unwanted marketing (including but not limited to robocalling) but also requirements that commercial and corporate speakers provide listeners with information about the quality of goods and services, about the terms and conditions of commercial transactions, and about listeners' available legal rights.

But some assessments of utility are considerably more contested.

Recall, for example, that both the majority and the dissent in *Citizens United v. Federal Election Commission* agreed that the First Amendment protects political speech in large part because of its great value to listeners. For this reason, an 8–1 Court upheld the government's campaign disclosure and disclaimer requirements – that is, speech that discloses the source of certain campaign communications or contributions – because they require speech that is useful to listeners.[7]

But the majority and dissent vigorously disagreed about whether listeners experience unfettered corporate political speech as useful. Their differing views turned on their differing assessments about how listeners actually process information. In striking down governmental limits on corporate campaign speech, the majority implicitly adopted the "rational actor" model – that is, that listeners carefully gather and listen to all relevant information and then make rational decisions based on that information. Under this approach, the more speech from all sources, the better for listeners.

Others, however, conclude instead that the "rational actor" model itself privileges idealism at the expense of realism. In the words of dissenting Justice Stevens:

> If individuals in our society had infinite free time to listen to and contemplate every last bit of speech uttered by anyone, anywhere; and if broadcast advertisements had no special ability to influence elections apart from the merits of their arguments (to the extent they make any); and if legislators always operated with nothing less than perfect virtue; then I suppose the majority's premise would be sound.[8]

Contested assessments of utility are by no means limited to the realm of political speech. Alan Morrison, for example, worries that the Court's commercial speech doctrine has lost sight of listeners and their utility: "I had hoped that, as the commercial speech doctrine developed, the utility of the information to the consumer would be part of the balance, instead of simply asking whether the challenged statements were truthful."[9] He finds instead that courts protect a great deal of commercial speech that serves only the interests of commercial speakers and not that of their listeners. As examples, he asserts that – despite current case law to the contrary – a genuine concern for listeners' utility would permit government to require retail establishments near schools and playgrounds to place cigarette advertisements at least five feet from the floor (i.e., above a child's eye level), as well as to restrict tobacco advertisers' use of color and graphics. I wonder whether Collins and Skover would find those visual embellishments to be of utility to those who find them more pleasant or entertaining than more lackluster alternatives.

I don't think for a minute that Collins and Skover make the idealistic mistake of assuming that listeners' assessments of utility are necessarily rational. Instead, listeners' assessments are often based on aesthetic, intuitive, and other arational judgments, and so we shouldn't be surprised when their tastes diverge. But sometimes listeners' assessments of utility don't just differ from each other; sometimes listeners' experiences of utility are in direct conflict with each other. Think of trolling, for example. As Whitney Phillips explains, "trolls take perverse joy in ruining complete strangers' days. They will do and say absolutely anything to accomplish this objective, and in the service of these nefarious ends deliberately target the most vulnerable – or as the trolls would say, exploitable – targets."[10] To be sure, the trolls' targets are listeners who find this speech of no utility and often of great harm. But some number of the trolls' listeners include other members of the trolling community who derive pleasure and excitement in watching each other "ruin[] complete strangers' days." They consider trolling to be enjoyable – of utility – precisely because others find it so unpleasant.

Relatedly, Nathaniel Persily has examined how robot trolls' ability to disseminate fake news serves the utility of some listeners at the expense of others:

> The power [if any] of fake news is determined by the virality of the lie that it propagates, by the speed with which it is disseminated without timely contradiction, and by how many people receive and believe the false statement. As with other information or rumors in the offline world, many factors can drive a story's popularity: its entertainment value, novelty, salaciousness, and the like. But the pace with which lies can travel in the on-line world is much greater, and different strategies and techniques, such as automated social-media bots, can spread those lies to the right people ... Bots can serve many purposes, some beneficent and others nefarious. They can be used to skew on-line polls and to write favorable on-line reviews for restaurants or hotels. They can even be used to automatically generate YouTube videos based on other online content. Of greatest relevance here, bots can spread information or misinformation, and can cause topics to 'trend' online through the automated promotion of hashtags, stories, and the like. During the 2016 campaign, the prevalence of bots in spreading propaganda and fake news appears to have reached new heights ... The "search for truth" is necessarily far down the list of priorities for the social network, just as it is for its users, who will often find false, negative, bigoted, or other outrageous speech to be more meaningful and engaging.[11]

In other words, that the nasty and pernicious features of certain speech can strip it of utility for some listeners is precisely why other listeners find it useful.

This is the dark side of utility.

Relatedly, our assessments as listeners of our own utility are sometimes shaped – even coerced – by powerful speakers. For example, Collins and Skover suggest that listeners may be adapting to tolerate more defamation and privacy invasion in exchange for the greater utility of technology, that we "are willing to risk more harm in exchange for the benefit conferred by new communications technologies." But the notion that these are entirely our own choices reflects at least as much idealism as realism, as commercial and other powerful entities don't just accommodate and serve our interests as listeners – they invest huge amounts of time and money to influence and even manufacture our preferences. We will adapt, the authors say. But not all adaptations are healthy, and not all tradeoffs are truly free. Listeners may "adapt" to the loss of privacy protections the way that a frog placed in a pot of hot water "adapts" to its boiling: not necessarily as a matter of choice and not necessarily to our benefit.

In earlier work, I've explored related problems, urging that sincere attention to listeners' interests requires that we refrain from idealizing all speaker–listener relationships and instead recognize that speakers sometimes enjoy information and power advantages that increase the likelihood and severity of the harms that they may inflict upon their listeners. These harms include the harms of deception, manipulation, and coercion – which describe different ways in which a speaker may seek to bend her listener's will for her own purposes through power and the distortion of information.[12] Consumers, workers, clients, and patients exemplify listeners in such asymmetrical relationships. Attention to these asymmetries can support the government's choice to privilege listeners' interests over speakers' consistent with the First Amendment – for example, in the commercial and professional speech settings, where government imposes duties of honesty, accuracy, and disclosure upon comparatively powerful and knowledgeable speakers.

But listeners' interests don't always win out in these settings. Morgan Weiland, for example, asserts that the contemporary Court's approach to free speech problems has included a significant and potentially damaging (perhaps even hypocritical) change in its concept of "listeners":

> In the republican tradition, listeners are a stand-in for the public, whose interest in free expression is to achieve collective self-determination and self-government ... Leaving this tradition behind, the Court's new approach narrowly conceived of listeners as individual consumers or voters whose interest in free expression is to make informed choices in the market for goods or candidates ... [L]isteners' rights are subordinated to corporate speech rights. It is deeply ambiguous whether the Court's deregulatory holdings actually benefit listeners, though corporate interests are always served.[13]

Weiland explains that the Court's turn now enables plausible First Amendment attacks on regulations that we would formerly have viewed as furthering listeners' interests – such as privacy regulations that prohibit commercial entities' use of certain consumer information for marketing purposes, antidiscrimination regulations that prohibit Internet service providers from limiting users' access to certain sources of Internet traffic, and regulations that ban certain misrepresentations by corporate and commercial actors.

My sense is that, in grappling with the foregoing challenges, Collins and Skover would choose to err on the side of coverage, such that they would find speech to be covered by the First Amendment so long as *any* listener subjectively experiences it as useful, and that such speech would then be protected unless and until it inflicts harm that exceeds some objective measure: "[O]ur utility-based free-speech jurisprudence is neither obligated to justify censorship nor compelled to legitimate hypocrisy. This is so because it ratchets upward for more First Amendment coverage and often for more constitutional protection, provided there is no empirically provable overwhelming harm." In other words, negative theory provides the tie-breaker when listener assessments of utility are in conflict: close coverage calls go against the government that seeks to regulate contested speech.

This then invites a discussion of "empirically proven overwhelming harm" (or, as Collins and Skover assert elsewhere, "serious and immediate" or "widespread individual or collective" harm). Empirically proven to whom (and how)? Overwhelming (or serious and immediate, or widespread) to whom? The law has long struggled with these questions of objectivity – of identifying the "reasonable person" who will make these judgments for us. For example, "censorship" is a value-laden term that assumes the value (or utility) of the targeted expression: we generally talk of "censoring" speech that challenges political, religious, and artistic orthodoxy. "Regulation" is another value-laden term that instead emphasizes the nonutility (or harm) of the targeted speech: for example, we generally speak of "regulating" fraud, perjury, blackmail, and related expression. Our choice of terms reveals our assumptions about the contested expression's utility (or harm). In the hard cases, of course, these assumptions are contested. One woman's censorship is another man's regulation. Those who are quick to see utility in contested speech may well be those least likely to experience, and thus see, its harm. And vice versa.

The new norm of utility is in great part a celebration of listeners' freedom to choose that which they find useful. It is a powerful and attractive tool for thinking about the speech we value and why. But the utility norm is neither simple nor objective. I've sought to complicate the concept of utility, as I think that realism requires that we acknowledge that listeners themselves can and do disagree about the utility (and harm) of contested speech, that some listeners (as well as speakers) see other listeners simply as means to their own ends of utility, and that assessments of utility (and harm) can be shaped by the powerful to the detriment of those less powerful. Exactly what, if anything, free speech law should do about this complicated reality is a vexing challenge that has long confounded many of us. What's new is old again. And vice versa.

Reply

Robotica Refined

Ronald K. L. Collins and David M. Skover

Dialogic engagement – that robust exchange of ideas – is one of the revered aspirational tenets of the First Amendment. As evidenced by our first book together, *The Death of Discourse* (1996), it is one that we have long valued. And so too with some of our subsequent books such as *On Dissent: Its Meaning in America* (2013). Now with *Robotica*, we are again fortunate to have the informed engagement of several learned individuals. Such engagement helps shape our thinking with an eye to improving it.

In this way, our dialogue mimics, in modern times, the kind that Socrates sought out in his various oral encounters in ancient Athens. As any careful reader of the Platonic dialogues knows, their ultimate worth stems not simply from Socrates' comments but also from his interlocutors' responses. It is in that spirit that we first invited and then welcomed the commentaries of Ryan Calo, Jane Bambauer, James Grimmelmann, Bruce Johnson, and Helen Norton. Their thoughtful contributions – sometimes novel and nuanced – are especially beneficial given the relative scarcity of scholarship concerning the First Amendment and robotic expression. Interestingly, their reactions fall on a spectrum from praise to peril. Whereas Professor Bambauer finds *Robotica* to be a "forceful and convincing defense of wide speech protection for robotic expression," Mr. Johnson views our tract as pointing to a dystopian "Brave New World."

Of course, on some points, we differ from our colleagues, but that comes with any healthy exchange. Hence, we appreciate the input even when we take exception to it. In the end, what matters most are the best reasoned arguments. On that score, we leave it to our readers to judge for themselves.

&

Professor Ryan Calo's introduction kindly describes our give-and-take approach in *Robotica* – replete with commentators who are "little predisposed to take a sympathetic view" of some of our arguments – as "a model for future inquiry in robotics law and policy." We hope so. After all, some hearty intellectual rough-and-tumble is not only true to free speech principles, it also expands the borders of one's thinking. "Given the thoroughly interdisciplinary character of robotics law and policy," notes Calo, "it might also be interesting to hear from scholars in computer science and engineering who study and inform the design of robotics." Yes, most assuredly. At this intersection between law and technology, the science of law stands to learn much from laws of science and vice versa. More is better.

Imagine what you cannot imagine; such is the robotic domain of the future. "Many of the most exciting contemporary uses of artificial intelligence," says Calo, "involve recognizing patterns that people cannot." Indeed. Someday, no doubt, robotic responders may test the soundness of our logic in future books. But until that day arrives, we need, in Professor Calo's words, human thinkers to tee up those "critical question[s] for our time" and likewise issue "a warm invitation to the remainder of the community to weigh in." That is our way, the First Amendment way.

We turn next to Aristotle, for there is merit in what he once wrote: "what we are all inclined to do [is] direct our inquiry not by the matter itself, but by the views of our opponents."[1] And so let us now consider those views that in one way or another took issue with ours. We will do so by way of five tenets offered to further clarify and, in some instances, refine what we have said thus far.

Tenet #1: On Technology and Theory

Robotica was not inspired by a desire to propound a new and generalized theory of free speech. Rather, our aim was always to address the relationship between robotic technologies and the First Amendment. Thus, our primary focus is on the potential of robotic expression to reconfigure free speech theory. Imagistically put, such technologies add a transformative dye into the beaker of First Amendment waters. Ever since 1990, when we published an article entitled "The First Amendment in an Age of Paratroopers,"[2] we have fixed on the connection between emerging communications technologies and First Amendment freedoms. This book is a continuation and expansion of that. Insofar as our work is constructed within those parameters, any application of our free speech thinking outside of them is beyond our purview.

Tenet #2: Commentary In, Commentary Out – The Coverage vs. Protection Distinction

Central to our project is the distinction between those activities that might be *covered* by the First Amendment as distinguished by from what speech is *protected* by it. To ignore this, or to conflate the two, is to muddle and mistake our meaning. Accordingly, we cannot overstate the importance of this dichotomy.

So let us return to our argument, this in the name of enhanced clarity. In the context of robotic expression, Part II presents a theory of when a claim of First

Amendment *coverage* can reasonably be made, which we name "intentionless free speech" (IFS). Inspired by reception theory, we argue that when a reasonable receiver understands a transmission of information to be a meaningful expression, First Amendment coverage exists. In other words, unless the receiver finds some expressive meaning that comports with IFS, the transmission will not be deemed to be speech at all. Only if a robotic transmission satisfies the IFS standard will First Amendment *protection* analysis come into play. Part III proposes that First Amendment *protection* may be determined by a contextualized evaluation of the utilities secured and disutilities or harms incurred by the robotic expression in question. At that point, the norm of utility operates as a rationale or a justification for First Amendment protection. Whether utilities are offset by governmental demonstrations of harm will ultimately determine whether the robotic expression is given First Amendment protection.

Confusion over this dichotomy is most manifest in Professor James Grimmelmann's commentary. His misunderstanding is evidenced at the very beginning of his piece when he argues, "A few seconds' reflection shows that sometimes robotic transmissions are speech and sometimes they aren't, so the proper question is not 'whether and why' but 'when?'" It is true that sometimes robotic transmissions are speech and sometimes they aren't. That is what IFS is all about. Our discussion of IFS directly answers the "when" question: First Amendment speech coverage is accorded *when* a reasonable receiver understands a robotic transmission to be meaningful expression. To overlook this based on "a few seconds' reflection" is to mischaracterize our thesis at the outset and thereafter to derive misguided conclusions. Speech will not "eat the world" under a maxim of utility, as Professor Grimmelmann asserts, because speech is not to be defined by utility but rather by IFS, and protected speech is not to be determined by utility alone but rather by evaluation of competing utilities and harms.

Let us focus more centrally on the following passage from Part II of our work (again, our *coverage* analysis), because Professor Grimmelmann declares that "it represents the precise point at which the argument goes wrong":

> Even when robots or robotic components communicated with one another, there was still "meaningful" information being conveyed back and forth – all in exchanges that were set into motion by the human investor and that culminated in his or her reception of the robotrader's report. In short, the interrobotic communicative exchange worked at the behest of and in the service of human objectives. Assuming that the investor's purposes and goals were lawful, the robotrader's exchanges of information alone made those commercial objectives possible. Why, then, should the intermediate stages in the process – the communicative steps – be viewed as any less deserving of First Amendment *coverage*? (emphasis added)

Against that conceptual backdrop, let us consider Grimmelmann's claim: "The argument, as best as I can understand, seems to be that the lack of human involvement in generating or receiving 'interrobotic communicative exchange' is no obstacle to First Amendment *protection*" (emphasis added). On the one hand, if by this he means only that lack of human involvement at every step of the interrobotic exchange, which is not necessarily an obstacle to *coverage*, is then quite logically no necessary obstacle to *protection*, we agree. On the other hand, if by this he means that there will or is likely to be First Amendment protection in all such cases, we disagree.

He then adds the following, which leads us to believe that he confuses coverage with protection: "the practical reality is that such communications will be *protected* as speech whenever they are 'at the behest of and in service of human objectives'" (emphasis added). Again, the latter passage is from Part II, the *coverage* portion of our analysis. That is, before there can be any First Amendment utility-protection analysis (Part III), there must be some real coverage analysis, which may well preclude the former. Or to state it differently, once robotic expression is First Amendment covered under IFS (not utility) analysis, only then does the evaluative process begin with utility and related inquiries. After IFS analysis, the activity is analyzed to determine if it *qualifies* for protection.

On a related point, in Section VIII of his piece, Professor Grimmelmann acknowledges that First Amendment speech protection has and can be recognized for activities that, although not directly experienced by humans, bear a sufficient nexus to other activities with clear communicative meaning to a human. For purposes of First Amendment coverage, can it not be said that application of our IFS theory to the robotrader's interrobotic exchanges that culminate in a report received by a human resonates with such nexus analysis, even if the nexus involves several interrobotic connections?

Professor Grimmelmann's analytical problem is compounded when he draws on Robert Post's arguments concerning "First Amendment *coverage*" (emphasis added). It is in that precise context that the reader is advised that "Collins and Skover set up the norm of utility in opposition" to Professor Post's coverage claims. But we do not. Our utility analysis is not a measure of coverage. To put it metaphorically: this is a case of mixing apples with oranges. When that occurs, the methodical flaw becomes yet more apparent: to transform IFS reception coverage analysis into utility protection analysis is to equate a prerequisite with a conclusion.

The problem here is that if one starts off on the wrong footing, one is certain to stumble. At one point, Professor Grimmelmann appears to have understood our coverage–protection dichotomy: "I think Collins and Skover have it right when they claim that a listener's experience is sufficient to *ground* a *legally*, morally, and politically *cognizable* speech interest" (emphasis added). Had he not strayed from that point, he would not have stumbled.

Tenet #3: On Utility – A Conceptual Framework for Protecting Robotic Speech

In order to clear away some analytical brush, it may be useful to stress what our utility norm is not. It is:

- Not exclusionary: Our utility norm can work in tandem with other First Amendment normative theories. In that sense, it does not exclude consideration of other theories of free speech value.
- Not hypocritical: Our utility norm aims to avoid trading in hypocrisy – the kind that occurs, for example, when Enlightenment theories of First Amendment value are stretched to the breaking point in order to protect outlier forms of expression.
- Not absolute: Our utility norm is checked by the harm principle, insofar as claims of technological benefits may be overcome by demonstrations of disutilities and harms (e.g., physical, economic, and environmental injuries or national security harms, etc.).
- Not synonymous with other norms or principles: Our utility norm ought not be understood to collapse into other more confining normative value theories. A robotic expression that serves even private interests, as con-trasted with public ones, might be protectable in the absence of any significant competing disutility or harm. Moreover, our utility norm does not focus on desires and wants that fall far afield from functional-ity. The more utility bends to mere pleasure, the more self-gratification dilutes its conceptual value. Though the presence of pleasure alone may not negate utility, the utility norm should not be consumed by an all-devouring pleasure principle.

  Mr. Johnson seems to be unmindful of this point when he critiques us for failing to address the "bedrock principle" providing heightened First Amendment protection to "speech relating to matters of public concern." To this charge, we offer several responses.

  First, "public concern" is not an inquiry that is relevant to First Amend-ment coverage for robotic expression under our IFS theory. It only becomes relevant under our utility calculus for First Amendment protection. The more robotic expression is useful for the general public, the more protectable it may be; or the more the public interest is harmed, the less protectable it may be.

  Second, as the foregoing suggests, notions of public interest may be already subsumed within the utility calculus. This is reinforced by our earlier observation that the utility norm is not exclusionary but may work in tandem with other First Amendment normative value theories.

  Third, public interest is a concept that is not infrequently defined vis-à-vis other First Amendment norms, such as Alexander Meiklejohn's theory of self-governance. The Supreme Court suggested as much in

Garrison v. Louisiana when it equated "speech concerning public affairs" with "the essence of self-government."[3] To the extent that this occurs, public interest analysis may dilute the utility norm and thereby diminish the domain of First Amendment protection.

Fourth, as Mr. Johnson concedes, public interest is an "unruly" norm inviting confusion. Indeed, some of Professor Norton's line-drawing concerns could be equally applicable to Mr. Johnson's public interest analysis.

Fifth, given the First Amendment's aegis, the public interest in robotic communications technologies may well be defined primarily as the maximizing of the free flow of digitized information, ideas, and opinions.

Finally, insofar as the utility norm may invite a Huxleyan dystopia, the same may be said – and we stressed as much in *The Death of Discourse* – of existing First Amendment doctrines. Moreover, as discussed more fully in Tenet #4 that follows, a governmental "cure" to such a problem might itself be viewed as a form of Orwellian tyranny.

- Not canonical: Our utility norm, like all other theories, must have some play in the joints to be effective. Because of that play, there will always be hard questions of line drawing. What we propose in Part III is more a conceptual framework for First Amendment evaluation of robotic expression than uncompromising jurisprudential dictates. Thus it is that we offer mainly generalized principles for analyzing specific issues of protection and dedicate but several pages to such preliminary determinations.

Not oblivious to this point, Professor Norton is nonetheless troubled by the "hard line-drawing problems" that "the dark side of utility" poses. We need emphasize, however, that there are meaningful limitations built into our robotic free speech analysis. In addition to the IFS threshold elaborated in Tenet #2, there is the harm principle. In other words, evaluation of one person's utilities and another person's dis-utilities and harms are all part of the calculus of First Amendment protection, and the precise point at which a line is drawn is often too contextualized to be determined *a priori*.

Of course, the idea of rights-in-conflict is not new to First Amendment inquiry. Just consider, for example, the conflict between press rights and the fair trial rights of an accused that gave rise to *Nebraska Press Association v. Stuart*. As Chief Justice Warren Burger put it:

the guarantees of freedom of expression are not an absolute prohibition under all circumstances, but the barriers to prior restraint remain high and the presumption against its use continues intact. We hold that, with respect to the order entered in this case prohibiting reporting or commentary on judicial proceedings held in public, the barriers have not been overcome; to the extent that this order restrained publication of such material, it is clearly invalid. To the extent that it prohibited publication based on information gained from other sources, we conclude that the heavy burden imposed as a condition to securing a prior restraint was not met.[4]

In other words, not all rights (or interests) are created equal. Sometimes the thumb on the scale weighs more heavily for one right than for another. Put into our context, one person's utilities may be more functional and less harmful to society than another's. If so, the First Amendment utility norm (supplemented by other doctrines such as content discrimination, vagueness, substantial overbreadth, etc.) may point to enhanced protection for one rights claimant.

Moreover, recall our primary focus on the relationship between robotic technology and free speech law examined in Tenet #1. Hence, one must be mindful of the potential that new technologies have to reconfigure old legal tests. In that regard, the Internet functionally obliterated much of the First Amendment obscenity doctrine. Something of the same might be said of *Brandenburg v. Ohio*'s incitement test: "the constitutional guarantees of free speech and free press do not permit a State to forbid or proscribe advocacy of the use of force or of law violation except where such advocacy is directed to inciting or producing imminent lawless action and is likely to incite or produce such action."[5] Given the nature of robotic expression – its mind-boggling speed and its wide-ranging reach – *Brandenburg's* imminence test may have to be revised with much more emphasis on the "likely to produce such action" prong and all that implies. The magnitude of harm and the impracticability of governmental checks may call for a technological fix, perhaps even a governmentally sanctioned one that could very well raise new First Amendment challenges and issues. All told, our key point here is that emerging technology will drive much of future First Amendment analysis.

In the end, it is well to ponder the sage advice of François-Marie Voltaire: "Doubt is not a pleasant condition, but certainty is an absurd one."[6]

Tenet #4: On Functional Fixes – Technological and Regulatory Responses

The negative liberty secured by the First Amendment inveighs generally against governmental intervention in the communications marketplace. This might be so even when robotic expression causes real and substantial harms. The law typically disfavors regulatory responses when private-sector technological fixes ("less burden-some means") are both available and adequate. Such may likely be the case, as we noted in our utility discussion earlier, when robotic technologies have the capacity to outstrip the pragmatic potential of regulatory responses.

When Professor Norton bemoans the dissemination of "fake news" by "robot trolls," our tenet takes on enhanced force. On the one hand, false statements or misinformation about private individuals or commercial products are already regu-lated by numerous federal and state consumer protection and defamation laws. On the other hand, the problem is much more complicated when it comes to "fake news" in the political arena. If nefarious groups deploy trolls to spread misinfor-mation there, it may be incumbent on opposing groups to respond in technological kind and employ antitrolls to correct the record with truthful information. In a sense, this robotic warfare is akin to real warfare, with anti–ballistic missile technol-ogy checking enemy ballistic missiles. Similarly, when Mr. Johnson decries "the destruction of American democratic discourse" by robots that "may completely escape government controls," we cry out for robotic fixes that trump the potential of regulatory responses alone.

Notably, the technological fix is an instantiation of Justice Louis Brandeis's First Amendment maxim that the answer to false speech is not censorship but counter-speech.[7] Even if entities spend "huge amounts of time and money to influence and even manufacture our preferences," as Professor Norton laments, should we admit to governmental regulation of such political campaigns? Would this not be a stark example of governmental paternalism running amok?

As the authors of *The Death of Discourse*, we greatly sympathize with Mr. John-son's angst over the electronic pollution of enlightened and rational political discourse. Our cultural critique in that book notwithstanding, as a legal matter we nod to the compelling arguments against the governmental monitoring of bot-generated political falsehoods. Of course, falsehoods have long been purveyed by human agents of political campaigns using earlier electronic technologies rather than robotics; to be sure, radio and television ushered in an era of far more wide-spread political misinformation than the printing press. Surely, the First Amend-ment would prevent government from censoring false political speech regardless of the technology.[8] Ours is a First Amendment that abhors a governmental ministry of truth.

Tenet #5: On Thinkers – Safeguarding the Producers and Products of Knowledge

In her insightful Commentary, Professor Jane Bambauer invites us to reflect on "thinker innovations" and how those new technologies might be harnessed to expand the domain of human knowledge. Related to that concern is the need to safeguard the informational output of "robot thoughts." It is those thought products that Bambauer wishes to place under the jurisprudential umbrella of First Amend-ment law. She makes intriguing points to which we want to add a few of our own.

It is a stunning fact about data: "From the beginning of time until 2002, the world created five exabytes (five billion gigabytes) of information; today, we create that much data in about 10 minutes."[9] As if data generation were not astounding enough, consider also the storage, analysis, and sharing of this data. The new intelligence, of course, is artificial intelligence; the new Enlightenment is light-years beyond the imagination of Francis Bacon, the father of empiricism, and his scientific colleagues. It is within that domain that Jane Bambauer urges us to think about "freedom of thought" associated with the "private development of new insights" about oneself and one's world. How will First Amendment law protect that domain – one that focuses less on communication and more on knowledge?

Justice Benjamin Cardozo once said that "freedom of thought ... is the matrix, the indispensable condition, of nearly every other form of freedom. With rare aberrations a pervasive recognition of this truth can be traced in our history, political and legal."[10] But efforts to protect that freedom – and the bounties of knowledge created in an electronic era – reveal the wide gulf between rhetorical endorsement and doctrinal enforcement.

It is in this setting that we are asked to shift conceptual gears and move away from "dialogical" paradigms and toward "thinker" ones; that is, to focus more on "thinker innovations" rather than confining our analysis to "communications innovations." This move entails withdrawing *communication* from the blend, or doing so in a more direct context. Or as Bambauer emphasizes later: "Machine thinkers are not necessarily communicators. They do not necessarily transfer knowledge to a human or even to another machine." In other words, how do we protect thought and its byproducts when communication is not expressly in the mix? To cast the question in her own words: "So should Collins and Skover's call to recognize First Amendment protection for useful robot communications apply equally to useful robot thoughts?" She asks this because, as she sees it, "it is not immediately clear why communication is always a *vital* part of a robot's conceptual mix."

Importantly, the thinker–communicator divide may not be as stark as Professor Bambauer suggests. Whether generated by humans or robots, a thinker's research is integrally related to communication, at least insofar as the information being collected has already been expressed. That is, roboticized collection and analysis of data is virtually impossible without some real measure of communicative inter-action with humans or other computers. In this sense, the robot is distinguishable as a technology from binoculars or a telescope. To function effectively, neither bin-oculars nor telescopes need to interact with other binoculars or telescopes, and a government ban on a type of binoculars would more easily constitute a takings or due process issue than a free speech claim. The information that Professor Bambauer would vest with First Amendment significance comes from somewhere, and when that information is transmitted to a robot and ultimately transferred to its human receiver, communication has transpired. In that sense, the robot is simultaneously a "thinker" and a "communicator."

All of this prompts us to consider washing machines. Let us explain. Washing machines, as Professor Bambauer asserts, are useful. We turn a knob and, presto, the "ultra white cycle" begins. By doing so, do we *communicate* with our washing machine? Or think of the old tub-and-wringer variety. Do we communicate with the wringer when we crank it and it responds by pushing garments between its two rollers? Now, what if we add a computer chip? We push buttons, and it all happens electronically. Is pushing the button communication? But what if we had an AI washing machine that asked questions about everything from the volume and heat of the water to the speed of the spin cycle and operated according to our vocal responses? Unless such washing machine conundrums are solved, Grimmelmann might argue, speech will eat the world. But will it? Or, to rephrase the question, will the new technological world eat speech if we remain oblivious to how such innovations affect freedom of expression?

Before putting our discussion through an analytical wringer, it is helpful to restate the obvious: with ever-increasing frequency, communication is digitalized as data make their way across endless wireless byways. As that occurs, how we understand the contours of speech and intelligence will change. Seen in this light, the problem will hardly be speech devouring the world. Rather, the problem is far more likely to be the new technological world devouring speech and the protections once accorded to it. To the extent that we allow that to occur, the problem of the past will be repeated – censorship will once again demand its due in shackling the latest technology.

Let us tap into the mindset of how we use our words in everyday language to help us resolve the washing machine riddle. For example, consider the following:

- "I spoke to my tub and wringer today."
- "I talked with my washing machine earlier today when I turned the knob to cold water."
- Or, "after breakfast, I conversed with my washing machine when I pushed the electronic long-cycle button."

Such "conversations" are of the kind that invite psychological counseling. People of sound mind don't typically speak to or with washing machines or tables or cars. But wait. What if the car is equipped with a speech-recognition device? In that context might conversing with one's car make some sense? Consider, for example, the following statements:

- "My new car is so cool. I can place my Starbucks order by using its voice-command feature and then have it tell me when my order will be ready."
- Or what if I said, "I just love my new AI washing machine. It asks me just how I want my delicates done, and it even tells me when the wash is done."

Now, ask yourself: Are the latter statements of a different order than the previous three? If so, why? Might the answer have much to do with the fact that in the latter instances, there is communication going on? Surely, it might not be of the traditional type envisioned by Socrates and championed by Meiklejohn. But it is communication nonetheless; a message is being sent and received and even replied to. To that extent, is a demarcating line not drawn? And if so, is this not the point at which our IFS theory enters into the picture to do its conceptual spade work?

So, Professor Bambauer, yes. It is possible to speak with your washing machine *provided* you talk to the right one ... much as we just spoke with Siri on our laptop to find an article in *The Guardian* about talking washing machines and other home devices.[11]

◈

We come to our closing words. Yet ours is a strange ending, if only because it comes at the dawn of a new day in our First Amendment jurisprudence. What tomorrow will bring we can but imagine, and then only vaguely and partially so. After all, we see tomorrow through the lens of today. Or to paraphrase Marshall McLuhan: We drive into the future with our eyes fixed on the rearview mirror.[12] In that light, we have tried, where appropriate, to cast some of our arguments with a wide net, if only to allow ample room for future analytical maneuvering. Of course, future technologies, different economies, cultural changes, and the vagaries of an ever-burgeoning free speech jurisprudence will all shape the contours of what is to come, say, in 2044 – the 400th anniversary of *Areopagitica*. Will our world today look as strange to those living tomorrow as Milton's looks to us now? Yes, in all likelihood. Then again, certain ideas last over time, not so much because they are fixed but because they are adaptable. It is precisely that evolutionary principle – of which Justice Oliver Wendell Holmes was acutely aware – that gives staying power to the most lasting ideas. If an idea does not evolve, it will not endure. Perhaps more than all else, we have crafted our arguments against the backdrop of that maxim.

Evolution does not respect constitutions, customs, or creeds. It washes over them like waves erode shorelines. Beyond metaphorical messages, what does that mean? It means that we must approach robotic communication with a certain open-mindedness, a preparedness to question our presuppositions,[13] and a willingness to embrace, albeit guardedly, what seems inevitable. That is, the inevitable may not always sync well with today's view of law or even with today's values associated with what it means to be a human being engaged in communication. But recall Socrates and his critique of writing. If we are to be honest, we cannot deny, *carte blanche*, the merit of much of what he said: something was lost in the transition from orality to scribality. And yet, as Plato had the foresight to realize, something was also gained – such is the measure of "man." Until we understand that, roboticized communication will produce more dizzying paradoxes in the law than standards by which a free society can live and flourish.

Modernity never grows old. This explains why there will always be some "crisis of modernity," *ad infinitum*. When we think in such terms, names like François-Marie Voltaire and Denis Diderot or more recently Michel Foucault and Jean Baudrillard spring to mind. But we might as well think of Johannes Gutenberg (Western inventor of the printing press), Tim Berners-Lee (inventor of the Internet), or Martin Cooper (inventor of the handheld cellular mobile phone). Technologies – and, more specifically, communications technologies – are inextricably linked to modernity. Thus, there will always be some "crisis" swirling around them. And why is that so?

As we have seen, the mechanisms of communication affect the way we think and interact and therefore influence the law of free speech governing them. Whenever a profoundly new communication technology emerges, its effects on how we comprehend our world and communicate knowledge will be far reaching, as will the emerging law governing it. Both benefits and harms are blended in the crucible. Moreover, in the process, the very notions of benefit and harm are reconfigured. Thus, what Socrates deemed to be harmful Plato demonstrated to be beneficial. If utility is a suitable free speech norm, it is because its value is not static; it is dynamic.

Mindful of what we have just sketched out, one can sense something of the subterranean side of what we have offered up in *Robotica*. That something might be understood as a *philosophy of technology*, a more wide-ranging way of thinking about life and law. Given how vital technology is to culture and how it dominates it in so many ways, a philosophy that speaks to such concerns would seem natural.[14] But that is hardly the case, and it is certainly not the case when it comes to legal philosophy. Ironically, this absence is even more striking when one thinks of how technology impacts our conceptions of knowledge and truth – matters central to the First Amendment. To be sure, much more would need to be said to give real and full significance to this seedling of a philosophical point. For now, however, we trust that what we have outlined concerning the architectonic qualities of technology will suffice to indicate that there is more at stake here than law alone, even constitutional law. This brings us to a related point, our final one.

Artificial. It is what humans, rather than what God or nature, create. It is our mortal contribution to existence. Think of it as our attempt to be God-like. In that sense it is both presumptuous and wondrous. Thus, if more and more of our modern collective intelligence tends toward the artificial, it is because it is all-too-human to do so. It is, if you will, our Promethean predisposition. By that mythological gauge, we ask: Will the free-speech jurisprudence of the future be bound or unbound? Probably more the latter. If so, hail Prometheus!

– *finis* –

Notes

PART I THE PROGRESS AND PERILS OF COMMUNICATION

1 Plato, *Phaedrus* 274D–275B, trans. Alexander Nehamas and Paul Woodruff (Indianapolis, IN: Hackett Publishing Co., 1995), pp. 79–80.

2 G. R. F. Ferrari, *Listening to the Cicadas: A Study of Plato's Phaedrus* (New York: Cambridge University Press, 1990), p. 220.

3 In his account of preliterate Greek culture, Professor Eric Havelock notes that "usage as it is recorded in the political, religious, or family sphere can itself often turn into a kind of technique ... [M]uch of social behavior and deportment had to be ceremonial, or had to be recorded ceremonially, which may amount to very much the same thing." Eric Havelock, *Preface to Plato* (Cambridge, MA: Harvard University Press, 1963), p. 80. Accounting for religious practice as an invented craft. Havelock explains that "Greek religion was a matter not of belief but of cult practice, and cult practice was composed of an accumulated mass of procedures which had to be performed skillfully in order to be performed dutifully and properly and piously." *Ibid.*, p. 81.

4 M. T. Clanchy, *From Memory to Written Record: England 1066–1307* (Cambridge, MA: Harvard University Press, 1979), p. 203. According to Professor Clanchy, "William the Conqueror went one better and jokingly threatened to make one donee 'feel' the conveyance by dashing the symbolic knife through the recipient abbot's hand saying, 'That's the way land ought to be given.'" *Ibid.*

5 See, e.g., Marc Bloch, *Feudal Society*, trans. L. A. Manyon (New York: Routledge Press, 1962), pp. 113–114; Clanchy, *From Memory to Written Record*, p. 208; Harold J. Berman, "The Background of the Western Legal Tradition in the Folklaw of the Peoples of Europe," *University of Chicago Law Review* 45: 553, 563 (1978).

6 Bloch, *Feudal Society*, p. 114.

7 Berman, "The Background of the Western Legal Tradition," p. 561. See also Clanchy, *From Memory to Written Record*, pp. 232–233; J. E. A. Jolliffe, *The Constitutional History of Medieval England: From the English Settlement to 1485* (London: Adam and Charles Black, 4th edn., 1961), pp. 2–4, 9–10, 58–59; M. E. Katsh, *The Electronic Media and the Transformation of Law* (New York: Oxford University Press, 1989), pp. 60–63;

F. W. Maitland, *The Constitutional History of England*, edited by H. A. L. Fisher (New York: Cambridge University Press, 1908), pp. 115–118.

8 Berman, "The Background of the Western Legal Tradition," pp. 562–563.

9 See, e.g., Jolliffe, *The Constitutional History of Medieval England*, pp. 23–24 ("Law is not in the king's mouth" but spoken by lawful men in the "folkmoots"); Berman, "The Background of the Western Legal Tradition," pp. 564–567. Like its trials by oaths, the oral culture's rules were often expressed in poetic ways. "Phrases like 'unbidden and unbought, so I with my eyes saw and with my ears heard', 'foulness or fraud', 'house and home', 'right and righteous', 'from hence to thence' – were common." *Ibid* at 562.

10 See, e.g., James Bryce, *Studies in History and Jurisprudence* (Oxford: Clarendon Press, 1901), 1: 275–276; Michael Gagarin, *Early Greek Law* (Berkeley: University of California Press, 1989), pp. 10, 131.

11 See, e.g., Florian Coulmas, *The Writing Systems of the World* (Hoboken, NJ: Wiley, 1989), p. 11; M. T. Clanchy, "Remembering the Past and the Good Old Law," *History* 55: 165, 168–170 (1970). See also Katsh, *The Electronic Media and the Transformation of Law*, p. 25 (explaining the consequences of using speech to pass on traditions in oral societies). Eric Havelock posits that oral communication may have operated on three levels in ancient Greek society:

"There would be the area of current legal and political transactions; the issuance of directives which would accumulate as precedents. Here the governing class bore the main responsibility for oral formulation of what was necessary. Then there would be the continual re-telling of the tribal history, the tale of the ancestors and how they behaved as models for the present. This historical task would be the special province of the minstrels. And finally there would be the continual indoctrination of the young in both tale and precedent through recital." Havelock, *Preface to Plato*, pp. 120–121.

For a pathbreaking exploration of the classical art of memory that employed mnemonic techniques for rhetorical purposes, see Frances A. Yates, *The Art of Memory* (Chicago: Chicago University Press, 1966).

12 Jolliffe, *The Constitutional History of Medieval England*, p. 13. The oral preservation of *nomoi* (customary norms) in Greek society was important to the survival of the group identity of the people: "[T]he tradition, the continuity of law, custom, and usage must be maintained, or the scattered groups would disintegrate and their common tongue be lost. The essential vehicle of continuity was supplied by a fresh and elaborate development of the oral style, whereby a whole way of life, and not simply the deeds of heroes, was to be held together and so rendered transmissible between the generations." Havelock, *Preface to Plato*, p. 119, footnote omitted.

13 Professor Walter Ong astutely observes, "Oral utterance thus encourages a sense of continuity with life, a sense of participation, because it is itself participatory." Walter Ong, *Interfaces of the Word: Studies in the Evolution of Consciousness and Culture* (Ithaca, NY: Cornell University Press, 1977), p. 21.

14 Ong, *Interfaces of the Word*, p. 20.

15 See, e.g., Maitland, *The Constitutional History of England*, pp. 115–116; Berman, "The Background of the Western Legal Tradition," pp. 561–562 (oaths to be repeated "without slip or trip"). The purportedly rigid forms of oral pleading in illiterate societies, however, may be exaggerated. Clanchy suggests that formulaic oaths or pleas, "held in memory

alone, ... probably did change in ways imperceptible to the users. Even in the earliest recorded pleadings changes took place." Clanchy, "Remembering the Past," p. 175. Clanchy draws a telling analogy between the remembrancer in the early Western oral cultures and the professional oral pleader in the English courts of the thirteenth century:

In the thirteenth century, and perhaps earlier, the litigant sometimes used a professional pleader to make the claim on his behalf. This pleader is described in French as a *conteur* and in Latin as a *narrator*. The claim is called a *conte*, a *narratio*, or a " tale" in English. So the pleader's art is described in the same terms as that of the medieval minstrel, the "singer of tales." This could be a coincidence. On the other hand it may indicate the pleader's original function as an illiterate remembrancer using the poetic technique of the singer of tales to recall the forms of his "tales" or pleadings and make them sound right. In the few surviving fragments of early English pleadings rhythmical and alliterative formulas are very evident. *Ibid* (footnotes omitted).

16 Professor Katsh argues that preliterate society was "conservative and hence profoundly antiprogressive when seen through the framework of our contemporary culture." Katsh, *The Electronic Media and the Transformation of Law*, p. 23. As qualified, the statement contains a measure of truth. Orality, however, provided a degree of flexibility in preliterate society that may have disappeared in the subsequent scribal and typographic eras.

17 In their penetrating work on the cultural traditions in preliterate societies, Professors Jack Goody and Ian Watt observe that such societies are "homeostatic" in the sense that their members tend to remember that which continues to be of social value and to forget selectively that which ceases to be of contemporary relevance. Goody and Watt label this process the "social function of memory." Jack Goody and Ian Watt, "The Consequences of Literacy," in Jack Goody, editor, *Literacy in Traditional Societies* (New York: Cambridge University Press, 1968), pp. 27, 30–34, 44. See also Jack Goody, *The Interface between the Written and the Oral* (New York: Cambridge University Press, 1987), pp. 167–190 (discussing memory and learning in oral and literate cultures).

18 Clanchy, *From Memory to Written Record*, p. 233. See also Clanchy, "Remembering the Past," pp. 165, 171–172, 176.

19 Theodore F. T. Plucknett, *A Concise History of the Common Law* (London: Butterworth, 5th edn., 1956), p. 308 (quoting René Wehrlé, *De La Coutume Dans Le Droit Canonique* (1928), pp. 139–140).

20 See, e.g., Coulmas, *The Writing Systems of the World*, pp. 11–12 (when memories are passed on to the next generation, "legend and memory become indistinguishable"); Clanchy, "Remembering the Past," pp. 162–168, 172.

21 See, e.g., Havelock, *Preface to Plato*, p. 121 ("The inhibition against new invention, to avoid placing any possible strain upon the memory, continually encouraged contemporary decisions to be framed as though they were also the acts and words of the ancestors."); Fritz Kern, *Kingship and Law in the Middle Ages*, trans. S. B. Chrimes (Oxford: Basil Blackwell, 1939), p. 179 (stating that customary law was a "perpetual grafting of new on to old law").

22 Clanchy, "Remembering the Past," p. 171.

23 See generally Sotheby's, *The Magna Carta* (New York: private printing, December 18, 2007); Featured Documents, "The Magna Carta," *The National Archives*, at www.archives.gov/exhibits/featured-documents/magna-carta; A. E. Dick Howard, *The Road from Runnymede: Magna Carta and Constitutionalism in America* (Charlottesville:

University of Virginia Press, 2015); J. C. Holt, *Magna Carta* (New York: Cambridge University Press, 3rd edn., 2015).

24 Robert K. Logan, *The Alphabet Effect: The Impact of the Phonetic Alphabet on the Development of Western Civilization* (New York: William Morrow, 1986), pp. 19–25; Ong, *Orality and Literacy*, pp. 83–84.

25 Warren Chappell, *A Short History of the Printed Word* (New York: Knopf, 1970), pp. 59–83; Elizabeth A. Eisenstein, *The Printing Revolution in Early Modern Europe* (New York: Cambridge University Press, 1983), pp. 12–13.

26 See Coulmas, *The Writing Systems of the World*, pp. 11–13; Harold A. Innis, *Empire and Communications* (Toronto: University of Toronto Press, 1972), p. 711 (discussing the temporal and spatial aspects of media); Katsh, *The Electronic Media and the Transformation of Law*, pp. 28, 63–67 (explaining how writing was a tool for acquiring power and how those in power resisted societal change); Logan, *The Alphabet Effect*, pp. 104–105 (discussing the model of abstraction provided by the alphabet); Rosamond McKitterick, *The Carolingians and the Written Word* (New York: Cambridge University Press, 1989), pp. 36–37 (explaining how the Carolingians used the written word to supplement memory and to consolidate authority); Marshall McLuhan, *The Gutenberg Galaxy: The Making of Typographic Man* (Toronto: University of Toronto Press, 1962), p. 238 (discussing the authoritative power of print); Ong, *Interfaces of the Word*, pp. 21–22 (discussing the separation of "the word from man and man from the word" which necessarily takes place in both writing and print), 86–87 (discussing the informational advantage of treatises and how the availability of such treatises remade oral speech), 243 (discussing the shift in consciousness from past to present); Ong, *Orality and Literacy*, pp. 101–112 (discussing writing's artificial, distancing effect), 177 (discussing writing as a "one-way informational street"); Walter Ong, *The Presence of the Word: Some Prolegomena for Cultural and Religious History* (New Haven, CT: Yale University Press, 1967), pp. 35–47 (discussing temporal-spatial and distancing effects of alphabet and print).

27 "Enframing" is an activity that depicts a person, object, event, or idea and simultaneously sets boundaries around the representation of these things. When we enframe an event, we describe it in some way (for example, by an oral or written account); as we describe this event, we fix the terms by which we understand it. In the case of the oral or written account, we locate the event within a setting of words, thus fixing our understanding of the event in terms of the words selected to describe it. Had we chosen instead to draw a picture, the same process would occur, but within the field of pictorial representation. Any technique that portrays reality enframes or shapes reality. Enframing, therefore, is a quality of any mode of representation and varies according to the selected mode. Different modes of representation, with their different types of enframing, will set different boundaries. Throughout Part I, we argue that the oral, written, print, and electronic modes of representation enframe reality in radically different ways. We have adapted the word "enframing" from William Lovitt's translation of Martin Heidegger's term *Gestell*, although we do not use the translated word in quite the same sense. We find the word "enframing" suggestive of the manner in which modes of representation alter reality and use it for our own purposes. See Martin Heidegger, *The Question Concerning Technology and Other Essays*, trans. William Lovitt (New York: Harper & Row, 1977), p. 19 and n.17; William Lovitt, Introduction, *ibid* pp. xiii, xxix.

28 As Professor Brian Stock describes this phenomenon: "[T]he new use of texts is not merely "the graphic counterpart of speech." It has a structure and logical properties of its own. In societies functioning orally the advent of the written word can disrupt previous patterns of thought and action, often permanently ... When written models for conducting human affairs make their appearance, a new sort of relationship is set up between the guidelines and realities of behaviour: the presentation of self is less of a subjectively determined performance and more of an objectified pattern within articulated norms. One no longer responds through inherited principles handed down by word of mouth. The model is now exteriorized. Individual experience still counts, but its role is delimited; instead, loyalty and obedience are given to a more or less standardized set of rules which lie outside the sphere of influence of the person, the family, or the community." Brian Stock, *The Implications of Literacy: Written Language and Models of Interpretation in the Eleventh and Twelfth Centuries* (Princeton, NJ: Princeton University Press, 1983), p. 18 (footnote omitted).

Goody and Watt observe that the early recording of previously oral cultural traditions in Greek society enabled two phenomena that had not been present to the same degree before literacy: a historical consciousness (i.e., an awareness of the past as different from the present) and a critical consciousness (i.e., a deliberate rejection and reinterpretation of social dogma to reconcile inconsistencies in inherited beliefs and conventions of understanding). See Goody and Watt, "The Consequences of Literacy," pp. 48, 56.

29 The historical correlation between the growth of literacy and writing and the building of secular and ecclesiastical empires is not coincidental. See generally Eisenstein, *The Printing Revolution* (Carolingian empire); Innis, *Empire and Communication* (Egypt, Babylonia, Greece, Rome, Western Europe, Confucianism, Buddhism, Islam, Christianity).

30 Goody and Watt argue that "writing establishes a different kind of relationship between the word and its referent, a relationship that is more general and more abstract, and less closely connected with the particularities of person, place and time, than obtains in oral communication." Goody and Watt, "The Consequences of Literacy," p. 44; Goody, *The Interfaces between the Written and the Oral*, pp. 75–76 (stating that written records strip away the individual and reveal general and universal relations).

31 Sue Curry Jansen, *Censorship: The Knot That Binds Power and Knowledge* (New York: Oxford University Press, 1991), p. 41. See also V. Gordon Childe, *Man Makes Himself* (New York: New American Library, 1951); Yu-t'ang Lin, *A History of Press and Public Opinion in China* (Chicago: University of Chicago Press, 1936).

32 Jansen, *Censorship*, pp. 41–42.

33 See, e.g., Marilyn Rye, "The Index Librorum Prohibitorum," *The Journal of Rutgers University Libraries*, 43: 66–81 (1981); Jansen, *Censorship*, p. 47.

34 Stock, *The Implications of Literacy*, p. 18.

35 See John Man, *The Gutenberg Revolution: How Printing Changed the Course of History* (London: Transworld Publishers, 2010), pp. 163–280.

36 Mitchell Stephens, *The Rise of the Image and the Fall of the Word* (New York: Oxford University Press, 1998), p. 29, citing to Elizabeth L. Eisenstein, "Printing as a Divine Art," Oberlin Library Lecture, November 4, 1995.

37 See Richard Abel, *The Gutenberg Revolution: A History of Print Culture* (New Brunswick, NJ: Transaction Publishers, 2011), pp. 23–126.

38 Elizabeth L. Eisenstein, *The Printing Press as an Agent of Change* (New York: Cambridge University Press, 1980), p. 3.

39 Francis Bacon quoted in Eisenstein, *The Printing Press as an Agent of Change*, pp. 3–4.

40 Eisenstein, *The Printing Press as an Agent of Change*, pp. 306–307.

41 Katsh, *The Electronic Media and the Transformation of Law*, p. 142.

42 Arthur G. Dickens, *Reformation and Society in Sixteenth-Century Europe* (San Diego, CA: Harcourt, 1966), p. 51. For additional discussion of this point, see William J. Bouwsma, *John Calvin: A Sixteenth-Century Portrait* (New York: Oxford University Press, 1988), pp. 98–100; Eisenstein, *The Printing Revolution in Early Modern Europe*, p. 147; H. G. Haile, *Luther: An Experiment in Biography* (Princeton, NJ: Princeton University Press, 1980), pp. 164–174; Logan, *The Alphabet Effect*, pp. 217–223.

43 Voltaire quoted in John Morley, *Diderot and the Encyclopaedists* (London: Chapman and Hall, 1878), I: 162.

44 Ong, *Interfaces of the Word*, p. 239.

45 *Ibid.*, pp. 82–83.

46 See Coulmas, *The Writing Systems of the World*, pp. 11–14 (mass production, abstraction, control); Eisenstein, *The Printing Revolution in Early Modern Europe*, pp. 51 (mass production and uniformity), 63 (systematization and abstraction), 72 (systematization), 73–74 (reliability and authority), 79–80 (mass production and preservation), 83 (permanence); Katsch, *The Electronic Media and the Transformation of Law*, pp. 33–35 (reliability, authority, and mass production), 85–86 (systematization), 215 (uniformity), 217–218 (abstraction); McLuhan, *The Gutenberg Galaxy*, pp. 125 (permanence), 156 (certainty and authority), 208–209 (uniformity); Ong, *The Interfaces of the Word*, pp. 89 (control), 330–332 (closure); Ong, *Orality and Literacy*, pp. 101–102 (systematization), 117–138 (closure, systematization, control, and abstraction); Ong, *The Presence of the Word*, pp. 47–53 (mass production, systematization), 63–66 (abstraction).

47 See Eisenstein, *The Printing Revolution in Early Modern Europe*, p. 71.

48 See Howard Jay Graham, "Our Tong Maternall Maruellously Amendyd and Augmentyd: The First Englishing and Printing of the Medieval Statutes at Large, 1530–1533," *University of California at Los Angeles Law Review* 13: 58, 58–59 (1965).

49 See *ibid.*, pp. 59–60.

50 Dyer was one of the first reporters after the scribal Year Book period. See Plucknett, *A Concise History of the Common Law*, p. 280.

51 Plowden's reports covered almost exactly the same period as Dyer's and were considered "highly authoritative." *Ibid.*

52 Plucknett notes that the thirteen volumes of Coke's Reports, so highly regarded that they were cited simply as The Reports, synthesized and organized the principles of English law as they arose from the cases Coke observed. The report of each case thoroughly summarized all relevant legal authority to date. Even in Coke's day, however, the case report mingled presentation of the facts and law with commentary, criticism, and legal history. *Ibid.*, pp. 280–281.

53 The publication of Burrow's Reports established the format for official reporting. His reports "discriminat[ed] between facts, arguments and decision," *ibid.*, p. 281, a form that still exists in today's typical first-year law student's case briefs.

54 Among the first English treatises on legal philosophy, the work of the English barrister Christopher St. Germain (1460–1540) was one of the most important. Apparently published in Latin in 1523, St. Germain's book was published again in English in 1530. A criticism of the common law, the treatise is most notable for its discussion of notions of equity in English legal thought. *Ibid.*, p. 279.

55 Issued in 1628 (First Institute), 1642 (Second Institute), and 1644 (Third Institute and Fourth Institute), Coke's works "embodied the bulk of English law in the form of decisions, or comments upon decisions." *Ibid.*, p. 282.

56 William Blackstone's *Commentaries* has been called "a great, readable, reasonable book about English law as a whole." In his work, Blackstone "attempt[ed] to explain and justify the common law in the eyes of the laity." *Ibid.*, p. 286. Partly because Blackstone's treatise organized a mass of legal materials, doctrines, and concepts in one book, his work traveled to eighteenth-century America and was especially influential there. *Ibid.*, p. 287.

57 *Ibid.*, p. 263.

58 An Act for the Prevention of Frauds and Perjuries, 29 Car. 2, ch. 3 (England: 1677).

59 The preamble of the Statute of Frauds reads: "For prevention of many fraudulent practices, which are commonly endeavored to be upheld by perjury or subordination of perjury, be it enacted . . ." *Ibid.*

60 Charles W. Hawkins, "Where, Why and When Was the Statute of Frauds Enacted?," *American University Law Review* 54: 867, 872 (1920). See also John Edward Murray, Jr., *Murray on Contracts* § 68 (Dayton, OH: Lexis Publications, 3rd edn., 1990), p. 301; Philip Hamburger, "The Conveyancing Purposes of the Statute of Frauds," *Journal of Legal History* 27: 354, 356–357, 372–373 (1983).

61 *Hotchkiss v. National City Bank of N.Y.*, 200 F. 287, 293 (S.D.N.Y. 1911) (Judge Learned Hand's religious reference occurred in his discussion of objective versus subjective approaches to contract law).

62 See generally Arthur Linton Corbin, *Corbin on Contracts*, 2: § 275 (Eagan, MN: West Publishing, 1963 & Supp. 1991); Hugh Evander Willis, "The Statute of Frauds: A Legal Anachronism," *Indiana Law Journal* 3: 427, 528 (1928).

63 See Eisenstein, *The Printing Revolution in Early Modern Europe*, p. 83 ("It was no longer possible to take for granted that one was following 'immemorial custom' . . . Struggles over the right to establish precedents became more intense as each precedent became more permanent and hence more difficult to break."). See also Katsh, *The Electronic Media and the Transformation of Law*, p. 87 (discussing the increased business for common law courts and a growing attention to rule-oriented solutions). But cf. Plucknett, *A Concise History of the Common Law*, p. 349 (explaining that, although the printing of the sixteenth-century case reporters increased the number of citations to cases, precedent was not generally treated as binding authority until the 1800s).

64 See Duncan Kennedy, "The Structure of Blackstone's Commentaries," *Buffalo Law Review* 28: 205 (1979); cf. Neil Postman, *Amusing Ourselves to Death* (New York: Penguin Books, 1984), p. 57 (referring to United States Supreme Court Chief Justice John Marshall as the "Typographic Man").

65 *Entick v. Carrington*, 19 Howell's State Trials 1029 (Michaelmas Term, 1765).

66 Lucien Febvre and Henri-Jean Martin, *The Coming of the Book: The Impact of Printing, 1450–1800*, trans. David Gerard (London: Verso, 1990), pp. 191–192.

67 *Ibid.*, p. 246.

68 William Blackstone, *Commentaries on the Laws of England* (London: Strahan, 1803), IV: pp. 151–152.

69 Much of the Benjamin Bache account was adapted from Ronald Collins and David Skover, *On Dissent: Its Meaning in America* (New York: Cambridge University Press, 2013), pp. 104–107. For source materials regarding the account, see Geoffrey R. Stone, *Perilous Times: Free Speech in Wartime from the Sedition Act of 1798 to the War on Terrorism* (New York: W. W. Norton & Co., 2004), pp. 35–36; Jeffrey A. Smith, *Franklin & Bache: Envisioning the Enlightened Republic* (New York: Oxford University Press, 1990); James Tagg, *Benjamin Franklin Bache and the Philadelphia Aurora* (Philadelphia: University of Pennsylvania Press, 1991); Peter Charles Hoffer, *The Free Press Crisis of 1800* (Lawrence: University Press of Kansas, 2011); James Morton Smith, *Freedom's Fetters: The Alien and Sedition Laws and American Civil Liberties* (Ithaca, NY: Cornell University Press, 1956).

70 Jansen, *Censorship*, p. 65.

71 See Haynes McMullen, *American Libraries before 1876* (Westport, CT: Greenwood Press, 2000) and Donald Davis, Jr. and John Mark Tucker, *American Library History: A Comprehensive Guide to the Literature* (Santa Barbara, CA: ABC-CLIO, 1989).

72 See American Library Association, "Number of Libraries in the United States (circa 2015)," at www.ala.org/tools/libfactsheets/alalibraryfactsheet01.

73 See Kerry Close, "The Most Popular TV Show of 2016 Was Not from a Big Network," *Fortune.com* (January 4, 2017), at fortune.com/2017/01/04/netflix-popular-tv-show/.

74 Neil Postman, *Amusing Ourselves to Death: Public Discourse in the Age of Show Business* (New York: Viking Penguin, 1985), pp. 78, 87.

75 See Statistica, "Number of TV Households in the United States from Season 2000–2001 to Season 2014–2015," at www.statista.com/statistics/243789/number-of-tv-households-in-the-us/.

76 David Hinckley, "Average American Watches 5 Hours of TV per Day, Report Shows," *New York Daily News*, March 5, 2014.

77 See Nielsen, *The Total Audience Report*, 3rd Quarter 2016, at www.marketingcharts.com/television/are-young-people-watching-less-tv-24817/.

78 The statistics on global Internet usage from 2000 to 2016 derive from "Internet," *Wikipedia*, July 25, 2015, at https://en.wikipedia.org/wiki/Internet and *Internet World Stats: Usage and Populations Statistics*, "World Internet Users and 2016 Population Stats," at www.internetworldstats.com/stats.htm.

79 The statistics in this paragraph can be found in the Webroot report, "Internet Pornography by the Numbers," at www.webroot.com/us/en/home/resources/tips/digital-family-life/internet-pornography-by-the-numbers and in "Porn Sites Get More Visitors Each Month Than Netflix, Amazon and Twitter Combined," *Huffington Post*, May 4, 2015, at www.huffingtonpost.com/2013/05/03/internet-porn-stats_n_3187682.html. Other significant studies on Internet usage and demographics include Top Ten Reviews, "Internet Pornography Statistics Overview," at www.toptenreviews.com/software/articles/internet-pornography-statistics-overview/ and Jason Chen, "Finally, Some Actual Stats on Internet Porn," at gizmodo.com/5552899/finally-some-actual-stats-on-internet-porn.

80 "Pornography Statistics: Annual Report 2015," *CovenantEyes*, July 26, 2015, at www
.covenanteyes.com/pornstats.

81 *Ibid.*

82 Dated April 28, 1917, President Wilson's Executive Order stated: "WHEREAS the existence of a state of war between the United States and the Imperial German Government
makes it essential to the public safety that no communication of a character which would
aid the enemy or its allies shall be had, THEREFORE, by virtue of the power vested in me
under the Constitution and by the Joint Resolution passed by Congress on April 6, 1917,
declaring the existence of a state of war, it is ordered that all companies or other persons,
owning, controlling or operating telegraph and telephone lines or submarine cables, are
hereby prohibited from transmitting messages to points without the United States, and
from delivering messages received from such points, except those permitted under rules
and regulations to be established by the Secretary of War for telegraph and telephone
lines, and by the Secretary of the Navy for submarine cables. To these Departments,
respectively, is delegated the duty of preparing and enforcing rules and regulations under
this order to accomplish the purpose mentioned."

83 Senate Bill 1705, *Intelligence Authorization Act for Fiscal Year 2016*, July 7, 2015. The
relevant provision of the proposed measure is Section 603: "Requirement to report terrorist
activities and the unlawful distribution of information relating to explosives." Subsection
(a) of section 603 provides: "Whoever, while engaged in providing an electronic communication service or a remote computing service to the public through a facility or means of
interstate or foreign commerce, obtains actual knowledge of any terrorist activity ... shall,
as soon as reasonably possible, provide to the appropriate authorities the facts or circumstances of the alleged terrorist activities." Subsection (c) of section 603 provides: "The facts
or circumstances described in this subsection ... involves distribution of information
relating to explosives, destructive devices, and weapons of mass destruction." Subsection
(d) of section 603 concerns privacy protection and provides: "Nothing in this section
may be construed to require an electronic communication service provider or a remote
computing service provider—(1) to monitor any user, subscriber, or customer of that
provider; or (2) to monitor the content of any communication of any person."

84 Laura Wittern-Keller and Raymond J. Haberski, Jr., *The Miracle Case: Film Censorship
and the Supreme Court* (Lawrence: University Press of Kansas, 2008), p. 11.

85 343 U.S. 495 (1952) (also known as "The *Miracle* Case").

86 Of course, other laws regulated electronic media for reasons other than national security
or obscenity. See, e.g., 47 U.S.C. §223 (harassing telephone calls) and 47 U.S.C. §227
(robo calls).

87 18 U.S.C. §1464, upheld in *FCC v. Pacifica Foundation*, 438 U.S. 1726 (1978).

88 47 U.S.C. §609.

89 47 U.S.C. §223, invalidated in *Reno v. ACLU*, 521 U.S. 844 (1997).

90 47 U.S.C. §231, invalidated in *Ashcroft v. ACLU*, 542 U.S. 656 (2004).

91 413 U.S. 15 (1973).

92 See Ronald Collins and David Skover, "The Pornographic State," *Harvard Law Review*
107: 1374 (1994), expanded in *The Death of Discourse*, pp. 139–200.

93 Kiddie porn is the major exception. See *New York v. Ferber*, 458 U.S. 747 (1982)
(upholding state child pornography statute against First Amendment challenges); *Osborne*

v. Ohio, 495 U.S. 103 (1990) (upholding state statute regulating the mere possession of child pornography against First Amendment challenges); *United States v. Williams*, 553 U.S. 285 (2008) (upholding federal law prohibiting the pandering of child pornography).

94 In May of 2016, one of Siri's cofounders and the current CEO of Viv Labs, Dag Kittlaus, introduced at a New York tech show the newest AI assistant to come on the scene. Called "Viv," the technology is designed to work across any digital device (such as an IPhone or an Android), to handle "stacked" inquiries such as follow-up questions relating to the original query, and to be open to third-party developers who can bring new capabilities and services into the system. Once Viv is launched, whether she will succeed in overcoming the popularity of her rivals is yet to be seen. See Elizabeth Dworkin, "Siri's Creators Say They've Made Something Better That Will Take Care of Everything for You," *Washington Post*, May 4, 2016, at www.washingtonpost.com/news/the-switch/wp/2016/05/04/siris-creators-say-they've-made-something-better-that-will-take-care-of-every thing-for-you; Lucas Matney, "Siri-Creator Shows Off First Public Demo of Viv, 'the Intelligent Interface for Everything'," *Techcrunch.com*, May 9, 2016, at https://tech crunch.com/2016/05/09/siri-creator-shows-off-first-public-demo-of-viv-the-intelligent-inter face-for-everything/; and Justin Connolly, "Meet Viv – Your New Artificial Assistant," *Manchester Evening News*, May 14, 2016, at www.manchestereveningnews.co.uk/news/artificial-intelligence-assistant-viv-siri-11331679.

95 As we use the term, "robot" includes at least two basic categories: robotic functions (e.g., Siri) and a mechanical humanoid, both of which embed artificial intelligence.

96 Harry Surden, "Autonomous Agents and Extension of Law: Policymakers Should Be Aware of Technical Nuances," *Concurring Opinions*, February 16, 2012, at concurring opinions.com/archives/2012/02/autonomous-agents-and-extension-of-law-policymakers-should-be-aware-of-technical-nuances.html, pp. 3, 5–6 (article in a symposium on Samir Chopra and Laurence White, *A Legal Theory for Autonomous Artificial Agents* (Ann Arbor: University of Michigan Press, 2011)).

97 *Ibid.*

98 "Machine learning" is a term in computer science that refers to a computer's capacity to comb through gigantic amounts of data in order to make future predictions. It is used to identify economic trends, perform medical diagnoses, navigate planes and cars, translate documents, filter spam, interpret pictures, and recognize voices, among many other functions. There are substantially different machine learning approaches. "Reinforcement learning" is a trial-and-error strategy that reinforces positive results and avoids negative results, typically used in advanced economic applications (e.g., finding a Nash equilibrium) or in sequenced tasks (e.g., playing a game). In contrast, "unsupervised learning" involves a process of "clustering" data and analyzing its hidden categories (i.e., gathering unlabeled data and inferring informational structures). See Yaser S. Abu-Mostafa, "Machines That Think for Themselves," *Scientific American*, July 2012, pp. 78–81 (describing the concept of "machine learning" and explaining and illustrating its primary approaches). See also Ian Barker, "What You Need to Know about Deep Learning," *BetaNews.com*, November 2, 2016, at betanews.com/2016/11/02/deep-learning-breakdown/ (deep learning processes data "through a number of layers, usually in a neural network, the output from one layer forming the input for the next"; sometimes

called hierarchical learning or deep structured learning, it "seeks to model data in order to solve problems like object and facial recognition, natural language processing and speech recognition"); "Learning about Deep Learning," *Re/Code*, May 4, 2016, at recode .net/2016/05/04/learning-about-deep-learning/ ("A key point to understanding deep learning is there are two critical but separate steps involved in the process. The first involves doing extensive analysis of enormous data sets and automatically generating 'rules' or algorithms that can accurately describe the various characteristics of different objects. The second involves using those rules to identify the objects or situations based on real-time data, a process known as inferencing."); Kevin Murnane, "What Is Deep Learning and How Is It Useful?," *Forbes.com*, April 1, 2016, at www.forbes.com/forbes/welcome/? toURL=http://www.forbes.com/sites/kevinmurnane/2016/04/01/what-is-deep-learning-and-how-is-it-useful/ (deep learning is used in everything from powerful image recognition and tagging and analyzing satellite imagery to repurposing known and tested drugs for use against new diseases); Jim Romeo, "The Emergence of Deep and Machine Learning," *Digital Engineering*, February 2, 2016, at www.digitaleng.news/de/the-emergence-of-deep-and-machine-learning/ (the rapid development of machine learning has been applied in categories such as targeted advertising, recommendations systems, fraud detection, and spam detection and has advanced the development of autonomous or self-driving cars); Sue Halpern, "How Robots & Algorithms Are Taking Over," *New York Review of Books*, April 2, 2015 (review of Nicholas Carr, *The Glass Cage: Automation and Us* (New York: W.W. Norton, 2014) ("While these machines cannot think, *per se*, they can process phenomenal amounts of data with ever-increasing speed and use what they have learned to perform such functions as medical diagnosis, navigation, and translation among many others. Add to these self-repairing robots that are able to negotiate hostile environments like radioactive power plants and collapsed mines and then fix themselves without human intercession when the need arises.").

Deep learning sensationally returned to the news headlines when Google's *AlphaGo* program mastered the art of the highly complex board game Go and crushed the professional champion Lee Sedol at a highly publicized tournament in Seoul. See "Artificial Intelligence and Go: Showdown," *Economist.com*, March 12, 2016, at www .economist.com/node/21694540/print ("A Go board's size means that the number of games that can be played on it is enormous: a rough-and-ready guess gives around 10^{170} ... [AlphaGo's big idea] is to develop its own intuition about how to play – to discover for itself the rules that human players understand but cannot explain.").

99 Alan Winfield, *Robotics: A Very Short Introduction* (Oxford: Oxford University Press, 2012), pp. 14–16. See also Curtis E. A. Karnow, "The Application of Traditional Tort Theory to Embodied Machine Intelligence," at https://works.bepress.com/curtis_karnow/9/, pp. 3–4, 6–7 (delivered at the Robotics and the Law Conference, Center for Internet and Society, Stanford Law School, April 2013). ("The notion of intelligence as applied to machines is often just shorthand for 'I don't know how they do that so quickly,' an amazement borne of ignorance ... [But] true autonomy involves self-learning: where the program does not simply apply a human-made heuristic ..., but generates its own heuristic ... [Robots] operate in the physical environment, and may be exposed to a more highly varied type of inputs which must be accounted for as they occur – the pace of the world cannot be

dismissed as inconvenient. It is this rich set of unpredictable real time data which presents the challenges for robots and creates the desire for autonomy.").

100 Winfield, *Robotics*, pp. 15–16.

101 "The Dawn of Artificial Intelligence," p. 2.

102 See "AARON the Artist – Harold Cohen," *PBS: Ask the Scientists*, at www.pbs.org/safarchive/3_ask/archive/qna/3284_cohen.html (interview with Harold Cohen, the creator and mentor of AARON).

103 See Tia Ghose, "A New Bot-ticelli? Robot Painters Show Off Works at Competition," *LiveScience.com*, May 19, 2016, at www.livescience.com/54794-robot-art-contest-winners .html; "Roboart – The $100,000 Robot Art Competition!," *Robotart*, at robotart.org/.

104 See William Hochberg, "When Robots Write Songs," *The Atlantic*, August 7, 2014, at www.theatlantic.com/entertainment/archive/2014/08/computers-that-compose/374916/. See also Tim Adams, "David Cope: 'You Pushed the Button and Out Came Hundreds and Thousands of Sonatas'," *The Guardian*, July 10, 2010, at www.theguardian.com/technology/2010/jul/11/david-cope-computer-composer (released in 2010, the first album of Emily Howell, the computer, titled *From Darkness, Light*, was "composed in six movements and performed on two pianos").

105 See Olivia Goldhill, "The First Pop Song Ever Written by Artificial Intelligence Is Pretty Good, Actually," *Quartz.com*, September 24, 2016, at https://qz.com/790523/daddys-car-the-first-song-ever-written-by-artificial-intelligence-is-actually-pretty-good/; Jesse Emspak, "Robo Rocker: How Artificial Intelligence Wrote Beatles-Esque Pop Song," *LiveScience .com*, September 30, 2016, at livescience.com/56328-how-artificial-intelligence-wrote-pop-song.html.

106 See Evgeny Morozov, "A Robot Stole My Pulitzer!," *Slate*, March 19, 2012, at www .slate.com/articles/technology/future_tense/2012/03/narrative_science_robot_journalists_customized_news_and_the_danger_to_civil_discourse.html. Regarding the First Amendment implications of computer-created art, music, and journalism, see, e.g., John Frank Weaver, "Robots Deserve First Amendment Protection," *Future Tense: The Citizen's Guide to the Future / Slate*, May 15, 2014, p. 14, at www.slate.com/blogs/future_tense/2014/05/15/robots_ai_deserve_first_amendment_protection.html. ("[T]here is the serious potential for art, music, and commentary that is offensive, thought-provoking, and possibly even dangerous in the same way that human-created art, music, and commentary have been forever. In that case, local, state, and federal governments may want to limit robot speech.")

107 Jennifer Hicks, "Artificial Intelligence Beats a Path to Ecommerce," *Forbes.com*, September 23, 2016, at www.forbes.com/forbes/welcome/?toURL=http://www.forbes.com/sites/jenniferhicks/2016/09/23/artificial-intelligence-beats-a-path-to-ecommerce/ ("Online retailers are scrambling to partner with or adopt new AI technologies to help facilitate customer interaction to try and match and even surpass the typical in-store experience."); Ben Rossi, "3 Ways Artificial Intelligence Is Transforming E-Commerce," *Information Age.com*, July 18, 2016, at www.information-age.com/3-ways-artificial-intelligence-trans forming-e-commerce-123461702/ (replacing precise search engine queries with natural-language searching; developing personal virtual shopping assistants; amassing and amalgamating information on a customer's shopping behaviors, preferences and tastes).

108 See, e.g., Elaine Ou, "Why Hire a Lawyer When a Robot Will Do?," *Bloomberg.com*, September 22, 2016, at www.bloomberg.com/view/articles/2016-09-22/why-hire-a-lawyer-when-a-robot-will-do (search engine Luminance "studies thousands of documents and contract clauses" and "organizes massive piles of legal documents into smaller piles based on their relevance"); Dan Mangan, "Lawyers Could Be the Next Profession to Be Replaced by Computers," *CNBC.com*, February 17, 2017, at www.cnbc.com/2017/02/17/lawyers-could-be-replaced-by-artificial-intelligence.html ("The legal profession — tradition-bound and labor-heavy — is on the cusp of a transformation in which artificial-intelligence platforms dramatically affect how legal work gets done. Those platforms will mine documents for evidence that will be useful in litigation, to review and create contracts, raise red flags within companies to identify potential fraud and other misconduct or do legal research and perform due diligence before corporate acquisitions. Those are all tasks that – for the moment at least – are largely the responsibility of flesh-and-blood attorneys."); Charlie Sorrel, "Robot Lawyers Are Here to Get You Out of Parking Tickets, Protect You from Cops," *Fastcoexist.com*, June 30, 2016, at www.fastcoexist.com/3061404/robot-lawyers-are-here-to-get-you-out-of-parking-tickets-protect-you-from-cops (the chatbot lawyer, DoNotPay, which advises the user wanting to appeal a parking ticket and generates the documentation required for appeal, "has so far gotten 160,000 tickets dismissed in the U.K. and New York in 21 months"); and Shannon Liao, "'World's First Robot Lawyer' Now Available in All 50 States," *The Verge*, July 12, 2017, at www.theverge.com/2017/7/12/15960080/chatbot-ai-legal-donotpay-us-uk; Amanda Huntley, "Law Firm Hires First Ever Artificial Intelligence Lawyer," *Inquisitr.com*, May 13, 2016, at www.inquisitr.com/3090963/law-firm-hires-first-ever-artificial-intelligence-lawyer/ ("Ross," a computer system that uses highly sophisticated levels of natural language processing and pattern recognition machine learning, is now being used by the New York corporate law firm Baker & Hostetler to assist its human staff lawyers in handling its bankruptcy practice); Monidipa Fouzder, "Artificial Intelligence Mimics Judicial Reasoning," *The Law Society Gazette*, June 22, 2016, at www.lawgazette.co.uk/law/artificial-intelligence-mimics-judicial-reasoning/5056017.article (decision-making algorithm helps make legal reasoning "faster, more efficient and consistent").

109 See, e.g., Chris Neiger, "Google Sees a World Rife with Futuristic Robots," *The Motley Fool*, August 4, 2014, at www.fool.com/investing/general/2014/08/04/google-sees-a-world-rife-with-futuristic-robots.aspx (Google has purchased eight robotics companies over the past two years and is working on artificial intelligence for robots used in domestic service, such as care for the elderly.).

110 See Angad Singh, "'Emotional' Robot Sells Out in a Minute," *CNN*, June 22, 2015, at www.cnn.com/2015/06/22/tech/pepper-robot-sold-out ("Pepper the humanoid robot is so hot that he sold out within a minute, according to his Japanese creator, SoftBank Robotics Corp ... With his array of cameras, touch sensors, accelerometer and other sensors in his 'endocrine-type multi-layer neural network,' Pepper has the ability to read your emotions as well as develop his own ... Pepper has his own evolving emotions which 'are influenced by people's facial expressions and words, as well as his surroundings,' according to SoftBank.").

111 See, e.g., Alyssa Newcomb, "Hello Barbie: Internet Connected Doll Can Have Conversations," *ABC News*, February 17, 2015, at abcnews.go.com/Technology/barbie-internet-connected-doll-conversations/story?id=29026245; Jingyi Low, "Could This Talking AI Barbie Be the Future of Children's Toys," *Vulcan*, March 17, 2015, at https://vulcanpost .com/195981/hello-barbie-talking-future-toy/; Andrew Tarantola, "Realdoll Invests in AI for Future Sexbots That Move, and Talk Dirty," *Engadget*, June 12, 2015, at www.engadget .com/2015/06/12/realdoll-robots-ai-realbotix/; George Gurley, "Is This the Dawn of the Sexbots?," *Vanity Fair*, May 2015, at www.vanityfair.com/culture/2015/04/sexbots-realdoll-sex-toys.

112 See, e.g., Matthew Hutson, "Our Bots, Ourselves," *The Atlantic*, March 2017, at www.theatlantic.com/magazine/archive/2017/03/our-bots-ourselves/513839/.

113 See, e.g., Richard Lardner, "5 Things to Know about Artificial Intelligence and Its Use," *ABC News*, July 28, 2015, at abcnews.go.com/Technology/wireStory/things-artificial-intelli gence-32743981 (Humanoid robots "are at least 25 years away and perhaps decades beyond that to realize," according to experts. "The most challenging aspect of a [humanoid] robot is the hardware," said Toby Walsh, a professor of artificial intelligence at the University of New South Wales in Sydney, Australia."); Jonathan Vanian, "Why Artificial Intelligence Is Still a Work in Progress," *Fortune.com*, May 23, 2016, at fortune.com/2016/05/23/google-baidu-research-artificial-intelligence/ (because machine learning today is "still 99% human work," according to AI expert Oren Etzioni, far better models in software development are needed before machines can both autonomously and accurately learn from data).

114 See generally Collins and Skover, *The Death of Discourse*, pp. 69–135 ("Commerce and Communication").

115 Mark Stockley, "Artificial Intelligence Could Make Us Extinct, Warn Oxford University Researchers," *Naked Security*, February 17, 2015, at https://nakedsecurity.sophos.com/ 2015/02/17/artificial-intelligence-could-make-us-extinct-warn-oxford-university-researchers/; Samuel Gibbs, "Musk, Wozniak and Hawking Urge Ban on Warfare AI and Autonomous Weapons," *The Guardian*, July 27, 2015, at www.theguardian.com/technology/2015/jul/27/ musk-wozniak-hawking-ban-ai-autonomous-weapons.

116 Among the threats posed by "truly intelligent robots" that concern AI researchers, fears of vast disruption within labor markets (as smart machines obsolesce blue-collar and lower-skilled white-collar jobs in everything from manufacturing to administrative office work to healthcare) and panicked nightmares of "killer robots" (as machines without effectively coded ethics engage in destructive foreign warfare or domestic terror) loom large. See, e.g., Eric Horvitz, "AI, People, and Society," *Science*, July 7, 2017, p. 7 ("Excitement about AI has been tempered by concerns about potential downsides … For example, data-fueled classifiers used to guide high-stake decisions in health care and criminal justice may be influenced by biases buried deep in data sets, leading to unfair and inaccurate inferences. Other imminent concerns include … threats to civil liberties through new forms of surveillance, … criminal uses of AI, destabilizing influences in military applications, and the potential to displace workers from jobs and to amplify inequities in wealth."); Ben Hirschler, "Robots and Artificial Intelligence Erase 5.1 Million Jobs by 2020: D Report," *Reuters*, January 18, 2016, at www.rawstory.com/2016/ 01/robots-and-artificial-intelligence-could-erase-5-1-million-jobs-by-2020-davos-report/ (the

loss of approximately 65 percent of the world's total workforce in fifteen global economies); Cecillia Tilli, "Killer Robots? Lost Jobs? The Threats that Artificial Intelligence
Researchers Actually Worry About," *Slate.com*, April 28, 2016, at www.slate.com/articles/
technology/future_tense/2016/04/the_threats_that_artificial_intelligence_researchers_
actually_worry_about.html ("According to a study by Carl Frey and Michael Osborne of
the University of Oxford, almost 50 percent of jobs in the U.S. and U.K. are susceptible of
automation."); Douglas Bonderud, "Artificial Intelligence, Real Security Problems? Meet
Frankenstein's Children," *SecurityIntelligence.com*, January 20, 2016, at https://securityin
telligence.com/artificial-intelligence-real-security-problems-meet-frankensteins-children/
(Even if a robot revolution is exaggerated, "the increasing use of artificial systems in
business poses two key challenges: honest mistakes and deliberate sabotage … AI that's
tasked with too much, too soon or compromised by malicious actors could mean big
problems for corporations … A bigger attack surface means bigger problems and
demands higher priority on the IT security list."); David Faggella, "Artificial Intelligence
Risks – 12 Researchers Weigh in on the Dangers of Smarter Machines," *Huffingtonpost.
com*, March 1, 2016, at www.huffingtonpost.com/daniel-faggella/artificial-intelligence-r_
b_9344088.html ("From AI-influenced oppression via laws put in place by corrupt
leaders, to destructive capitalism, to unexplained and unverifiable AI that we can't fully
comprehend, the potential risks vary but are nonetheless disturbing."). For arguments
emphasizing the significant positive welfare effects of AI in the balance, see Gonenc
Gurkaynak, Ilay Yilmaz, and Gunes Haksever, "Stifling Artificial Intelligence: Human
Perils," *Computer Law & Science Review*, May 3, 2016, at dx.doi.org/10.1016/j.
clsr,2016.05.003. ("It is very early to begin thinking about regulating AIs or AI studies,
particularly if such regulations may hinder developments that could prove essential for
human existence."). Although we are fully conscious of the raging controversies over AI
threats, we need not and do not stand behind any of the sides in these debates. Suffice it to
say that we find no serious First Amendment ramifications in governmental efforts to
regulate the AI–impacted economy or to control AI dangers to public welfare and
national security such as those threats mentioned here.

PART II ROBOTS AND THEIR RECEIVERS

1 In an article on the history of the First Amendment's free press clause, Professor Eugene
Volokh has argued that the freedom of the press was not understood at the time of the
1791 framing of the Bill of Rights (as well as the time of the Fourteenth Amendment's
ratification) as protecting a right of the press *as industry* (thus limiting the right to reporters
and publishers), but rather as protecting a right of the press *as technology* (thus according
the right of all persons to use mass communications technologies). See Eugene Volokh,
"Freedom for the Press as an Industry, or for the Press as a Technology? – From the
Framing to Today," *University of Pennsylvania Law Review* 160: 459 (2012). Professor
Volokh's technology-centered approach to the free press clause resonates with our own
medium-centric approach to the First Amendment as a whole – regarding both the
historical evolution of communications media and the future development of free speech
doctrine and theory in the era of robotics. For another insightful work on the revitalization

of the press clause, see Sonja R. West, "Awakening the Press Clause," *UCLA Law Review* 58: 1025 (2011).

2 In earlier works, we considered the relationships that exist between law in its various forms and its technological methods of creation and transmission. Recognizing that little attention has been paid to the significance of law's dissemination, we argued that any profound understanding of our legal culture requires a real appreciation of the role played by its modes of communication – whether oral, scribal, print, or electronic. The increasing prevalence of electronic audiovisual technology, we concluded, stands to reconfigure legal interpretation, institutions, and theories. See Ronald K. L. Collins and David M. Skover, "Paratexts," *Stanford Law Review* 44: 509 (1992). See also Ronald K. L. Collins and David M. Skover, "Paratexts as Praxis," *Neohelicon* 37: 33 (2010) (charting out the technological, operational, institutional, commercial, and theoretical implications of moving from a print-based casebook paradigm to an electronic course book model for legal studies).

3 See Jeff John Roberts, "Ban on Drone Photos Harms Free Speech, Say Media Outlets in Challenge to FAA," *Gigaom*, May 6, 2014, at https://gigaom.com/2014/05/06/ban-on-drone-photos-harms-free-speech-say-media-outlets-in-challenge-to-faa/; Margot Kaminski, "Drones and Newsgathering at the NTSB," *Concurring Opinions*, May 9, 2014, at concurring opinions.com/archives/2014/05/drones-and-newsgathering-at-the-ntsb.html.

4 See Stephen Kiehl, "FAA Grants CNN Permission to Test Drones in News Gathering," *GlobalPolicyWatch*, January 13, 2015, at www.globalpolicywatch.com/2015/01/faa-grants-cnn-permission-to-test-drones-in-news-gathering/.

5 The new FAA rules require a nonhobbyist operator to register his drone with the FAA, to pass a background national security check, and to obtain a remote pilot certificate (a far less expensive or strenuous process than acquiring a commercial pilot license). The most burdensome restrictions involve limitations on usage: a drone must be operated only during daylight hours, kept within sight (unaided by binoculars), and flown no faster than 100 mph and no higher than 400 feet in altitude. Because these constraints exceed those of other probusiness drone policies within the European Union, some commercial drone enthusiasts have criticized the FAA for falling short of what is practical and desirable. See Federal Aviation Administration, "Fact Sheet – Small Unmanned Aircraft Regulations (Part 107)," June 21, 2016, at www.faa.gov/news/fact_sheets/news_story.cfm?newsId=20516; Kevin Baird, "New FAA Rule Simplifies Commercial Drone Process," *News-Miner*, June 23, 2016, at www.newsminer.com/news/local_news/new-faa-rule-simplifies-commercial-drone-process/article_595d696e-3856-11e6-b834-a3f1b86a1669.html; Tero Heinonen, "Here's What's Missing from the New Drone Regulations," *TechCrunch.com*, June 29, 2016, at https://tech crunch.com/2016/06/28/heres-whats-missing-from-the-new-drone-regulations/ (visual line-of-sight drone flights are not enough).

6 See Kelly Moffitt, "As New Rules Go into Effect for Commercial Drone Operations, Here's What You Need to Know," *St. Louis Pubic Radio News*, August 31, 2016, at news.stlpublicradio.org/post/new-rules-go-effect-commercial-drone-operations-heres-what-you-need-know#stream/0 (quoting Matt Waite); Will Coldwell, "High Times: The Rise of Drone Photography," *The Guardian*, 17 June 2016, at www.theguardian.com/travel/2016/jun/17/why-drone-photography-offers-a-different-view-of-travel. A more comprehensive description and analysis of the increasing use of drones for researching and newsgathering

purposes is given in Phillip Chamberlain, *Drones and Journalism: How the Media Is Making Use of Unmanned Aerial Vehicles* (New York: Routledge, 2017).

7 See Eugene Volokh and Donald M. Falk, "Google: First Amendment Protection for Search Engine Results," *Journal of Legal Economics and Policy* 8: 883 (2012) (scholarly description of the Google controversy); Richard G. Marcil, "Do Robots and Computers Have Free Speech Rights under the First Amendment? The Day Is Coming (Bad Idea!) When They Might," *Macomb Township Patch*, at patch.com/michigan/macomb/bp-do-robots-and-computers-have-free-speech-rights-ub133d295b2#.U_fhKrdOXVg (newsletter report summarizing the FTC's investigation into Google's potential antitrust monopoly violations and the company's First Amendment defenses).

8 See Federal Trade Commission, "Google Agrees to Change Its Business Practices to Resolve FTC Competition Concerns," *Federal Trade Commission Press Release*, January 3, 2013, at www.ftc.gov/news-events/press-releases/2013/01/google-agrees-change-its-business-practices-resolve-ftc. *Fortuna* did not smile as kindly upon Google in Europe, however, where European Union's antitrust officials imposed a record $2.7 billion fine – the largest penalty of its kind – for "unfairly favoring" some of the company's own services over those of rivals. See Mark Scott, "Google Fined Record $2.7 Billion in E.U. Antitrust Ruling," *New York Times*, June 17, 2017, at www.nytimes.com/2017/06/27/technology/eu-google-fine.html. See also Aoife White, "Google Fine Is Small Change Compared with EU's Bigger Threat," *Bloomberg*, June 27, 2017, at www.bloomberg.com/news/articles/2017-06-27/google-gets-record-2-7-billion-eu-fine-for-skewing-searches ("While the penalty will barely make a dent in its $90 billion cash hoard, Google faces the prospect of less ad revenue and a regulatory backlash targeting other services from maps to restaurant reviews as well as the threat of even more penalties.").

9 In an insightful article, Professor Frederick Schauer similarly highlights the important conceptual differences between First Amendment coverage and protection. See Frederick Schauer, "The Boundaries of the First Amendment: A Preliminary Exploration of Constitutional Salience," *Harvard Law Review* 117: 1765, 1771 (2004) ("[T]his article concerns itself with the logically prior and long-neglected issue of speech that is not encompassed by the First Amendment in the first place ... Questions about the boundaries of the First Amendment are not questions of strength – the degree of protection that the First Amendment offers – but rather are questions of scope – whether the First Amendment applies at all.").

Moreover, Professor Schauer explores, in an admittedly preliminary fashion, significant nonlegal reasons for the categories of speech that fall within or outside of the First Amendment's purview. *Ibid.* at 1787–1800 ("[T]he most logical explanation of the actual boundaries of the First Amendment might come less from [free speech doctrine and theory] and more from the political, sociological, cultural, historical, psychological, and economic milieu in which the First Amendment exists and out of which it has developed."). In several ways, our project resonates with Professor Schauer's thesis. We, too, concern ourselves more with the First Amendment coverage of robotic expression than with protection for particular types of robotic speech. We, too, believe that First Amendment coverage of robotic expression is justified more by socioeconomic and cultural dynamics than by the tenets of traditional free speech law and theory alone. That said, there is an important distinction between our work and Professor Schauer's. His work is speech-centric, insofar as he aims to explain why content-based regulations in certain categories of expression – such as securities law, antitrust law, labor law, sexual harassment law, intellectual property law, and others – fall outside First Amendment boundaries. Our book, however, is medium-centric, insofar as we strive to explain why expression generated by robotic technology should rightfully fall within First Amendment boundaries to begin with.

10 See Tim Wu, "Machine Speech," *University of Pennsylvania Law Review* 161: 1495 (2013); Tim Wu, "Free Speech for Computers?," *New York Times*, June 19, 2012, p. A29. ("If we call computerized decisions 'speech,' the judiciary must consider [antitrust and consumer protection] laws as potential censorship, making the First Amendment a formidable anti-regulatory tool [for companies such as Google, YouTube, Yahoo, Facebook, Microsoft, and Apple]."); Oren Bracha and Frank Pasquale, "Federal Search Commission: Access, Fairness, and Accountability in the Law of Speech," *Cornell Law Review* 93: 1149 (2008).

11 Wu, "Free Speech for Computers?," p. A29.

12 Bracha and Pasquale, "Federal Search Commission," p. 1195.

13 Bracha and Pasquale, "Federal Search Commission," pp. 1148–1149.

14 Wu, "Machine Speech," pp. 1496–1497.

15 Eugene Volokh and Donald M. Falk, "First Amendment Protection for Search Engine Results," *UCLA School of Law Research Paper No. 12–22*, April 20, 2012, p. 3 (Google-commissioned white paper).

16 Stuart Minor Benjamin, "Algorithms and Speech," *University of Pennsylvania Law Review* 161: 1445, 1479 (2013).

17 Josh Blackman, "What Happens If Data Is Speech?," *Journal of Constitutional Law* 16: 25, 34 (2014). See also Timothy B. Lee, "Do You Lose Free Speech Rights If You Speak Using a Computer?," *Ars Technica/Law & Disorder*, June 22, 2012, at arstechnica.com/tech-policy/2012/06/do-you-lose-free-speech-rights-if-you-speak-using-a-computer/ ("The question isn't whether Google's *computers* have First Amendment rights. Obviously they don't. Rather, the people who own and operate Google's computers – its engineers, executives, and shareholders – have First Amendment rights. And regulating the contents of Google's website raises First Amendment issues regardless of how Google might have used software to generate that content ... So it's true that computers don't have First Amendment rights ... [N]either do printing presses. But *people* have free speech rights, and those rights apply even if we use computers to help us speak.").

18 Volokh and Falk, "First Amendment Protection for Search Engine Results," p. 4–5.

19 Benjamin, "Algorithms and Speech," p. 1475. For a commonsensical statement of this proposition, see Lee, "Do You Lose Free Speech Rights?" ("It wouldn't make sense to say that the government can freely regulate the computer-generated sections of [the *New York Times*] – like [Nate] Silver's [election] projections or the 'most e-mailed list' – because they are software-generated ... Regulating these sections of the site raises exactly the same First Amendment issues as regulating the content or placement of traditional news stories.").

20 Benjamin, "Algorithms and Speech," p. 1461 (citation omitted), 1471.

21 Volokh and Falk, "First Amendment Protection for Search Engine Results," p. 17 (citations omitted).

22 See, e.g., Stanley E. Fish, "Literature in the Reader: Affective Stylistics," in Jane P. Tompkins, editor, *Reader-Response Criticism: From Formalism to Post-Structuralism* (Baltimore, MD: John Hopkins University Press, 1980), pp. 70–100 (early articulation of Fish's reader-response critical theory positing that the experience of a text is its meaning and not the illusionary objectivity of its sentences or words); Stanley E. Fish, "Interpreting the Variorum," in Tompkins, *Reader-Response Criticism*, pp. 164–184 (maturation of Fish's reader-response theory with the development of his notion of the interpretive community); Norman Holland, *The Dynamics of Literary Response* (New York: W. W. Norton & Co., 1975) (application of psychoanalytic psychology to model the literary work); Norman Holland, *The Nature of Literary Response: Five Readers Reading* (Piscataway, NJ: Transaction Publishers, 2011) (readers respond to literature in terms of their own lifestyles, characters, personalities, or identities); Wolfgang Iser, "The Reading Process: A Phenomenological Approach," in Tompkins, *Reader-Response Criticism*, pp. 50–69 (insofar as readers fill in the "gaps" left by the text, they reveal the indeterminacy and inexhaustibility of the text); Hans Robert Jauss, *Toward an Aesthetic of Reception*, trans. Timothy Bahti (Minneapolis: University of Minnesota Press, 1982) (the foundational writings of the leading proponent of the aesthetic of reception develop categories to channel conventional literary history into a history of aesthetic experience, including exemplary readings in the comparative analysis of literature).

23 See generally Jane P. Tompkins, "An Introduction to Reader-Response Criticism," in Tompkins, *Reader-Response Criticism*, pp. ix–xxvi (providing an excellent synthesis of the school of reader-response criticism and a useful comparison of the competing theories within the school). More recently, reader-response criticism has evolved (or been absorbed) into "reception study" (or "reception theory" relating to more general cultural studies). An important collection of works for reception study is James L. Machor and Philip Goldstein, editors, *Reception Study: From Literary Theory to Cultural Studies* (New York: Routledge, 2001).

24 Tompkins, "An Introduction to Reader-Response Criticism," p. xvii (quoting Stanley Fish).

25 The original "wave poem" hypothetical was cocreated by former UCLA English professors Steven Knapp and Walter Benn Michaels to demonstrate that it would be radically counterintuitive to claim that "intentionless writing" and "intentionless meaning" are possible. Their case study posits that a beach walker comes across "a curious sequence of squiggles in the sand" that spell out the first stanza from William Wordsworth's poem, "A Slumber Did My Spirit Seal." If a wave washed up and left in its wake the second and final verse from the poem, the observer would either "ascribe these marks to some agent capable of intentions (the living sea, the haunting Wordsworth, etc.)" or "count them as nonintentional effects of mechanical processes (erosion, percolation, etc.)." In the second case, however, the observer's conclusion would be that these accidental marks were not words but "will merely seem to *resemble* words." The point being, of course, that authorial intentionality is critical to deciphering meaning: "[T]o deprive [the words] of an author is to convert them into accidental likenesses of language. They are not, after all, an example of intentionless meaning; as soon as they become intentionless they become meaningless as well." Steven Knapp and Walter Benn Michaels, "Against Theory," in W. J. T. Mitchell, editor, *Against Theory: Literary Studies and the New Pragmatism* (Chicago: University of Chicago Press, 1985), pp. 11, 15–17.

For our purposes, the relevance of the "wave poem" hypothetical and of Knapp's and Michaels's analysis of it become more obvious when the coauthors proceed to ask: "Can computers speak? Arguments over this question reproduce exactly the terms of our example. Since computers are machines, the issue of whether they can speak seems to hinge on the possibility of intentionless language. But our example shows that there is no such thing as intentionless language; the only real issue is whether computers are capable of intentions." The remainder of our essay challenges Knapp's and Michael's thesis, at least insofar as we would extend First Amendment coverage to intentionless robotic expression that is invested with meaning and significance by its receivers.

26　The answer to this question was quite clear to the philosophical pragmatist Richard Rorty, who sharply critiqued Knapp's and Michaels's analysis of their "wave poem" hypothetical. Rejecting their claim that authorial intent is critical to textual meaning, Professor Rorty replied: "Knapp and Michaels' claim that meaning is identical with intention suggests that we put in the text whatever context we find useful and then call the result a discovery of the author's intention. But why call it anything in particular? Why not just put in a context, describe the advantages of having done so, and forget the question of whether one has got at either its 'meaning' or 'the author's intention?'" Richard Rorty, "Philosophy without Principles," in W. J. T. Mitchell, editor, *Literary Studies and the New Pragmatism* (Chicago: University of Chicago Press, 1985), p. 132, 134. As will soon become obvious, we believe that Rorty has the better of the debate with Knapp and Michaels – at least insofar as our intentionless free speech theory also considers questions about authorial personhood or intentionality to be largely irrelevant with regard to constitutional protection for robotic expression.

27　See Leslie Kendrick, "Free Speech and Guilty Minds," *Columbia Law Review* 144: 1255 (2014). Kendrick has targets other than robotic speech in her sights, primarily the contentions of those First Amendment theorists who deem that intention (or the speaker's mental state) is, strictly speaking, irrelevant to First Amendment coverage. See, e.g., Larry Alexander, *Is There a Right of Freedom of Expression?* (New York: Cambridge University Press, 2005); Frederick Schauer, *Free Speech: A Philosophical Enquiry* (New York: Cambridge University Press, 1982); Martin H. Redish, "Advocacy of Unlawful Conduct and the First Amendment," *California Law Review* 70: 1159 (1982).

28　Kendrick, "Free Speech and Guilty Minds," pp. 1256–1260.

29　*Ibid.*

30　*Ibid.*

31　Compare Jane Bambauer, "Is Data Speech?," *Stanford Law Review* 66: 57 (2014) and James Grimmelmann, "Speech Engines," *Minnesota Law Review* 98: 868 (2014). It should be noted that three other First Amendment theorists have written to explain that foundational free speech theories and doctrines do not present serious conceptual barriers to coverage of "strong AI speakers," defined to be the "as-yet-hypothetical machines that would think and generate expressive content independent of human direction." Toni M. Massaro, Helen Norton, and Margot E. Kaminski, "Siri-ously 2.0: What Artificial Intelligence Reveals About the First Amendment," *Arizona Legal Studies Discussion Paper No. 17–01*, January 2017 (forthcoming in *Minnesota Law Review*). Unlike Bambauer and Grimmelmann, who strongly advocate for First Amendment coverage of robotic expression, Massaro, Norton, and Kaminski reveal deep concerns over their discovery of "surprisingly few barriers to First Amendment coverage of strong AI speech" and the "unfamiliar and uncomfortable, or even dangerous, places" to which such coverage might carry us. *Ibid.* at 6–7, 45.

32 Bambauer, "Is Data Speech?," pp. 63, 90–91.

33 Grimmelmann, "Speech Engines," pp. 874–875, 923, 931–932.

34 Bambauer, "Is Data Speech?," p. 61.

35 Grimmelmann, "Speech Engines," p. 924.

36 In a related regard, the Supreme Court in *Sorrell v. IMS Health Inc.*, 131 S. Ct. 2653 (2011), held that a Vermont law that restricted the sale, transfer, disclosure, and use of computerized pharmacy records revealing the prescribing practices of individual doctors, which had been enacted to thwart privacy invasions by data miners, violated the First Amendment. In imposing heightened judicial scrutiny, the Court recognized that the creation and dissemination of such computer-generated information constituted more than mere commercial conduct; rather, "speech in aid of pharmaceutical marketing . . . is a form of expression protected by the Free Speech Clause of the First Amendment." 131 S. Ct. at 2659.

37 In this regard, consider the discussion of robotic creation of paintings, music, and stories, *supra* pp. 29–30.

38 Bambauer, "Is Data Speech?," p. 86.

39 See *infra* p. 42. For an ironic treatment of the unviability of a First Amendment right to know, see Ronald K. L. Collins and David M. Skover, *The Death of Discourse* (Durham, NC: Carolina Academic Press, 2nd edn., 2005), pp. 111–112 ("There is no right to know . . . in a highly commercial [and advanced capitalistic] culture . . . The public's right to know could never have been more than what it has become – an idle slogan.").

40 We purposefully use the term "intentionless," because it conveys a meaning different than "unintentional."

41 319 U.S. 141 (1943) (a city ordinance forbidding the door-to-door distribution of literature by knocking or ringing doorbells violated the First and Fourteenth Amendments).

42 See, e.g., *Board of Education, Island Trees Union Free School District No. 26 v. Pico*, 457 U.S. 853 (1982) (the First Amendment imposes limitations upon a local school board's exercise of its discretion to remove books from high school and junior high school libraries) and *U.S. v. American Library Association* (2003) (because public libraries' use of Internet filtering software does not violate their patrons' First Amendment rights, the Children's Internet Protection Act does not induce libraries to violate the Constitution and is a valid exercise of Congress's spending power).

43 Although the Supreme Court's obscenity cases strongly concentrate on the definition of the unprotected speech category, the Justices have been virtually silent on the reasons for protecting nonobscene pornography or the nature and significance of governmental interests that justify suppression of obscene expression. Perhaps this is due to the Court's acceptance in *Roth v. United States*, 354 U.S. 476, 485 (1957) of the premise that "implicit in the history of the First Amendment is the rejection of obscenity as utterly without redeeming social importance." Given such a premise, judicial consideration of the meaning and value of the pornographic experience or the character and substantiality of

the state's interests become somewhat irrelevant. One notable exception, however, is *Stanley v. Georgia*, 394 U.S. 557 (1969), in which the Court held that the mere possession of obscene material cannot constitutionally be criminalized. In his opinion for the Court, Justice Thurgood Marshall's reasoning resonates, although not consciously or explicitly, with the reader-response and reception theory's valuation of the receiver's experience. The "right to receive information and ideas, regardless of their social worth ... is fundamental to our free society," Marshall wrote. "[A]lso fundamental is the right to be free, except in very limited circumstances, from unwanted governmental intrusions into one's privacy." In that light, the "mere categorization of these films as 'obscene' is insufficient justification for such a drastic invasion of personal liberties," for "[i]f the First Amendment means anything, it means that a State has no business telling a man, sitting alone in his own house, what books he may read or what films he may watch. Our whole constitutional heritage rebels at the thought of giving government the power to control men's minds." *Ibid.* at 564–565.

44 413 U.S. 15 (1973).

45 413 U.S. at 24.

46 425 U.S. 748 (1976) (invalidating under the First and Fourteenth Amendments a state statute that prevented the dissemination of prescription drug information). Earlier in *Bigelow v. Virginia*, 421 US 809 (1975), the Court struck down a Virginia law that made it a misdemeanor for "any person, by publication, lecture, advertisement, or by the sale or circulation of any publication, or in any other manner, [to encourage] or [prompt] the procuring of abortion or miscarriage." In justifying its ruling, the *Bigelow* Court noted that the abortion clinic advertisement in question contained important information in the "public interest." 421 U.S. at 821, 822, 826.

47 425 U.S. at 765.

48 113 S. Ct. 1505, 1517 (1993) (Blackmun, J., concurring).

49 113 S. Ct. at 1520–1521.

50 517 U.S. 484 (1996).

51 517 U.S. at 503. See also Ronald Collins and David Skover, *The Death of Discourse* (Boulder, CO: Westview Press, 1996), p. 101 (citations omitted): "Indeed, of the major commercial speech cases in which governmental regulation has been invalidated, nearly all 'involved restrictions on either purely or predominantly informational speech, such as bans on price advertising'. By comparison, governmental regulations were sustained in cases not involving 'predominantly informational advertising'."

52 131 S. Ct. 2729 (2011) (invalidating a California law that prohibited the sale or rental of "violent video games" to minors).

53 131 S. Ct. at 2733.

54 131 S. Ct. at 2733, quoting Chief Judge Richard Posner in *American Amusement Machine Assn. v. Kendrick*, 244 F.3d 572, 577 (C.A.7 2001) (striking down a similar restriction on violent video games).

55 See, e.g., *Florida Star v. B.J.F.*, 491 U.S. 524 (1989) (crime victims); *Oklahoma Publishing Co. v. District Court*, 430 U.S. 308 (1977) (juvenile offenders); *U.D. Registry, Inc. v. State*, 40 Cal. Rptr. 2d 228, 230 (Ct. App. 1995) (evicted tenants).

56 131 S. Ct. 2653 (2011). We referenced *Sorrell* for a different purpose earlier in note 36.

57 131 S. Ct. at 2659.

PART III THE NEW NORM OF UTILITY

1 Alexander Meiklejohn, *Free Speech and Its Relation to Self-Government* (New York: Harper & Brothers, 1948).

2 Alexander Meiklejohn, "The First Amendment Is an Absolute," *Supreme Court Review* 1961: 245 (1961).

3 Toni M. Massaro, Helen Norton, and Margot E. Kaminski, "Siri-ously 2.0: What Artificial Intelligence Reveals About the First Amendment," *Minnesota Law Review* 101: 2481, 2497 (2017).

4 *Ibid.* at 2499.

5 *Ibid.* at 2488–2491.

6 *Ibid.* at 2512.

7 See generally Lucien Febvre and Henri Jean Martin, *The Coming of the Book: The Impact of Printing 1450–1800* (New York: Verso, 1976); Paul F. Grendler, "Printing and Censorship," in Charles B. Schmitt, editor, *The Cambridge History of Renaissance Philosophy* (New York: Cambridge University Press, 1988), p. 45.

8 *Mutual Film Corporation v. Industrial Commission of Ohio*, 236 U.S. 230 (1915), overruled in *Joseph Burstyn, Inc. v. Wilson*, 343 U.S. 495 (1952). *See generally* Laura Wittern-Keller, *Freedom of the Screen: Legal Challenges to State Film Censorship, 1915–1981* (Lexington: University Press of Kentucky, 2008).

9 Alexander Meiklejohn, *Political Freedom: The Constitutional Powers of the People* (New York: Oxford University Press 1965) (foreword by Malcolm P. Sharp), pp. xv, xvi.

10 John Stuart Mill, *On Liberty*, edited by David Bromwich and George Kateb (New Haven, CT: Yale University Press, 2003), p. 81.

11 376 U.S. 254 (1964).

12 The quote has been attributed to Heraclitus of Ephesus (*circa* 535 BC–475 BC).

13 354 U.S. 476, 485 (1957).

14 413 U.S. 15, 36 (1973).

15 521 U.S. 844 (1997) (striking down the anti-indecency provisions of the Communications Decency Act).

16 *Ibid.* at 850 (notes omitted).

17 *Ibid.* at 885.

18 535 U.S. 564 (2002).

19 *Ibid.* at 566.

20 *Ashcroft v. ACLU, II*, 542 U.S. 656 (2004).

21 Harry M. Clor, *Public Morality and Liberal Society: Essays on Decency, Law, and Pornography* (Notre Dame, IN: University of Notre Dame Press, 1996).

22 Walter Berns, *Freedom, Virtue and the First Amendment* (New York: Gateway Books, 1965).

23 See, e.g., Catharine MacKinnon, *Only Words* (Cambridge, MA: Harvard University Press, 1996).

24 See, e.g., Andrea Dworkin, *Pornography: Men Possessing Women* (New York: Perigee Trade, 1981).

25 Frederick Schauer, *Free Speech: A Philosophical Inquiry* (New York: Cambridge University Press, 1982), p. 182.

26 Quoted in Ronald Collins and David Skover, *The Death of Discourse* (Durham, NC: Carolina Academic Press, 2nd edn., 2005), p. 188 (referring to the sexually-explicit photography of Robert Mapplethorpe).

27 *Ibid.*

28 Frederick Schauer, "Harm(s) and the First Amendment," *Supreme Court Review*, 2011: 81 (2011).

29 *Ibid.* at 83 ("by and large, not very much of the Court's rhetoric and doctrine has directly faced the issue of speech-created harm.")

30 250 U.S. 616 (1919) (two leaflets thrown from windows of a building, one of which was in Yiddish, held to violate Espionage Act and impede national war effort).

31 130 S.Ct. 2705 (2010) ("material support or resources" to even the nonviolent activities of a designated terrorist organization held to be unprotected under First Amendment).

32 564 U.S. 552 (2011) (Vermont statute that restricted the sale, disclosure, and use of records that revealed the prescribing practices of individual doctors violated the First Amendment).

33 134 S.Ct. 1434 (2014) (invalidating "aggregate contribution limits" of the Federal Election Campaign Act).

34 See, e.g., *Ocala Star-Banner Co. v. Damron*, 401 U.S. 295, 301 (1971) (White, J, concurring) (defamation of public officials), and *Monitor Patriot Co. v. Roy*, 401 U.S. 265, 301 (1971) (White, J, concurring) (defamation of public officials).

35 *R.A.V. v. St. Paul*, 505 U.S. 377 (1992).

36 See, e.g., *City of Renton v. Playtime Theaters, Inc.*, 475 U.S. 41 (1986) and its "secondary effects" progeny; *Garcetti v. Ceballos*, 547 U.S. 410 (2006) (public employee speech).

37 See *United States v. Stevens*, 559 U.S. 460 (2010); *Snyder v. Phelps*, 562 U.S. 443 (2011); *Brown v. Entertainment Merchants Association*, 564 U.S. 786 (2011).

38 Rebecca Brown, "The Harm Principle and Free Speech," *Southern California Law Review*, 89: 953, 955 (2016) (footnote omitted).

39 *Ibid.* at 1008.

40 *Ibid.* at 1009.

41 Erich Muehlegger and Daniel Shoag, "Cell Phones and Motor Vehicle Fatalities," *Science Direct* (2014), at scholar.harvard.edu/files/shoag/files/cell_phones_and_motor_vehicle_fatalities.pdf.

42 A useful summary of Section 230 of the Communications Decency Act and judicial applications of that provision is provided in "Immunity for Online Publishers under the Communications Decency Act," *Digital Media Law Project*, at www.dmlp.org/legal-guide/immunity-online-publishers-under-communications-decency-act.

43 Bob Sullivan, "Study: Social Media Polarizes Our Privacy Concerns; Facebook and Its Competitors Are Challenging Long-Held Perceptions of Privacy," *NBCNews.com*, March 10, 2011, at www.nbcnews.com/id/41995992/ns/technology_and_science/t/study-social-media-polarizes-our-privacy-concerns/#.WJ-sskozXIU.

44 See Mary Madden, "Public Perceptions of Privacy and Security in the Post-Snowden Era," *PewResearchCenter.com*, November 13, 2014, at www.pewinternet.org/2014/11/12/public-privacy-perceptions/.

45 See, e.g., Polly Sprenger, "Sun on Privacy: 'Get Over It,'" *Wired.com*, January 26, 1999, at archive.wired.com/politics/law/news/1999/01/17538.

46 Madden, "Public Perceptions."

47 For historical accounts of Anglo-American prior restraint laws and their relationship to the First Amendment, see, e.g., David Rudenstine, *The Day the Presses Stopped: A History of the Pentagon Papers Case* (Berkeley: University of California Press, 1996); Lucas Powe, *The Fourth Estate and the Constitution: Freedom of the Press in America* (Berkeley: University of California Press, 1992); Thomas I. Emerson, *The System of Freedom of Expression* (New York: Random House, 1970).

48 403 U.S. 713 (1971).

49 *Id.* at 726–727 (Brennan, J., concurring).

50 Floyd Abrams, *Speaking Freely: Trials of the First Amendment* (New York: Penguin Books, 2006), pp. 239–240.

51 See *Arkansas v. Bates*, Defendant's Memorandum of Law in Support of Amazon's Motion to Quash Search Warrant (Cir. Ct., Benton, County, Ark., #CR-2016–370-2) (February 17, 2017). The court never ruled in the controversy, because the defendant eventually authorized Amazon to release the Alexa recordings. See, e.g., Sylvia Sui, "State v. Bates: Amazon Argues That the First Amendment Protects Its Alexa Voice Service," *Jolt Digest*, March 25, 2017, at jolt.law.harvard.edu/digest/amazon-first-amendment.

52 See, e.g., "In re Grand Jury Subpoena to Kramerbooks & Afterwords," *Media Law Report*, 26: 1599 (D.D.C., 1998) and *Tattered Cover, Inc. v. City of Thornton*, 44 P.3d 1044 (Colorado, 2002).

53 See, e.g., *Riley v. California*, 134 S. Ct. 2473, 2489 (2014) (electronic devices and the data they contain that "reveal much more in combination than any isolated record" and expose "the sum of an individual's private life").

54 See, e.g., *In re Grand Jury Subpoenas Duces Tecum*, 78 F.3d 1307, 1312 (8th Cir., 1996); *In re Faltico*, 561 F.2d 109, 111 (8th Cir., 1977); *In re Grand Jury Investigations of Possible Violations of 18 U.S.C. §1461*, 706 F.2d 11 (D.D.C., 2005).

55 *Amazon.com LLC v. Lay*, 758 F. Supp., 1154, 1168 (W.D., Washington, 2010).

56 "U.S. Robocall Volume Reaches 1.45 Billion Calls in December, Breaking New Record for YouMail National Robocall Index Report," *PRNewswire.com*, January 19, 2016, at www.prnewswire.com/news-releases/us-robocall-volume-reaches-145-billion-calls-in-decem ber-breaking-new-record-for-youmail-national-robocall-index-report-300205468.html.

57 John W. Schoen, "Which Cities Receive the Most Robocalls," *CNBC.com*, January 15, 2016, at www.cnbc.com/2016/01/15/which-cities-receive-the-most-robocalls.html.

58 *Ibid.*

59 See Ben Smith, "O'Connor Backs Off Robocalls," *Politico*, October 28, 2010, at www.politico.com/blogs/bensmith/1010/OConnorbacksoffrobocalls.html. Apparently, Justice O'Connor did not authorize the use of her statement as part of the robocall campaign.

60 For only one example, an online company named "Robotalker" offers its services in prepaid blocks for automated texts and phone calls. Voice messages up to two minutes in length can be transmitted at high volume pricing of 2.2 cents per call. Written messages can be sent even more cheaply, at high-volume pricing of 1.1 cent per text. See "Robotalker," at www.robotalker.com/.

61 *Ibid* (FTC investigations); "'ROBOCOP' Bill Seeks to End Annoying Calls," *Half Moon Bay Review*, April 27, 2016, at www.hmbreview.com/news/robocop-bill-seeks-to-end-annoying-calls/article_8475dba2-0cb6-11e6-8938-37216c790dde.html (over three million complaints received by FTC).

62 "FCC Signs Robocall Agreement with Canadian Regulator: Commission Continues International Enforcement Partnerships," *FCC News Release*, November 17, 2016, at https://apps.fcc.gov/edocs_public/attachmatch/DOC-342223A1.pdf.

63 See H.R. 4932 – ROBOCOP Act, 114th Congress 2nd Session, *Congress.gov*, April 13, 2016, at www.congress.gov/bill/114th-congress/house-bill/4932/text; Denise Riley, "Fight Back against Robo Calls," *MyEasternShoreMD.com*, May 8, 2016, at www.myeasternshoremd.com/opinion/article_61a92597-542e-5341-80e4-4f0622ea056c.html.

64 See "All Actions – H.R. 4932," *Congress.gov*, April 15, 2016, at www.congress.gov/bill/114th-congress/house-bill/4932/all-actions?overview=closed#tabs.

65 The facts and figures in this paragraph derive from the compendium of state laws regulating automated calling maintained by *Robo-Calls.net*, at www.robo-calls.net/robo-call-laws.php. Only nine states – Alabama, Alaska, Arizona, Delaware, Georgia, Ohio, Vermont, West Virginia, and Wisconsin – are listed as having no restrictions on robocalls at the state level.

66 Such states include California, Colorado, Indiana, Minnesota, New Jersey, and North Dakota.

67 Such states include Hawaii, Idaho, Illinois, Maine, Mississippi, New York, Oklahoma, Oregon, and Tennessee.

68 Such states include Maryland, Massachusetts, Michigan, Missouri, New Mexico, Pennsylvania, Rhode Island, South Dakota, Utah, Virginia, Washington, and the District of Columbia.

69 Such states include Kentucky and North Carolina.

70 Such states include Maine and Texas.

71 See, e.g., *Van Bergen v. Minnesota*, 59 F.3d 1541 (8th Cir., 1995) (upholding a Minnesota antirobocalling statute that explicitly prohibited "any call, regardless of its content," unless a prior business relationship existed between the caller and recipient); *Bland v. Fessler*, 88 F.3d 729 (9th Cir., 1996) (upholding a California antirobocalling statute similar to the Minnesota law validated in *Van Bergen*); *Oklahoma ex rel. Edmonson v. Pope*, 505 F. Supp. 2d 1098, 1106 (2007) (finding that Oklahoma's robocall disclosure requirements "curtail no more speech, or compel no more speech than necessary to accomplish their purpose"). Among the various prohibitions imposed in state antirobocalling legislation, the timing restrictions are unquestionably the most likely to survive given the U.S. Supreme Court's special solicitude for the government's interest in protecting residential privacy from uninvited and uniquely intrusive speech. See, e.g., *Frisby v. Schultz*, 487 U.S. 474, 471 (1988) ("[W]e have repeatedly held that individuals are not required to welcome unwanted speech into their own homes and that the government may protect this freedom."); *Hill v. Colorado*, 530 U.S. 703, 716–717 (2000) ("The right to avoid unwelcome speech has special force in the privacy of the home.").

72 135 S. Ct. 2218 (2015). *Reed* held that any governmental regulation that is content-based on its face must be subject to the highest level of judicial scrutiny, even if the subject

matter restriction is viewpoint neutral and even if the government's motivations bore no discriminatory animus against the regulated speech category. Justice Clarence Thomas's opinion for the Court explained that "[c]ontent based laws – those that target speech based on its communicative content – are presumptively unconstitutional and may be justified only if the government proves that they are narrowly tailored to serve compelling state interests." *Id.* at 2226. As the jurist described it, "the critical first step in the content-neutrality analysis" is "to determine whether the law is content neutral on its face." *Id.* at 2228. Even if the law passes this first step, it may be deemed content based if it "cannot be 'justified without reference to the content of the regulated speech'," or "[was adopted] by the government 'because of disagreement with the message [the speech] conveys'." *Id.* at 2227 (quoting *Ward v. Rock against Racism*, 491 U.S. 781, 791 (1989)).

73 See, e.g., *Gresham v. Rutledge*, 198 F. Supp. 3d 965 (E. D. Arkansas, 2016) (invalidating Arkansas's antirobocalling statute, which explicitly forbids automated calls "for the purpose of offering any goods or services for sale, ... or for soliciting information, gathering data, or for any other purpose in connection with a political campaign," as an unconstitutional content-based regulation of protected speech that is not narrowly tailored to further the government's asserted privacy and safety concerns); *Cahaly v. LaRosa*, 796 F.3d 399 (4th Cir., 2015) (invalidating South Carolina's antirobocalling statute, which facially prohibited only "unsolicited consumer telephone calls" and those "of a political nature including, but not limited to, calls relating to political campaigns," as an unlawful content-based regulation that cannot withstand strict scrutiny review).

74 In these regards, the *Cahaly* decision is illustrative. Judge Albert Diaz's opinion for the 4th Circuit panel described the overinclusiveness of the South Carolina robocalling statute in these terms: "The asserted government interest here is to protect residential privacy and tranquility from unwanted and intrusive robocalls. Assuming that interest is compelling, we hold that the government has failed to prove that the anti-robocall statute is narrowly tailored to serve it. Plausible less restrictive alternatives include time-of-day limitations, mandatory disclosure of the caller's identity, or do-not-call lists ... The government has offered no evidence showing that these alternatives would not be effective in achieving its interest." (796 F.3d at 405). As to the statute's underinclusiveness, Judge Diaz explained: "At the same time, the statute suffers from underinclusiveness because it restricts two types of robocalls – political and consumer – but permits 'unlimited proliferation' of all other types." *Id.* at 406 (citation omitted). For analyses of the *Gresham* controversy, see Venkat Balasubramani, "Anti-Robocall Statute Violates First Amendment – Gresham v. Rutledge," *Technology & Marketing Law Blog*, September 6, 2016, at blog.ericgoldman.org/archives/2016/09/anti-robocall-statute-violates-first-amendment-gresham-v-rutledge.htm; Linda Satter, "Political Consultant Sues State over 'Robocalls' Ban," *ArkansasOnline*, May 5, 2016, at www.arkansasonline.com/news/2016/may/05/political-consultant-sues-state-over-robocalls-ban.htm; Caleb J. Norris, "Note: Constitutional Law – First Amendment and Freedom of Speech – The Constitutionality of Arkansas's Prohibition on Political Robocalls," *University of Arkansas Little Rock Law Review* 34: 797 (2012).

75 For facts and figures on the End Robocalls campaign, see "Ending Robocalls," *FoxNews.com*, January 21, 2016, at www.foxnews.com/tech/2016/01/21/ending-robocalls.html.

76 See https://consumersunion.org/end-robocalls/.

77 For an account of the Robocall Strike Force, see Nick Statt, "Apple and Google Join 'Strike Force' to Crack Down on Robocalls," *The Verge,* August 19, 2016, at www.theverge .com/2016/8/19/12556698/apple-google-fcc-robocall-strike-force-call-blocking.

78 For an account of the Robocall Strike Force's first 60-day report, see Chris Morran, "After 60 Days, What Has the 'Robocall Strike Force' Accomplished?," *Consumerist,* October 27, 2016, at https://consumerist.com/2016/10/27/after-60-days-what-has-the-robo call-strike-force-accomplished/.

79 Karl Marx, *Capital: A Critique of Political Economy,* edited by Frederick Engels, trans. Samuel Moore and Edward Aveling (Moscow: Progress Publishers, 1887), part I, chapter 1, p. 30.

EPILOGUE

1 John Milton, *Selected Essays of Education, Areopagitica, The Commonwealth,* edited by Laura E. Lockwood (Boston, MA: Houghton Mifflin Company, 1911), p. 128 (words: "according to conscience").

2 See Jonathan Rosen, "Return to Paradise," *The New Yorker,* June 2, 2008.

3 *Ibid.*

4 *Areopagitica,* p. 139.

5 *Ibid.* at 106.

ROBOTICA IN CONTEXT

1 Ryan Calo, "Open Robotics," *Maryland Law Review* 70: 571 (2011).

2 M.C. Elish, "Moral Crumple Zones: Cautionary Tales in Human Robot Interaction," *Proceedings of We Robot 2016,* at papers.ssrn.com/sol3/papers.cfm?abstract_id=2757236.

3 Jack B. Balkin, "The Path of Robotics Law," *California Law Review Circuit* 6: 45 (2015), responding to Ryan Calo, "Robotics and the Lessons of Cyberlaw," *California Law Review* 103: 513 (2015).

4 I refer to this quality as their "social valence." *Ibid.,* p. 545.

5 Ryan Calo, "Robots as Legal Metaphors," *Harvard Journal of Law and Technology* 30: 209 (2016).

6 *Louis Marx & Co. v. United States,* 40 Cust. Ct. 610 (1958).

7 *Comptroller of the Treasury v. Family Entertainment Center of Essex, Inc.,* 519 A.2d 1337 (Md. 1987).

8 See Tim Wu, "Machine Speech," *Pennsylvania Law Review* 161: 1495 (2013) and Stuart Minor Benjamin, "Algorithms and Speech," *Pennsylvania Law Review* 161: 1445 (2013).

9 See, e.g., James Grimmelmann, "Speech Engines," *Minnesota Law Review* 98: 868 (2014); Toni M. Massaro and Helen Norton, "Siri-ously? Free Speech Rights and Artificial Intelligence," *Northwestern Law Review* 110: 1169 (2016).

10 Given the thoroughly interdisciplinary character of robotics law and policy, it might also be interesting to hear from scholars in computer science and engineering who study and inform the design of robotics. I intend to purchase copies of *Robotica* for some of my colleagues in those fields and ask them for their thoughts.

11 Frederick Schauer famously draws a distinction between the threshold question of whether speech is covered by the First Amendment and the question of what protection follows from that coverage. For a recent discussion, see Frederick Schauer, "The Boundaries of the First Amendment: A Preliminary Exploration of Constitutional Salience," *Harvard Law Review* 117: 1765 (2004). Of course, coverage may prejudge protection in some circumstances. Imagine that instead of a wave poem, the waves of a strange beach leave a swastika in the sand. Imagine further that the municipality rakes over the swastika for fear it will offend residents. If, and only if, the swastika of sand is covered speech, then the First Amendment prohibits the government from censoring it on the basis of its apparent message.

12 Daniel Victor, "Microsoft Created a Twitter Bot to Learn from Users; It Quickly Became a Racist Jerk," New York Times, 24 March 2016.

THE AGE OF SENSORSHIP

1 For how computers replicate basic human thinking, see Brian Christian and Tom Griffiths, *Algorithms to Live By* (New York: Henry Holt and Co., 2016). For a discussion of automated experiments, see Seth Stephens-Davidowitz, *Everybody Lies* (New York: Harper Collins, 2017), pp. 205–221.

2 See Steven Pinker, *The Blank Slate* (New York: Penguin, 2002), p. 219.

3 See Pedro Domingos, *The Master Algorithm* (New York: Basic Books, 2015).

4 See Matt Ridley, *The Rational Optimist* (New York: Harper Collins, 2010), p. 357.

5 See A. J. Angulo, *Miseducation: A History of Ignorance-Making in America and Abroad* (Baltimore: Johns Hopkins University Press, 2016).

6 For an overview of laws based on the data minimization principle, see Marc Rotenberg, "Fair Information Practices and the Architecture of Privacy (What Larry Doesn't Get)," *Stanford Technology Law Journal* 1–34 (2001).

7 Catherine O'Neil, *Weapons of Math Destruction* (New York: Crown Publishing, 2016).

8 See, e.g., Laurence H. Tribe, "Trial by Mathematics: Precision and Ritual in the Legal Process," *Harvard Law Review* 84: 1329–1393 (1971); Eli Pariser, *The Filter Bubble: How the New Personalized Web Is Changing What We Read and How We Think* (New York: Penguin Press, 2011).

9 *Stanley v. Georgia*, 394 U.S. 557, 566 (1969).

10 Oliver Wendell Holmes, *The Common Law* (Boston, MA: Little, Brown, 1881), p. 108.

11 *Food Lion, Inc. v. Capital Cities/ABC, Inc.*, 194 F.3d 505 (4th Cir. 1999).

12 Protection of Human Subjects, 46 CFR §§46.101 et seq.

13 *Wisconsin v. Mitchell*, 508 U.S. 476, 487–488 (1993) (finding that bias enhancement was a permissible content-neutral regulation of *conduct*, but curiously also noting that a hate-motivated crime is believed to inflict greater individual and societal harm – a justification that could presumably support reaching the same result under First Amendment scrutiny). See also *Tison v. Arizona*, 481 U.S. 137, 156 (1987) ("Deeply ingrained in our legal tradition is the idea that the more purposeful is the criminal conduct, the more serious is the offense, and, therefore, the more severely it ought to be punished.")

14 *Zemel v. Rusk,* 381 U.S. 1 (1965).

15 By the way, while I think it's obvious that the courts will endow Watson and other health advice apps with First Amendment protection, this is a proposition that the U.S. Food & Drug Administration has not accepted and is nowhere near prepared to handle. U.S. Food & Drug Administration, *Mobile Medical Applications Guidance for Industry and Food and Drug Administration Staff* (2013).

16 See Daniele Coen-Pirani et al., "The Effect of Household Appliances on Female Labor Force Participation: Evidence from Microdata," *Labour Economics* 17: 503–513 (2010).

17 See Adam Kolber, "Criminalizing Cognitive Enhancement at the Blackjack Table," in Lynn Nadel and Walter P. Sinnott-Armstrong, editors, *Memory and Law* (New York: Oxford University Press, 2012).

18 *Sorrell v. IMS Health Inc.,* 131 S. Ct. 2653, 2667 (2011).

19 *United States v. O'Brien,* 391 U.S. 367, 376–377 (1968).

20 *Ibid.*

21 I am reformulating Collins and Skover's text here.

22 In subsequent work, I have used a definition of "information" that is quite similar to Collins and Skover's definition of communication (though this later work made an altogether different argument about free speech theory). Jane Bambauer and Derek Bambauer, "Information Libertarianism," *California Law Review* 105: 335–393 (2017).

SPEECH IN, SPEECH OUT

1 Charles Babbage, *Passages from the Life of a Philosopher* (London: Longman, Green, Longman, Roberts, and Green, 1864), p. 67.

2 See A. K. Dewdney, "A Tinkertoy Computer That Plays Tic-Tac-Toe," *Scientific American*, October 1989, p. 120.

3 See Nicole Perlroth, "Why Automakers Are Hiring Security Experts," *New York Times,* June 8, 2017, sec. B, p. 4.

4 *Spence v. Washington,* 418 U.S. 405, 410–411 (1974).

5 Lee Tien, "Publishing Software as a Speech Act," *Berkeley Technology Law Journal* 15: 629 (2000).

6 *Texas v. Johnson,* 491 U.S. 397 (1989).

7 *Cohen v. California,* 403 U.S. 15 (1971).

8 *Erie v. Pap's A.M.,* 529 U.S. 277 (2000).

9 James Grimmelmann, "There's No Such Thing as a Computer-Authored Work — And It's a Good Thing, Too," *Columbia Journal of Law & the Arts* 39: 403 (2016).

10 *Stanley v. Georgia,* 394 U.S. 557 (1969).

11 *Lamont v. Postmaster General,* 381 U.S. 301 (1965).

12 857 F. Supp. 2d 599 (E.D. Va. 2012).

13 730 F.3d 368 (4th Cir. 2013).

14 Robert Post, "Encryption Source Code and the First Amendment," *Berkeley Technology Law Journal* 15: 713 (2000).

15 See, e.g., Robert Post, "Recuperating First Amendment Doctrine," *Stanford Law Review* 47: 1249 (1995).

16 Frederick Schauer, *Free Speech: A Philosophical Enquiry* (Cambridge: Cambridge University Press, 1982), pp. 6–7.

17 Amanda Shanor, "The New Lochner," *Wisconsin Law Review* 2016: 133 (2016).

18 *Spence*, 418 U.S. at 410–411.

19 Tien, "Publishing Software as a Speech Act."

20 Stuart Minor Benjamin, "Algorithms and Speech," *University of Pennsylvania Law Review* 161: 1445 (2013).

21 Jane Bambauer, "Is Data Speech?," *Stanford Law Review* 66: 57 (2014).

22 Tim Wu, "Machine Speech," *University of Pennsylvania Law Review* 161: 1495, 1496–1497 (2013).

AN OLD LIBEL LAWYER CONFRONTS *ROBOTICA*'S BRAVE NEW WORLD

1 Certainly, although the term is absent from the Collins and Skover discussion, "public concern" which seems to be human centered is consistent with the reader-response criticism and reception theory that underlines their thesis. In my experience as a libel lawyer, however, it is easier to convince courts that a particular publication involves matters of public concern if human beings are actively involved on both the sending and receiving ends of such communications. One person is not the "public," but the media certainly should be.

2 See Clay Calvert, "Defining Public Concern after *Snyder v. Phelps*: A Pliable Standard Mingles with News Media Complicity," *Villanova Sports and Entertainment Law Journal* 40: 39 (2012).

3 *Chandok v. Klessig*, 632 F.3d 803, 813 (2d Cir. 2011).

4 *Gertz v. Robert Welch, Inc.*, 418 U.S. 323, 346 (1974).

5 *Philadelphia Newspapers, Inc. v. Hepps*, 475 U.S. 676 (1986).

6 *Milkovich v. Lorain Journal Co.*, 497 U.S. 1 (1990).

7 *Hustler Magazine, Inc. v. Falwell*, 485 U.S. 46, 50 (1988).

8 *Bartnicki v. Vopper*, 532 U.S. 514, 525, 533–534 (2001).

9 *Snyder v. Phelps*, 562 U.S. 443 (2011).

10 *Richardson v. Mellish*, 2 Bing. 229, 252 (1824).

11 Another legal issue, of course, is nationality and personhood. Do the Macedonian teenagers generating fake news, whether for clicks or for Putin, have any First Amendment rights? Do the bots that transmit their messages to computers throughout the United States have any such rights? Collins and Skover, of course, focus on the receiver, not the senders, so they do not consider these questions.

12 See Boer Deng, "Machine Ethics: The Robot's Dilemma," *Nature*, July 1, 2015, at www.nature.com/news/machine-ethics-the-robot-s-dilemma-1.17881.

13 "Bernie Sanders' Campaign Faced a Fake News Tsunami. Where Did It Come From?" *Huffington Post*, March 13, 2017, at m.huffpost.com/us/entry/us_58c34d97e4b0ed71826 cdb36/amp.

14 "1,000 Paid Russian Trolls Spread Fake News on Hillary Clinton, Senate Intelligence Heads Told," *Huffington Post*, March 31, 2017, at www.huffingtonpost.com/entry/russian-trolls-fake-news_us_58dde6bae4b08194e3b8d5c4.

15 Emilio Ferrera, "Disinformation and Social Bot Operations in the Run Up to the 2017 French Presidential Election," *Arxiv.org*, July 1, 2017, at arxiv.org/abs/1707.00086.

16 *Ibid.*

17 See *Citizens United v. FEC*, 558 U.S. 310 (2010).

18 See *Susan B. Anthony List v. Driehaus*, 814 F.3d 466 (6th Cir. 2016) (striking down Ohio law that banned "false political speech"). The court said: "[A] law cannot be regarded as protecting an interest of the highest order, and thus as justifying a restriction on truthful speech, when it leaves appreciable damage to that supposedly vital interest unprohibited." While Ohio's interests "are assuredly legitimate, we are not persuaded that they justify [such an] extremely broad prohibition." Obviously, whether a narrower regulation, perhaps directed at specific abuses relating to false robotic speech, *might* survive judicial scrutiny will be of interest, but recent case law is not encouraging. See *281 Care Comm. v. Arneson*, 766 F.3d 774 (8th Cir. 2014) ("[N]o amount of narrow tailoring succeeds because [Minnesota's political false-statements law] is not necessary, is simultaneously overbroad and underinclusive, and is not the least restrictive means of achieving any stated goal."); *Commonwealth v. Lucas*, 34 N.E.3d 1242 (Mass. 2015) (striking down a Massachusetts law, which was similar to Ohio's). One of the first cases to address this problem was the *Rickert* case, decided by the Washington Supreme Court, which narrowly rejected the regulatory scheme, ruling: "The notion that the government, rather than the people, may be the final arbiter of truth in political debate is fundamentally at odds with the First Amendment." *Rickert v. State Pub. Disclosure Comm'n*, 135 Wn.2d 628, 168 P.3d 826 (2007) (striking down Washington's political false-statements law, which required proof of actual malice but not defamatory statement).

19 *Susan B. Anthony List.*

20 *United States v. Alvarez*, 567 U.S. 709 (2012).

21 *Ibid.* at 719.

22 *Quigley v. Yelp*, 2017 U.S. Dist. LEXIS 103771 (N.D. Cal. July 5, 2017).

23 Also, the Internet is part of an international communications system, which means that foreign governments (and their free speech rules) may become involved in regulating robotic communications. Whether any such actions constitute "judgments" that are not enforceable in the United States would be determined by the provisions of the SPEECH Act, 28 U.S.C. §4102.

24 472 U.S. 749 (1985).

25 Oliver Wendell Holmes, Jr., *The Common Law* (1881), p. 3.

26 According to some commentators, when adjudicating constitutional protections relating to matters of public concern, the courts have taken an "inconsistent approach," and the case law has failed "to offer helpful criteria in identifying what counts as a matter of public concern." Mark Strasser, "What's It to You: The First Amendment and Matters of Public Concern," *Missouri Law Review* 77: 1083, 1119 (2012).

27 As Collins and Skover note, so-called commercial speech is an anomalous category of protected communications: "The free-speech significance of an advertisement or

commercial lies entirely in its potential meaning or value to the consumer who experiences it." The extent to which commercial speech can also be considered public concern speech, including whether different First Amendment tests should apply in those circumstances, is an interesting First Amendment issue, which the Court considered but did not resolve in *Nike, Inc. v. Kasky*, 539 U.S. 654 (2003). *Sullivan*, for example, involved defamation claims arising out of an advertisement, but the Court ruled that the publication was not a "commercial" advertisement: "It communicated information, expressed opinion, recited grievances, protested claimed abuses, and sought financial support on behalf of a movement whose existence and objectives are matters of the highest public interest and concern." 376 U.S. at 266. One of the earliest First Amendment commercial speech cases held that an out-of-state advertisement for abortion services "did more than simply propose a commercial transaction" – "it contained factual material of clear 'public interest.'" *Bigelow v. Virginia*, 421 U.S. 809, 822 (1975).

28 Or, to put the point in Miltonic prose that Collins and Skover may appreciate: new IFS is but old strict liability writ large.

29 *Palsgraf v. Long Island RR Co.*, 248 N.Y. 339, 341 (1928).

30 *People v. Croswell*, 3 Johns. Cas. 337 (N.Y. 1804).

31 *Schenck v. United States*, 249 U.S. 47, 52 (1919).

32 *Brandenburg v. Ohio*, 395 U.S. 444 (1969).

33 376 U.S. 254, 270 (1964).

34 Arguably, Americans resisting the harshness of the English common law of libel goes back at least to the Zenger case in 1735.

35 Vincent R. Johnson, "The Declaration of the Rights of Man and of Citizens of 1789, the Reign of Terror, and the Revolutionary Tribunal of Paris," *British Columbia International and Comparative Law Review* 13: 1, 9–13 (1990).

36 N.Y. Const. Art. I, Sec. 8.

37 *Immuno A.G. v. Moor-Jankowski*, 77 N.Y. 2d 235, 249–250 (1991).

38 Jack M. Balkin, "The Three Laws of Robotics in the Age of Big Data," *Ohio State Law Journal* 78 (2017).

39 And "press" because there may be ways to invigorate the Press Clause, to protect those communications entities and individuals who are in the business of regularly providing information to the public, unlike the fly-by-night disinformation bots that went dark after Trump's victory in 2016 and then were activated in advance of the Macron election campaign in 2017. See Sonja West, "Favoring the Press," *California Law Review* 106 (2018); Sonja West, "The 'Press.' Then and Now," *Ohio State Law Journal* 77: 49 (2016).

40 I am reminded, of course, of Professor Gilmore's dire warning:

> Law reflects but in no sense determines the moral worth of a society. The values of a reasonably just society will reflect themselves in a reasonably just law. The better the society, the less law there will be. In Heaven there will be no law, and the lion shall lie down with the lamb. The values of an unjust society will reflect themselves in an unjust law. The worse the society, the more law there will be. In Hell there will be nothing but law, and due process will be meticulously observed.

Grant Gilmore, *The Ages of American Law* 110 (1977).

WHAT'S OLD IS NEW AGAIN (AND VICE VERSA)

1 Toni M. Massaro and Helen Norton, "Siri-ously? Free Speech Rights and Artificial Intelligence," *Northwestern University Law Review* 100: 1169 (2016).
2 Toni M. Massaro, Helen Norton, and Margot E. Kaminski, "Siri-ously 2.0: What Artificial Intelligence Reveals about the First Amendment," *Minnesota Law Review* 101: 2481 (2017).
3 *Ibid.*, p. 2483.
4 *Ibid.*, p. 2512.
5 Geoffrey Stone, *Sex and the Constitution* (New York: Liveright Publishing Co., 2017), pp. 47–73.
6 Felix T. Wu, "The Commercial Difference," *William and Mary Law Review* 58: 2005 (2017).
7 558 U.S. 310 (2010).
8 *Ibid.*, p. 472.
9 Alan B. Morrison, "No Regrets (Almost): After *Virginia Board of Pharmacy*," *William & Mary Bill of Rights Journal* 25: 949, 952–953 (2017).
10 Whitney Phillips, *This Is Why We Can't Have Nice Things: Mapping the Relationship between Online Trolling and Mainstream Culture* (Boston, MA: MIT Press, 2016), p. 10.
11 Nathaniel Persily, "Can Democracy Survive the Internet?," *Journal of Democracy* 28: 63, 70–74 (2017).
12 Helen Norton, "Truth and Lies in the Workplace," *Minnesota Law Review* 101: 31 (2016).
13 Morgan N. Weiland, "Expanding the Periphery and Threatening the Core: The Ascendant Libertarian Speech Tradition," *Stanford Law Review* 69: 1389, 1395 (2017).

ROBOTICA REFINED

1 Aristotle, *On the Heavens* (294-b) in Jonathan Barnes, editor, *The Complete Works of Aristotle* (Princeton, NJ: Princeton University Press, 1985), vol. I, p. 484.
2 Ronald Collins and David Skover, "The First Amendment in an Age of Paratroopers," *Texas Law Review* 68: 1087 (1990).
3 379 U.S. 64, 74–75 (1964).
4 427 U.S. 539, 570 (1976).
5 395 U.S. 444, 448 (1969).
6 François-Marie Voltaire, "Letter to Frederick William, Prince of Prussia (28 November 1770)," *Voltaire in His Letters: Being a Selection from His Correspondence*, trans. by S. G. Tallentyre (New York: G. P. Putnam's Sons, 1919).
7 *Whitney v. California*, 274 U.S. 357, 377 (1927) (Brandeis, J., concurring).
8 See generally *United States v. Alvarez*, 132 S. Ct. 2537 (2012).
9 Kirk Kardashian, "What If We Put Servers in Space?," *Fortune Magazine*, January 29, 2015, at http://fortune.com/2015/01/29/connectx-space-data/.
10 *Palko v. Connecticut*, 302 U.S. 319, 326 (1937).
11 "CES 2014: LG Unveils 'Talking' Washing Machines," *The Guardian*, January 7, 2014, www.theguardian.com/technology/2014/jan/07/ces-lg-talking-washing-machines-appliances.

12 See Philip Marchand, *Marshall McLuhan: The Medium and the Messenger* (New York: Ticknor & Fields, 1980), p. 209.
13 Consider F. M. Cornford and W. K. C. Guthrie, editors, *The Unwritten Philosophy and Other Essays* (Cambridge: Cambridge University Press, 1967), pp. viii, ix, 35, 38, 42.
14 See, e.g., Robert C. Scharff and Val Dusek, editors, *Philosophy of Technology: The Technological Condition: An Anthology* (Oxford: Wiley-Blackwell, 2nd edn., 2014); Val Dusek, *Philosophy of Technology: An Introduction* (Malden, MA: Blackwell Publishing, 2006); Martin Heidegger, *The Question Concerning Technology and Other Essays*, trans. by William Lovitt (New York: Garland Publishing, 1977).

Index